RECENT
STUDIES
INDICATE

THE BEST OF SARAH BIRD

—

Sarah Bird

UNIVERSITY OF TEXAS PRESS ⋎ AUSTIN

Copyright © 2019 by Sarah Bird
All rights reserved
Printed in the United States of America
First edition, 2019

Requests for permission to reproduce material from this work should be sent to:

> Permissions
> University of Texas Press
> P.O. Box 7819
> Austin, TX 78713-7819
> utpress.utexas.edu/rp-form

♾ The paper used in this book meets the minimum requirements of ANSI/NISO Z39.48-1992 (R1997) (Permanence of Paper).

LIBRARY OF CONGRESS CATALOGING-IN-PUBLICATION DATA

Names: Bird, Sarah, author.
Title: Recent studies indicate : the best of Sarah Bird.
Description: First edition. | Austin : University of
    Texas Press, 2019.
Identifiers: LCCN 2018040434
ISBN 978-1-4773-1868-3 (pbk. : alk. paper)
ISBN 978-1-4773-1869-0 (library e-book)
ISBN 978-1-4773-1870-6 (nonlibrary e-book)
Subjects: LCSH: Bird, Sarah. | Feminism in literature. |
    Women in literature.
Classification: LCC PS3552.I74 Z46 2018 |
    DDC 814/.54 [B] —dc23
LC record available at https://lccn.loc.
    gov/2018040434

doi:10.7560/318683

Contents

MOTHERHOOD: TWO SECONDS AFTER THE STICK TURNS PINK

WRITING: USE IT IN YOUR WORK

Introduction

As a pathologically shy child driven by an insatiable curiosity about the world and the fascinating human creatures who inhabit it, I was simultaneously compelled by two deeply opposing forces: (a) I desperately desired to never have to speak to anyone outside of my immediate family and (b) I yearned to quiz every stranger who crossed my path.

Only one profession had the power to grant both of these contradictory wishes. Writing. Herein you will find the evidence of where these schizophrenic desires led me: essays and journalism.

Essays, the province of the muttering malcontent, her head full of the counternarratives and snappy comebacks she is too shy to give voice to: you are here in abundance.

And journalism, specialty of the introvert who has learned to compensate, who uses her notepad to wedge her way into the galaxy of worlds that first intrigue and then obsess her: you're represented as well.

Even though, given the wiring I arrived with at birth, writing checked all the essential boxes for my temperament, I would be almost thirty, supporting myself as a writer for most of a decade, before the concept of writing as a career occurred to me. I blame this late-dawning awareness on having grown up in a military family, with a large chunk of my formative years spent on overseas bases. In Base World, virtually all career choices involved wearing a uniform, telling time in hundreds of hours, and having the ability to recite the alphabet in funny words like "foxtrot" and "zulu."

As a base kid, the movie *Peyton Place* provided me with all the information I had about becoming a writer. I have long since forgotten everything about the film except for one scene that made an indelible impression upon my young mind. Carol Lindley played a character in the movie who yearned to become a writer. In the movie, we watch Carol peck out a novel on her old Underwood, rip the last page out of the typewriter, add it to her manuscript, and ship the whole thing straight off to a New York publisher.

Obviously you don't have to rewrite in the movies. Nor do you have an editor who calls to say she is "intrigued" by your four-hundred-page manuscript told in the first person by your heroine, a plucky shopgirl in Victorian England. She wonders, though, if the story might not work better told in the third person. By a harem girl during the Ottoman Empire.

But, no rewrites in the movies, so a couple of scenes later, our heroine is collecting her mail at the Peyton Place Post Office and discovers a letter from New York! Breathless, Carol tears the letter open. It is from the publisher. (Parenthetically, since Carol had not visibly aged, I suffered for years under the cruel delusion that publishers might actually operate within the same time dimension as the one occupied by writers. But back to the movie.)

Carol reads the letter and calls out, "Hallelujah! They

want to publish my book." And then the moment, the galvanizing moment for me, occurred. Carol, in her skintight '50s skirt, ran, ran like a geisha with her knees hobbled together, ran through Peyton Place waving the letter above her head and yelling—"I'M A WRITER! I'M A WRITER! I'M A WRITER!"

The summer he was sixteen, one of my best friends decided to explore career options other than growing reefer in his parents' basement. He decided to become a doctor. Drawing upon unsuspected reserves of motivation, he came up with and implemented a "Game Plan." That very summer he got a job working in a vet's office. He started studying and making good grades. The next summer he went to Guatemala and gave indigent natives inoculations. In college he passed organic chemistry. He graduated with an undergraduate degree in biomedical engineering, took the MCAT, and got into medical school. He learned how to deliver babies and suture knife wounds. He became a doctor. He had a Game Plan.

Occasionally, he asked me what I planned to do with my life aside from working part-time as a receptionist at the Albuquerque Paint and Body Shop. Unfortunately, in a weak, semi-delusional, totally high-on-cheap-Mexican-pot moment, I revealed that I'd thought, actually more sort of considered, the notion of the possibility of, maybe, who knew, becoming a writer? From that point on, my highly focused friend took to grilling me about my Game Plan for becoming a published author. Appalled at my total lack of anything remotely resembling a career path, he suggested one for me. And a very good suggestion it was: "Sarah," he advised, "what you need to do is write a best-seller." A best-seller? Gosh, why hadn't I thought of that? What a great way to start.

Long ago, I had to accept that there is no certain career path to becoming a writer. I would never be board-certified as a writer. I would never pass the bar and be licensed to practice the alphabet in any state of the union. And, since I didn't live in Peyton Place, God was never going to reach down out of the clouds and hand me that writer's diploma.

I often read about famous writers who say that they always knew that they wanted to be writers. I too was coming to understand that I wanted to be a writer, but only in the vague, dreamy way that a kid today knows that he or she would like to be Beyoncé or LeBron James. This inchoate longing might have gone no farther had I not discovered that rainbow of pulp fiction: *True Confessions*, *True Love*, and *True Story*. Faster than you can say "Fifty cents a word," I was confessing that I was half a woman loving half a man; that I had kidnapped my own child; seduced my parish priest, lusted after my son's karate teacher; and stolen my mother-in-law's meatloaf recipe.

They say write what you know. I am damned grateful I didn't try to research any of these page-scorchers. At just about the time that I had established a comfortable little niche for myself as a producer (I would never have called myself a writer) of pulp fiction, having learned how to confess in the first person using a thoroughly authentic blue-collar voice, that entire world imploded. Printed on high-acid paper that crumbled before you were done reading, pulp fiction vanished overnight.

Freelance magazine writing was next, and week after week I barraged New York editors with query letters—as I had learned to call them in journalism graduate school—and, trust me, mine were among the queeriest. And week after week I would receive letters informing me of just how grateful various publications were that I was "thinking of them." It was not until years later, until I had published several books and magazine editors had begun calling me with assignments, that I put together the puzzle of magazine writing: magazine editors are like bad boyfriends—as long as you need them, they don't want you.

Throughout my career, I have taken strength and comfort from the words of Thomas McGuane who, when asked to what he attributed his success as a novelist, gave this reply: "No family business." Like McGuane, having absolutely nothing else to fall back on, I persisted until I finally landed some assignments.

I wrote about a gay student at Brigham Young University, about a female petroleum engineer working on an offshore oil rig, about a transsexual, about autism, about the Penitentes of Northern New Mexico, about dating moody men and vampire friends who suck up your energy. I did human guinea pig stories in which I signed up for drug trials. I went on personals dates in those long-ago days before Tinder. I hiked Kauai's Napali Coast trail, moved back into my college boarding house, and went trekking in Arizona's Superstition Mountains with a llama and a crew of paranoid survivalists who decided that I was a government plant and confiscated my notepad. I wrote first-person essays about being secretly married for three years and, after our son was born, about living through the world's worst case of colic.

I was on my way. The assignments were flooding in: *National Observer, New Times, Savvy, Nutshell, Third Coast, 13-30*. These names will be familiar to connoisseurs of the periodical publication, who will recognize them immediately as all destined to join *True Confessions* in that great magazine graveyard in the sky.

Still, with No Family Business, I continued to rely on

persistence, the quality that, in retrospect, I believe set me apart from the many, many talented writers I knew who fell by the wayside—and one that I came by naturally. Though I would be well into my career before I realized it, I grew up with a writer in disguise.

My father was an Air Force officer who ate cottage cheese at lunch and blended concoctions that contained Knox gelatin for breakfast so that he could keep his weight down and continue earning the flight pay that sent his six children to Catholic school. When he was a captain we lived in Japan, in a tiny house with paper sliding doors and two bedrooms. My father made a space in a closet large enough for a small table, a chair, a gooseneck lamp, an ashtray for the cigars he smoked, his Underwood typewriter, and a ream of onionskin paper.

He would get up at four in the morning, the only time his crowded house was not a riot of kid noise, and he would write. Those tissue-thin sheets that my father filled with words in a smoke-filled closet while the rest of the world slept disappeared long ago, during one of our innumerable moves. What is left is a medallion on a stand that depicts George Washington crossing the Delaware, the prize for winning an essay contest. That, and the memory of a year's worth of grape Fizzies.

For those fortunate enough not to remember them, a Fizzie was a tablet that you dropped into a glass of water that would transform it into a cross between Kool-Aid and Alka-Seltzer. When this product was launched in the late '50s, the company ran a contest to find a slogan. My father spent many predawn hours coming up with his entry: "Abracadabra! Fizzie!"

I don't know what first prize was, but my father won a year's supply of Fizzies. (And for the few short days it took my brothers and sisters and me to lay waste to our "year's" supply, we all had purple tongues and lips from the highly fade-resistant product.) Today I would give most of what I possess to be able to hold in my hands those almost transparent sheets of onionskin paper that my father filled with hunted-and-pecked keystrokes. And though it took me far too long to understand that he was a writer in the purest sense of the word, not a navigator who entered contests when he wasn't flying aerial reconnaissance missions over enemy territory, he was always my model of persistence.

I don't know if it was persistence that sustained me when my budding career as a freelancer tilted more and more dangerously into the "free" zone, or whether it was just that the alternative sounded worse than starving to death. Yes, I refer to law school. As with so many of us who have a cunning way with words and night terrors involving numbers, law school loomed on the horizon like Mordor. Just as the Law School Admission Test study guide was guiding me to an acute awareness of how deeply logic-challenged I was, the romance novel presented itself as a potential source of rent money. Law school or the romance novel? I was in a quandary. For roughly three seconds. Let the record show that the plaintiff chose love in the first degree.

Writing five romance novels taught me the single most important lesson a beginning writer has to learn: how to sit all alone by yourself for months at a time and turn blank pieces of paper into a story. Writing romances was, for me, the literary equivalent of an out-of-town tryout, of playing the Catskills, and for that I will always be grateful to the genre. Or "John Ray," as I heard it called so many times by fans that I came to think of my rent-paying gig as either a porn star or a serial killer. From the start, however,

I wanted more than the form could offer. More freedom, more surprises, more imperfection, more real life.

Before I left the pink ghetto, I wrote a novel based on my experiences living in a boarding house for University of Texas co-eds. I would now like to offer myself as inspiration to anyone who has ever spent a day in bed with the covers pulled up over her head after receiving a rejection letter. This novel of mine was rejected thirty-five times. I still find that figure hard to believe, as I don't think there were thirty-five publishers in New York at that time. I've always worried that there were editors out there who hated the book so much they wrote multiple letters of rejection. Finally, however, the manuscript was bought and published under the title *Alamo House*. Other essays, articles, even a decade-long adventure in the screen trade, followed. My tenth novel was published recently.

Since the era when I was confessing that I was cheating on my husband with a telephone lineman—"Love in the Wrong Area Code!"—the writing landscape has changed so fundamentally that, when I am asked to speak to writers, I worry that I have nothing of use to pass on. Still, I would imagine that the basic temperament that inclines a person toward the writing life—intense curiosity about people combined with a physiological need to be alone for a sweet eight to ten hours a day to create worlds on paper—remains intact. In the end I always tell the students, whether they are in a middle-school classroom or an assisted living facility, that I hope they find the same joy, the same rapturous engagement, in writing that I have. That, of course, there will be heartache and frustration, rejection and disappointment. But there will be fun.

I tell them I have had such fun. Such immense, unimaginable fun.

RECENT
STUDIES
INDICATE

WOMANHOOD

—

The Secret Delta

A Question of Gender

AUSTIN SUN, 1976

Author's note: It is worth noting that this piece, first in the collection since it is one of the first I wrote, is also, far and away, the most serious in this volume. Perfectly illustrating the odd collisions of a writing life, the next piece is an essay about my two weeks as a go-go girl in Tokyo.

When I wrote "A Question of Gender" in 1976, I nearly moved in for most of a month and a half with the extraordinary subject whom I called "Liz." As I hope this article makes clear, Liz was astonishingly articulate and prescient. Working within the near void of information that existed about gender identity forty-two years ago, she managed to parse out most of the key elements that would guide the discussions in the decades to come. I think often about Liz and have made many unsuccessful attempts to track her down. If I could ever speak to her again, I'd thank her for her openness and her patience in dealing with a newbie writer, and for what she taught me about telling a person's truth.

The great mystery is not that we should have been thrown down here at random between the profusion of matter and that of the stars; it is that, from our very prison, we should draw from our own selves images powerful enough to deny our nothingness.

ANDRE MALRAUX

E lizabeth Raphael is in the ladies' restroom getting ready for a TV interview at UT. She is "talent," having been recruited by a friend in the class who needs an interviewee. With nervous, uncertain jabs that leave lipstick scars on her square jaw and mascara bruises under her blue eyes, Liz is putting on her makeup.

The mascara brush freezes in its flight to her pale lashes when the restroom door opens. Liz darts a jittery glance at the intruder, a small, red-headed woman, intent on getting into an elaborate nineteenth-century costume for a production down the hall. Liz continues making-up. The redhead, outfitted now, joins her at the mirror.

"God, isn't this a trip?" the actress asks, getting out her cosmetics stash. "Putting on makeup in the bathroom. It's like junior high again, isn't it?"

Delight replaces Elizabeth's uneasiness and she answers with a lip-glossed grin, "Really."

Later, Liz remembers, "I was really nervous when she came in. But she obviously accepted me as another girl and then, wow, she related to me having a *past* as a girl. That was too much!"

Liz's pleasure in such an apparently pedestrian event stems from the fact that, much as she may want one, she has no junior high past that included making-up in girls' bathrooms.

Last March Liz started hormone therapy in preparation for the sex-change surgery that will allow her to escape from an unwanted maleness. In September she began living as a woman.

Transsexualism. In our current free-swinging era, it is hard to make headlines with any sort of sexual permutation. Yet who doesn't know Dr. Renée Richards, the tennis player who had some success on the professional circuit following male-to-female sex reassignment surgery? While transsexualism is no longer as internationally scandalous as it was in 1952 when pioneer sex changee Christine

Jorgensen's medical history became the story to have received the largest worldwide coverage in the history of newspaper publishing, it remains profoundly misunderstood territory.

Standing behind her pushcart on the Drag, Elizabeth is a puzzling presence hawking chocolate chip cookies and banana bread. The androgynous combination of her long denim skirt and budding breasts, topped by a face full of rough-hewn features—almost pugnacious when they're not animated by Liz's usual warmth and openness—and compounded by a husky tenor voice, leaves most pushcart customers groping for forms of direct address. "How much are the cookies, son? Ah, er . . . ma'am?"

As disconcerting as her chimerical anatomy may be to onlookers, it seems more natural to Liz than the unfeminized male physique she used to feel an imposter inhabiting.

Elizabeth was born Michael Raphael in San Benito, Texas, the third son of a career Air Force officer.

"I was always rambunctious as a kid. Always outgoing, doing things." Seated in her west Austin apartment, Elizabeth recalls her early childhood. "I liked to play no matter what it was: dolls, fire engines, what have you." Liz's face, absorbed in the effort of memory, is soap-and-water plain. Fashioning herself somewhat in the cosmic cowgirl mold, she only wears makeup for gala occasions like the TV interview.

NIGHTGOWNS AND SLIPS

By the time Michael was ten, he preferred presenting as female. (Elizabeth requested that she be referred to with feminine pronouns only when we're speaking about the period from when she started living as a female—this past

September.) One of the earliest incidents Liz can remember went like this:

"I and my brother had spent the night over at a friend's house. They didn't have my boy's pajamas for us, so we were dressed in girl's baby dolls. Oh, my brother and I were both going around acting very angry, very embarrassed, very pissed off. But I was actually digging it. I dug the shit out of it. I really liked them. I don't know why, but they were comfortable. There was no sex feeling. I was far too young for that.

"We spent the night, and the next morning they fed us breakfast. I was reluctant to give up the baby dolls, but eventually I got dressed and that was that."

"That," however, was not quite "that." Back home, Mike stole a cotton nightgown off a neighboring clothesline and kept it hidden in the bathroom where he would retreat to put it on at opportune moments. Visiting relatives and friends also provided Michael with sources for the petticoats, slips, and panties he felt more comfortable in than his own boy's jockey shorts.

In 1964, at the age of 11, Liz remembers "getting into this thing with some boys I didn't know and telling them that I'd trick-or-treated as a girl that year; then, for some reason, I couldn't get the party dress and several petticoats off. So, I told them, I had to go to school the next day as a girl and I continued the rest of the year as my cousin. The thing was, they didn't think I was weird and I got away with the story.

"I used to dress in my mother's clothes all the time, even down to a girdle. I slept in a nightgown, something I swiped from my mother and kept stashed under my bed. I also ripped off a bunch of slips from my mom and wore them under my male clothes."

The overriding motive for these early forays into femininity was always the feeling of ease they brought. With a candor that is still characteristic of Elizabeth, 11-year-old Michael confided his secret to a group of friends. "My friends asked me why I was doing this and I said, 'Because they're more comfortable. Girl's clothes feel better to me.'"

Breaking from her boyhood memories, Elizabeth takes a long swallow of the Guinness she has been nursing and attempts a synthesis. "I'd *like* to say," she begins slowly, weighing each word against the memory of the first half of her life, "that I *wanted* to be a girl at that time. Many transexuals are acutely aware of this desire from infancy. But," she pauses, "I can't ever remember materializing that desire in my head until later."

Puberty struck around the time Mike's family moved to Austin in 1966 and, like many an adolescent with a less unsettled gender identity, Mike dealt with his doubts with an outward show of brashness—he became the class clown.

Elizabeth explains the reality behind the wisecracking gregariousness he adopted:

"I was very, very distraught, very, very confused, and very, very unhappy. I used to go down by this creek near our house to be alone and fantasize about being a girl. My favorite outfit was a full skirt of my mom's with two or three petticoats to make it stand out, a gold belt, and a cotton blouse—anything with frills. My mother was an early fan of pantyhose, so I got into those too.

"I had sort of a crush on a girl across the street. She was the prettiest girl in the class: blonde hair, a year younger than me since I'd flunked a grade. I guess I didn't exactly have a crush on her, it was more like I longed to be her. I would fantasize about living her life . . . going to school in skirts and blouses and all."

At O'Henry Junior High, Michael became increasingly miserable as gender distinctions grew clearer. Gym class focused his misery. "I despised it, not because of the exercise, although I was terrible at football and baseball. No, what I despised was undressing in front of sixty boys, the whole locker-room thing. It was very uncomfortable."

As he watched "the other girls get breasts and start dating or going steady," Michael's unhappiness and confusion crystallized. "I began praying to God every night that I be made a girl. I would just beg him to let me wake up as a female. I felt I had never been any good as a boy and I was tired of trying."

The general and Mrs. Raphael began picking up the signs that all was not well with their curly-haired boy. "They found my nighties under the bed and sometimes they would come in to wake me in the morning and see the nylon film and realize that it wasn't boy's pajamas. Once my father saw the lace of my slip showing and told me to unbutton my shirt. I did and there was the slip."

Michael was sent to a psychiatrist. Reviewing this period is clearly more painful for Elizabeth than the younger years were. She scissors a clump of baby-fine blonde hair behind her ear and goes on. "My parents thought I was sick. I wanted help. I thought if I cooperated and was honest, they could see what was happening. Above all, I wanted to be a girl."

Psychiatry held no answer and no relief. After a battery of tests the psychiatrist determined that Mike was experiencing a "sexual identity crisis"; tranquilizers and a stay at a special boarding school were recommended.

Michael celebrated his fifteenth and sixteenth birthdays at the school. In the dorm he discovered drugs, homosexual sex, and the "Easy Rider" image he decided to cultivate ("boots, leather fringed jacket, flared bellbottoms, hair parted down the middle—the whole hippie freak look"). The psychotherapy, tranquilizers, and "peer companion-ship," which were prescribed for the treatment of his "sex-ual identity crisis," had much less impact on Michael.

"I would go downtown and see something pretty in a window and it made me sorrowful in my heart that I couldn't wear this pretty thing. I wanted to look pretty, not handsome, never handsome, and it just tore me up inside," Liz recalls.

In June 1970 the school released Michael. They felt there was nothing more they could do. He immediately began dressing in the way that brought him comfort.

"I got off to the cut and feel of women's clothing. Mastur-bation almost always accompanied the dressing. The feel-ing was probably similar to the one a transvestite relishes. But there was a difference—I wanted to *be* a girl, not just wear girls' clothing. I wanted breasts, a girl's body.

"Once my parents caught a glimpse of my panties while I was dressing. Later I overheard them talking in their room. The word 'transvestite' came through."

He didn't stay long in Austin. That December—just turned 17—he declared his independence and "split for Ber-serkeley." Berkeley offered Mike ample opportunity to play out the gay, hippie freak role he was experimenting with.

"I said I was gay because I didn't know any better. I knew I wasn't the hetero male even though I'd made love to a woman and enjoyed it more than with guys—I even gave her my favorite dress the next morning. My body said I wasn't a woman. And I hadn't heard enough about TS, so I said I was gay."

A year of panhandling, the Diggers, acid, and amphet-amines sent Mike back to Austin.

SEARCH FOR SPIRITUAL ANSWERS

The search for reasons and relief lead many transsexuals to explore the spiritual life, perhaps more fully than "normals" who have never questioned whether their souls were assigned to the proper body. Mike found a measure of relief with a group that espouses traditional Catholic beliefs.

The change "beyond words" that came over Michael prompted him, in March 1973, to live within his newfound spiritual community. He hoped the discipline and monastic setting would curb his compulsion to wear female clothing. It didn't. He was suspended from his church for a year when his box of lingerie was discovered.

The year of suspension was spent struggling with the obsession which had banned Mike from his church:

"I used to stand before an icon of Our Mother of Perpetual Help and beg her to help me understand my transvestism—to understand why this desire to dress was so overwhelming. I would end up by breaking down in tears and begging her, 'Why can't I just be a girl?'"

After a year Mike was reaccepted by his church. In August 1975 he took up the monastic life again. He chose as his order name Michael Christopher, after the archangel. Elizabeth still speaks of her namesake with a terrible longing for a state so blessed that the entity is spared the burden of a body.

Although prayer helped, it didn't end Michael Christopher's quandary any more than psychotherapy, drugs, or homosexuality had. "I didn't cross-dress at all during this time. After a time, though, I did buy a few items—some lingerie. I would go to work at the warehouse in my men's slacks and white men's shirt. Everyone there thought I was a regular good ole boy. Underneath I'd be wearing hose, a pants liner, a camisole, and panties, of course. Of course

I took all of this off before I returned to the monastery because if someone asked, I didn't want to lie. I didn't like what I was doing because it was sneaky. Finally I left the monastery so I could indulge in dressing in private without disturbing anyone."

The separation from her spiritual sustenance still grieves Elizabeth, and she dreams of readmission as a woman after surgery.

The church was Michael's last strong connection with maleness; when it was broken, the person he'd felt himself to be for years began to emerge—Elizabeth. Elizabeth started appearing at Pearl Street Warehouse, the Country, and the New Apartment Lounge, usually wearing a women's pantsuit she'd bought at Penney's.

STEPS TOWARD A SOLUTION

It was at Pearl Street around February first that she met "the first flesh and blood transsexual of my life. She had her own tits and everything. I wanted to find out everything: who her doctor was, how to get hormones, all about the surgery."

This quest for knowledge, however, was subverted by the transsexual's steady stream of boyfriends and desire to keep her new profile low. "She even had a roommate, a girl, who didn't know. It blew her away when she found out."

Mike devoured *The Transsexual Phenomenon*, Dr. Harry Benjamin's classic study of transsexualism and sex conversion, and went on to read biographies of Christine Jorgensen and Jan Morris.

The steps toward and mechanics of sex-conversion surgery were unfolded. Michael learned that surgery applicants are carefully screened to weed out those who are "homosexual, transvestite, or psychotic." Female hormones derived from the urine of pregnant mares are taken orally and intramuscularly to induce in male-to-female transsexuals a woman's secondary sexual characteristics: breasts, hips, waist—the hourglass. The estrogen also softens the male libido and skin. Physically prepared, the preoperative male must live at least a year as a woman. The ultimate step is surgery. Typically, the testes are removed and the empty scrotum is left to form the lips of a simulated vagina. The penis too is amputated and its skin inverted to line the new vagina created by cutting into the area between the rectum and prostate. The sensitive skin makes orgasm possible, but conception, of course, is not.

The understanding that Our Mother of Perpetual Help had given to Mike's inchoate yearnings began to form:

"I knew by then that I was not, and never really had been, homosexual. I did not enjoy having a man make love to me and treat me like another guy; it just wasn't complete. I never liked anal intercourse; it felt like having my shit shoved back up my intestines.

"A gay man desires another man. Even if he's a queen he may get off to dressing as a girl, he may even prefer the feminine or passive role, but, the thing is: he is still a man and his sexual preference is for another man who will treat him as such.

"In talking with some of the queens I've met at the Warehouse and the Country, I've been told, 'I don't want tits, I want a flat chest, a man's chest.' They may want to take hormones to enlarge their chests as a trippy thing to play with, but, basically, the source of their excitement, the thrill they get from dressing, is their male body hidden beneath.

"I knew that I wasn't like them, because the sight of my body being a man's body outraged me."

The means of ending that outrage presented itself in

March of last year in the form of Linda, a preoperative transsexual. Elizabeth recalls the night:

"I met Linda at the New Apartment Lounge. I bought her a drink and we started talking. I asked her about her trip and she showed me her driver's license which she had in the feminine appellate.

"I was very excited and very pleased to actually get to talk with a transsexual and I asked her, 'Oh, are you post-operative?' She said, "No," but showed me the papers for a legal change of name. We talked at length about the hormones and surgery. Linda explained to me how to use a gaff—a piece of cloth with elastic to pull up and hold back the genitals so that when I dressed I wouldn't have a big lump and look like something out of National Lampoon."

Linda proved to be the link to medical help for Michael. The next day she took Mike to see the family physician who was prescribing hormones for her in preparation for the $5,500 sex-change operation.

Mike explained to the doctor that he was seriously interested in surgery, had been through five years of intensive psychotherapy, and didn't feel more would be of any benefit. The doctor prescribed female hormones for Mike.

The conjugated estrogens and progesterone Liz took orally three times a day, combined with the more potent twice-weekly injections of estrogenic substances, resculpted Liz's body over the next half year.

"My chest had been flat." Elizabeth tries to illustrate her former male flatness by stretching the satiny material of her blouse tight over the nascent breasts. "I practically fill a B-cup now."

By September Elizabeth felt ready for the next step toward surgery—the period of real-life testing, living as a woman twenty-four hours a day.

"I was over at this bar. I'd been going over there because they took me as Elizabeth and I really got off on that. A few of them, though, started calling me 'he.' That unnerved me. Then, the other night, this guy calls me 'he.' Several times.

"Finally I said, 'Why do you keep calling me "he"? I'm not a "he."

"'You're not? What are you?'

"'I'm a she, I'm a *woman*.'

"'Physically?'

"'Yes.' And I'm not lying there. As far as I'm concerned, physically, I am becoming a woman. But I knew what he was implying.

"He goes on, 'Well, nobody else here seems to think that you're a woman.'

"That just really bummed me out first class. That just ruined that bar for me. I don't want to go back there anymore. I'd been asked to cook . . . *asked*, and they don't ask *guys* to cook there. I was really getting off. Then he tells me that." Near tears, Elizabeth stops.

Elizabeth's very existence seems to magically draw the closet moralist out of the most unexpected observers. Their pronouncements on the propriety or impropriety of Liz's decision to consciously determine her sex, and to reshape her genitals to ratify that decision, invariably say more about the observers than they do about the observed.

The idea of someone choosing their gender, like they would decide whether to go into law or sanitation engineering, raises all sorts of threatening questions about personal identity, masculinity and femininity, body and soul. At one end of the spectrum of responses lies a noted specialist in transsexualism who distinguishes his patients from the "monosexual" masses. At the other end is a taxi driver, exasperated by trying to "understand and accept" what he finally decided was "just some geek who wants to get his dick cut off."

It's never hard for Elizabeth to find out how someone feels about her. The pronouns, if nothing else, give it away every time.

HE

Those strongly against Liz's transition from male to female stubbornly refer to her with masculine pronouns. Liz has both friends and enemies in the group refusing to accede to her requests for feminine reference.

"You can prefer all you want to be called 'she,'" a drag vendor working next to Liz told her one day. "I'll call you what I like."

Later, in Liz's absence, the vendor, joined by two of his colleagues, explains his adamant position. "I don't call him 'her,' because when you pull his pants down he's a he." All three vendors find this position statement amusing. Another vendor contributes the observation that he has "never spent time in bed with a transsexual and never will." The third vendor allows that while he's "not going to stomp him into the earth," he can't understand why Liz is doing what she is doing, unless she wants recognition. He sums up with, "Besides, having skin flaps sewn on you doesn't make you the opposite sex."

Liz's parents also refuse to acknowledge her entry into femininity by formalizing it with feminine pronouns. In a letter that Liz keeps carefully stored in a drawer, her now-retired air force officer father writes that no matter what Liz may do, for the general and his wife, she will always be the son the Lord sent them. Liz recalls her last visit home, early this summer, which prompted that letter:

"I dressed very masculine except that I'd just had my

ears pierced and had posts in them that I couldn't take out. So, my mother comes in and starts in on me . . . pick, pick, pick. Finally, she says, 'You look like a fairy.'

"That hurt. That really hurt. That was hitting below the belt.

"So I said, 'Well, look, what the hell do you expect me to do? Continue the facade of being a man? I'm not a man. I don't care what my genitals say.'

"Then she starts this shit about ruining their lives. Their lives! What about my life? I'm not trying to ruin their lives. I use their name as little as possible. I'm just trying to live my life as best I can.

"I wish she could accept me as her daughter."

At this point that seems as likely as Liz's older brother, Franklin, accepting her as his sister. "It's a monstrosity and an abomination of the flesh," Franklin intones judgmentally. That harsh pronouncement is tempered by a large measure of love and concern for his brother Mike's well-being, particularly spiritual well-being. Seeing his younger brother in a skirt, hose, makeup, and jewelry and contemplating even more profound alterations is, for Franklin, "as scary as watching a good friend get into heroin."

The social climate which, "in the name of liberal humanity, not only allows but condones" what Franklin considers "an act of castration," angers and outrages him. He sees his brother not as a villain, but as a pawn of the destructive forces that power our society.

"I have a sense of what he's searching for. Anyone who delves very far into themselves will come across a reverse image, so I empathize with Mike's instincts but I disagree with his methods."

Franklin hopes that his brother will find that the way to deal with what he regards as "a karmic debt" is not through medical science, but through some form of enlightenment that will "cut him from the flesh track he's on."

Among the friends mixing concern for Liz with a refusal to call her "her" is a 36-year-old woman who believes that all transsexuals are dupes of the medical profession spending thousands on an unneeded operation that "panders to their illusions."

Gilbert, a friend of Liz's heavily into leather fringe and body odor, expresses affection for his friend but adds, "What he's doing should be declared illegal." Gilbert admits that he "may be something of a fascist, but I think all those people coming out saying, 'I'm a lesbian'; 'I'm a homosexual'; 'I'm a transsexual' should be declared illegal. All they do is disrupt society. This sex-change operation should be illegal because people don't know what they're doing. They need to be protected from themselves."

Gilbert makes this analogy to his feeling about Liz's desire to surgically reconcile body and spirit: "It's like me going to a doctor and saying, 'I think I'm an orangutan. Fix my body to match that.'"

Interestingly, that kind of antagonism veiled with humor, and the staunch refusal to honor Liz's requests to affirm her femaleness, are almost exclusively male reactions. Women rarely display overt animosity or deny her requests for feminine reference. "Females are more accepting," says Liz. "But then most guys are really hung up on their own sex anyway."

HE-SHE-IT?

Somewhere between Gilbert and his orangutan analogy and the specialist with his "monosexuals" fall the casual observers who don't know Liz and can't figure out if she's "a dike or a queen."

The reaction Liz most often provokes is "He? . . . she? . . . it?" with accompanying sniggers. Most can't decide whether to pay homage in their personal pronouns to Liz's genitals or gender choice. After the initial he-she-it inquiry, "he" is usually chosen.

Friends of Liz's who knew her as a man before she began her real-life testing and who basically support the switch may still have pronoun problems. Concerted effort will yield a few "she's" and "her's," but they generally lapse back into thinking and speaking of Liz as a man. "I first met Mike when he was a guy and it's hard to stop thinking of him that way," says one long-time acquaintance.

Within this limbo area of the unemotional response falls the reaction that pains Liz the most: "When somebody thinks of me as a man even though I'm overtly dressed as a woman, that's my least favorite reaction—when they don't do it on purpose, not trying to be particularly cruel or spiteful, but they just think of me as something of an effeminate guy. Simply having someone flash on me as a guy really bothers me. It doesn't happen very often, but sometimes it does."

SHE

Contrasting sharply with these unwitting denials of Liz's femininity is the threatened-macho reaction that causes some men to ask questions like, "How can you be so messed up that you'd want to cut your dick off?" But responses to Elizabeth as an attractive woman contrast even more sharply. These delight her.

"I love it when a guy comes up and puts his arm around me or kisses my neck. Like, a while back, I met a guy at the Country. He opened the door for me, kissed my hand and told me, 'Vous etes une jolie fille.' I loved it. I like to be treated as a desirable woman. This is especially important to me now because it reaffirms my womanhood."

For somewhat different reasons, doctors, electrologists, and others involved professionally in helping Michael become Elizabeth carefully avoid the masculine in referring to Liz or any of their clients. One of the reasons for their deference may be money. Liz anticipates spending $5,500 for surgery alone. No breast implants, hormones, or follow-up.

Male-to-female surgical candidates like Liz need the services of an electrologist to remove beards and body hair. Liz's electrologist reckons that the painful process will take five years. During that time Liz, along with the five other Austin transsexuals being de-barbed at that clinic, will visit the electrologist once or twice a month for a one- to two-hour session. At these sessions the face is probed with a hair-fine needle that transmits an electrical current to kill the follicle.

Fifteen minutes of the torturous treatment costs $7.50. Liz's electrologist always says "she."

Liz's other brother, Nat, a 29-year-old mental health worker, also makes a deliberate effort to regard her as a woman. "Liz needed to feel that I was supportive," says Nat, "so I took that posture. At first it was a gesture of warmth and tact. Then I consulted friends and read about transsexualism and now I'm just kind of tickled, not in a flippant way, to be a part of this somehow."

Nat's strongest feelings have to do with the treatment of transsexuals by a "homophobic society preoccupied by what's manly and what's womanly." It is this societal pressure that Nat sees as being at the base of all the campy Halloween trappings that often accompany transsexuals and make them seen as pathetic castoffs of intersex. He is distressed to see Liz wearing makeup, jewelry, and hose because those things represent to him a throwback in the evolution of womankind.

Nat's is a fairly representative liberal response. Above all it is "accepting of differences." Liz can expect to be called Elizabeth in a group like the one Nat probably hangs with—the kind that was the first to switch from "Mexican" to "Chicano" and would be the last to refer to any female out of braces as a "girl." Nat's friends, as a matter of fact, consider him "fortunate in a left-handed way to be able to observe Liz's transformation. They also kid him good-naturedly, Nat says, about getting the sister he's always wanted.

The gay reaction, Liz reports, is usually positive. "A lot of Austin gays can accept me. Austin has a fairly enlightened gay community, and because they understand themselves so well they can be quite friendly with straights and not put them on edge. They think of me as not completely straight but not gay either. But they understand. Although some gays may react negatively because I'm going to cut off their love object.

"Most men I'd go for are not fairy-like. I don't get off at all to the nelly type." Her ideal mate would share her spiritual interests and believe that marriage is absolutely sacred. Liz yearns for children and would like to adopt two.

Whether Liz will find love anywhere along the spectrum of response she's experienced, from vilification to acceptance, remains to be seen. At present it is a dream for the future. Her current reality consists more of hostility, curiosity, and running debates on "What constitutes a *real* woman?" and "Why is a body important?" and "When will transsexuals realize that they're just adopting the trappings of womanhood?"

Liz doesn't expect love or even acceptance yet. "All I ask

is, don't disrespect me. After trying everything else, I just feel I've got to do what I've got to do.

"I know that clothes and makeup do not a woman make. But I *am* a woman. The sight of my body being a man outrages me. I am more comfortable now taking hormones, but I still cannot be content until I am as much of a woman as medical science can make me. I think of myself as a woman, not a man. I *am* a woman, not a man."

Ready, Set, Go-Go!

TEXAS MONTHLY, JUNE 2009

I recently watched a documentary about a camp for kids whose entire lives had been devoted to getting into show business. When these kids played peeka-boo, they did Bob Fosse jazz hands; their first sentences consisted of the words "start spreading the news." Seeing how hard they worked—singing and dreaming and tapping their tiny hearts out—made me feel really crappy, because for me, getting into show business had been a breeze. Seriously. I was eighteen, and I did it without ever strumming a solitary guitar chord, without ever spinning a plate, without ever hitting a single note on-key—without, in fact, having any discernible talent whatsoever. I owe it all to one man: Joey Moynihan.

It was the late '60s, the summer after my first year of college, and I was visiting my family at Kadena Air Base on Okinawa, an island in the middle of the East China Sea. A fortress of the American military was a very odd place for me to end up. I was a newly minted hippie with official Trotskyite-in-training glasses and jeans with a peace sign embroidered onto the frayed hind end. My father, a colonel running the tiny island's military school system, described this particular fashion choice as "Your ass is hanging out."

I enjoyed doing three things while there. The first was holding my father responsible for the Vietnam War; the second was haranguing my mother about purchasing white sugar and informing her that she was feeding granulated death to her six children; and the third was mooning about my deliriously handsome, cheating rat of a boyfriend who was not only sleeping with all my slut-bunny girlfriends but had managed to convince me that I had gotten crab lice from the dog. (Somehow the nuns back at my old school never covered where either babies or crab lice really come from.)

After my mother told me that I was a giant pain in the patched ass and that anytime I felt like taking over the shopping and cooking I could just have at it, I stomped off to my bedroom to sulk. As I brooded about King Crab back in what the GIs called either "the world" or "the big PX," a deejay on Armed Forces Radio announced that there was going to be a dance contest and that the first prize was an all-expenses-paid, two-week trip to Tokyo. Every male on earth believes he has a sense of humor, and every female believes she can dance. The fact that I'd slopped around the floor a few times was enough to make me believe that I was a shoo-in. Suitably deluded, I signed up for the contest.

The judge was a stumpy fireplug of a man named Joey Moynihan, a comedian who dreamed of being Bob Hope, and he was looking for his Joey Heatherton, a dumb blonde to use as a foil during his act. Joey aspired to a Rat Pack coolness that translated into suits with a sinister midnight sheen, a diamond horseshoe pinkie ring, Wolfman Jack hair slicked straight back with Vitalis, and frequent drenchings in Brut cologne. His Filipino manager, Mickey,

turned out to be fond of patronizing prostitutes and sending his wife back in Manila 3-D postcards of the Blessed
Virgin Mary that made it appear that the Holy Mother was
crushing a serpent beneath her bare foot.

The contest was held at the base's Teen Center. Mickey
put on an album I'd brought containing the most dance-
able song of the day, "Brown Eyed Girl" by Van Morrison.
Because of my talent at being Caucasian, female, and of
legal age on an island where that combination was rare,
I won the contest.

My mother knew of a seamstress who lived far beyond
the barbed-wire fence encircling Kadena in a small vil-
lage set amongst a field of habu grass. The shoulder-high
grass was named for the venomous pit vipers that slithered
through its leafy confines. With only a photo torn from a
copy of *Seventeen* magazine to guide her, the talented
young woman stitched up a suitably fringed dress for me,
and I was off to Tokyo.

I spent two weeks with Joey and Mickey touring the
military clubs around Tokyo where, instead of a record
player, I was expected to dance along to whatever songs
the band could play that weren't "Moon River" or "Chatta-
nooga Choo Choo." The first night, I danced to the musical
stylings of Watty Watanabe and the Nabe Notes as they
played "Baby Elephant Walk" and "Watermelon Man," the
two most undanceable songs ever composed, except for
what the band played at the club the next night: "I Dig Rock
'n' Roll Music." It was impossible to explain to Joey that,
although a song might contain the words "rock and roll" in
the title, it was still, essentially, a folk song and, as such,
was impossible to dance to.

For his own Borscht Belt reasons, Joey called me Zelda.
I recall exactly one joke from his "act": "I'm gettin' old. I'm

gettin' old. Just this afternoon I was chasin' Zelda here around the room, and when I finally caught her, I couldn't remember why I was chasin' her." Rim shot, followed by my vaudeville look of maidenly outrage.

Years later, I ended up writing a novel that centered on my two weeks in show business, and afterward I found out that most people assumed I'd danced in a cage. I'd like to set the record straight: This bird was never caged. Or even shod. Though go-go boots were very popular among the lovely Okinawan ladies of the night, it was impossible to find a pair large enough to fit my Paul Bunyan–esque feet. So no cage, no go-go boots, and, most important of all, no skanky behavior. Even my employer believed that "go-go" was hippie-speak for "do me." Joey informed me regularly that he "shot blanks," as if my fear of giving birth to a pinkie-ringed Wolfman Jack baby was the lone reason I didn't succumb to his stumpy-armed embrace.

On the last night of the tour, knowing that I would never see Joey again, I asked him if it was possible to get crab lice from a dog. In retrospect, I admire his restraint when he told me that, no, this was not possible, and added, "Whoever told you that is a real jaboni" and that I could do better. He, for example, was available.

That night, while the house band tootled through the drunken blats and trills of "Baby Elephant Walk," I sang "Brown Eyed Girl" to myself and danced to the music in my head as I thought about my faithless boyfriend back in "the world." I popped and twirled the fringe on the dress sewn by a girl who lived amid pit vipers. I made my dance a prayer to the Blessed Virgin Mary—the one who saved the world from sin by crushing a serpent beneath her bare feet.

And I added some jazz hands.

My Surprise Wedding

MODERN BRIDE, DECEMBER 2009

I can't exactly say why I never wanted to be married. Maybe it was growing up in a large, rampaging family where one spouse did all the cooking, cleaning, shopping and child-rearing, and the other took out the garbage. The empirical data led me to conclude that marriage was a raw deal.

Besides which, given my temperamental proclivity toward the massive freak-out, my wedding would have been a catered nervous breakdown waiting to happen. So, although in theory I liked the idea of a gorgeous dress and a big party, I had to say thanks but no thanks to that Bridge to Indentured Servitude and get on with some serious shacking up.

I might still be living in sin to this day had issues of major deductibility not intervened. When an old back injury flared up and surgery looked imminent, George and I had to produce a marriage license before I could be added to his employer's group plan. And since we were both a little grumpy about having our lives dictated by the insurance industry, we didn't tell anyone.

My back healed, we used the money we would have blown on letterpressed invitations and a beaded cathedral train as a down payment on a sweet little house, and we carried on with our sweet little life together. Still, every time I listened to a wedding-planning friend debate the pros and cons of a chocolate fountain versus an espresso station, I experienced a tiny pang. Those *New York Times* fairy tales about some impossibly romantic union always made me a bit wistful, especially when I thought of how the write-up of my own special day would have read:

"The groom, double-parked on his lunch hour, helped his fiancé crabwalk up the steps of the courthouse. The bride was wearing sweat pants and hadn't washed her hair in a week. The groom sported an Ultimate Frisbee T-shirt and flip-flops. The county clerk slid a Declaration of Informal Marriage across the counter and said, 'That will be $7.50.' The groom pulled out his wallet, slapped down $3.75, looked at the bride, asked, 'Where's your half?,' and then they released the doves."

Three blissful years later, we began revealing our dirty secret: We were legal. Since this was Austin, Texas—a city whose ethos is captured by the bumper sticker "Keep Austin Weird"—no one blinked. Cohabitation. Marriage. Whatever. And wasn't that what I wanted? Still, when my three best friends from grad school—Mary Ellen, Nancy and Judy—invited us to dinner right after the announcement, my heart leapt. Then it sank when they added, "Oh, yeah, it's potluck. Bring a green salad." No mention was made of my marriage.

On Potluck Day, George and I knocked at Mary Ellen's door. My hair was still dripping wet from the shower, I had cramps, oil from the salad dressing had leaked onto my shorts and I was depressed because I'd gotten married and no one cared. And I was supposed to not care either.

Then the front door swung open, and I wondered if Midol might have hallucinogenic properties. Sixty friends wearing old bridesmaids' dresses and funky tuxedos from Goodwill jumped out of hiding and yelled, "Surprise!"

Still blinking, gasping, and close to needing defibrillation, I was relieved of the salad and whisked away for bridal adornment. Mary Ellen had the gown all picked out: hers. Fortunately the elegantly simple, V-neck, ivory dress was not only exactly what I would have chosen, but also made of God's one-size-fits-all gift to the Disco Era, ultra-stretchy Quiana fabric. Other than being half a foot shorter on me than on my friend, the dress was perfect. George donned an iridescent midnight-blue tux jacket that any lounge singer worth his ruffled cuffs would have killed for.

The theme chosen by my fairy godmothers was: "Your Wedding Cake, Flowers, and All the Decorations Came from the Grocery Store. And They're All Blue." There was an extravaganza of a sugar and Crisco cake that even had a bride and groom topper. The napkins were printed with swirly script that read, "Sarah and George: Just Married All These Years." A deaf international lesbian celebrity spoken-word artist performed the "ceremony." Reading from one of the romance novels I'd cranked out to pay the mortgage, she asked if I would pledge to honor the "swollen evidence" of George's "male desire." And if George would swear equal devotion to the "aching chasm" of Sarah's "secret delta of womanhood."

George and I promised that we do, we would.

Corks popped, bubbly flowed and there was laughter and good wishes. In the joyous faces that surrounded me, I finally saw just how much I needed to be feted, to have my marriage marked and celebrated by pals who were as happy as I was that I had found the right person to share my life with. I loved my surprise wedding. The biggest surprise, though, was finding out the surprising need it filled.

Princess of the Oil Rigs

CAMPUS VOICE, APRIL–MAY 1986

I suppose if you're not a man and if you are going to intrude upon a man's world, you really ought to do it by seaplane and helicopter.

That, at any rate, is what I'm thinking as we taxi down one of the numerous canals that worm through the Mississippi Delta. What with the soggy August heat and the curtains of green bamboo on either side of the canal, we could just as easily be skidding along the Amazon, trying to get the pontoon plane airborne before headhunters reach us.

We glide into the air, ascending as cleanly as the cattle egrets that flap beside us like a row of freshly washed sheets drying on a line. "How long you been flying?" I ask the pilot, a dapper and tanned fellow in his early sixties.

"Longer'n you been breathing," he laughs. "I flew for the Navy in the war. What're you going offshore for?"

Offshore. Around the Gulf of Mexico, in small Louisiana towns like Thibodaux, Venice, and Houman, life is divided into two parts. "The Beach" is that half lived with family on solid earth. "Offshore" represents the working half, isolated on an oil platform out in the petroleum-rainbowed waters of the Gulf for seven, fourteen, even twenty-one days at a time.

I raise my voice above the rush of wind. "I'm going to interview a petroleum-engineering student, Cheryl Henneford. She's working offshore for the summer."

"A gal?" The pilot's eyebrows jerk up and he grins, a fly-boy grin still jaunty after four decades. "Got to give them gals credit."

As we sweep out over the Gulf, a haze blends sky and water into one phlegm-colored blur. It's punctuated by an endless progression of metal structures, some of the nearly two thousand oil platforms squatting down in the Gulf, busily sucking up what the dinosaurs left behind.

All the tales of offshore labor I've ever heard come back to me, most of them making Devil's Island sound like a Club Med vacation. Sure, the money's good. But you work twelve hard, dirty hours a day under a killing sun with men who, more likely than not, consider reading a dangerously subversive habit.

And this is where Cheryl Henneford, 21, a junior from Montana Tech, has chosen to spend her summer vacation? Though women have been working offshore for a decade, they are still interlopers in what remains an overwhelmingly blue-collar, Southern, white male world. Stories abound about how women are welcomed offshore: with slurs, innuendoes, hostility, relentless come-ons, and pranks—like tacking their stolen panties to the platform bulletin board and drilling peepholes into their showers. I wonder how Cheryl has been accepted.

Conoco's Platform 45CQ looks minuscule from the air. Once we touch down, though, the place grows. It is painted safety yellow except for the silver intestines that coil through the rig, filled with some of the 4,000 barrels of oil that Conoco pumps from this platform each day.

As I wait for Cheryl, field supervisor Dan Southworth tells me that he has fifty people working for him. About 90 percent of them are southerners. Only one woman is employed year-round. Working hours are from six in the morning until six at night. As we talk, men pass by in the hallway outside. Large men. American-flag patches and tattoos are popular fashion accessories. Then, from behind this beefy, oil-grimed crew emerges a porcelain doll in a hard hat.

When they get around to crowning the Princess of the Platforms, Cheryl Henneford will win it in a walk. Five feet four inches tall, 120 pounds. Curly golden hair. Bottomless blue eyes. Perfect white teeth. Flawless peach skin. She's wearing blue jeans and a T-shirt that counsels HAVE A GOLDEN DAY. What is this person doing here?

Well, Cheryl answers, as she takes me on a tour around the platform, at the moment she's rushing to qualify for her crane operator's license before she leaves to return to Montana the day after tomorrow. I lag behind as she scampers up and down stairways and catwalks in her doll-size steel-toed safety boots and points out the galley, the dispatcher's office, and the men's quarters. (We're not allowed in that area, just as no men are allowed near the "ladies' room.") Everywhere we go, hungry eyes peering out from under hard hats follow us. It's an industrial-strength version of walking into a small-town Dairy Queen and getting X-rayed by the locals.

"You've really got to watch it out here," Cheryl tells me when we're alone. "Everyone's always checking you out. It could get bad, depending on how you carry yourself. I'm not the type who flirts."

Cheryl is, however, the type who would spend part of her previous summer vacation in the Dominican Republic helping her physician father provide medical care. Who would consider the 230-mile ride from her family home in Billings, Montana, to her college town of Butte just a fun bike outing. Who would live her life by uncompromising Christian standards. It is those standards and her demeanor, Cheryl asserts, that make her co-workers regard her as more of a little sister than a romantic possibility. I remember the decidedly *un*-brotherly gazes, and I wonder.

After a lunch of meatloaf, hot dogs wrapped in bacon, red beans and rice, canned green beans, cornbread, sweetened tea, and unlimited cake, ice cream, and pie, we continue the tour. Once we cross the catwalk from the living quarters to the working platform, we have to stop our ears with lime-green earplugs to shut out the noise, ceaseless and as loud as a jet taking off.

Amid the great loops of steel and the dwarfing machinery that pull oil from under the sea, Cheryl comes alive in a way she hadn't before. "Your nuts and bolts are over here," she says, pointing to rows of bins with labels like ¼ NPT HEX NIPPLES and ¼ FEMALE BRANCH TREE. "All that quarter-inch stainless-steel line is part of your safety system. And this is your pilot rack." She leads me to a panel of gauges with a Medusa's crown of tiny pipes snaking away from it. It's part of her job—along with swabbing the deck and checking and repairing gears, cables, oil filters, and bearings—to read these and dozens of other gauges every day and to make sense of what they say.

Starting with a basic premise—oil floats on water—she somehow manages to make the whole complicated separation process seem like something I could duplicate in my own kitchen, should the urge ever strike.

"I didn't even know what a pipe wrench was when I first came out here," Cheryl marvels, genuinely thrilled about her new understanding of flow-rate charts and the gravity and sediment rate of oil.

The desire to spend a summer offshore began with a yearning to learn everything she could about "getting your oil out of the ground." The $2,300 she grosses each month with overtime, and the $30,000 to $35,000 starting salary she'll probably earn as a petroleum engineer when she graduates, genuinely seem secondary to her passion to understand the machinery around us. "A lot of PEs [petroleum engineers] are real smart academically, but they have no common sense. I want to know what it is and how it works," she says.

By this time, I'm parched in a way that only standing on metal in the middle of the Gulf of Mexico under an August sun can make you. As we walk back to the galley, I ask about the problems Cheryl has had in working with men who for the most part make Rambo look like a sissy.

"They're always testing you," she says. "Like when I first got here, they told me to go change the spark plugs on a diesel engine. Luckily I just happened to know there aren't any plugs on a diesel engine. I just go with it and try to do what they ask. I want to be taken seriously, so I have to pull my own weight."

Contrary to the tales of merciless harassment I'd heard, all Cheryl can report is that someone once sneaked into her room and left a dirty magazine under her pillow. "Basically, I guess, the Lord was just watching out for me and put me on a real good platform." Halfway to the galley, we run into field supervisor Southworth, and I ask how well he feels his summer engineer has been accepted. "She's our little queen. We respect and love her," he says. "She's caused some attitude adjustment among the troops out here. It's because she's very straightforward in explaining her standards, and the men knew right away what she expected. They're not tormented, if you understand what I'm saying, because the possibility just isn't there."

I answer that I would have imagined that everyone on the platform would be in love with Cheryl. Southworth considers that for a moment, then comments, "They probably are."

By the time we reach the galley I've almost decided that Cheryl has managed the miracle of cracking some of the toughest chauvinists around. And I can understand how. Christianity is one creed that these men understand and respect. Her beliefs reinforce the shield of dewy innocence that glistens around her, making it all but bulletproof. Lewdly propositioning Cheryl would be like contemplating unnatural acts with Bambi.

It's cool and dark in the galley, and I'm starting on my second gallon of tea when the men, dressed in coveralls with the arms cut out to show off their tattooed biceps, begin filtering in. They sit at other tables, pretending to ignore us while in fact hanging on to our every word. I turn to a nearby table. One fellow listens with a particular avidity. He has pocked skin, crooked teeth, and the look of a runt who's had to scratch everything he's gotten from life with strappy muscle and a scrappy will. I ask him how he feels about having women on the platform.

He looks around at his *compañeros*, fixes his mouth into a scowl, and answers, "Ain't got no business out here. No place for 'em. They done ruint everything. Cain't talk like we want to. Cain't act like we want to. Cain't cuss. Cain't take a leak off the side and not have one of 'em looking at you. But the main thing is, they cain't tote the load. They cain't do the work. With 'em around we don't get no work done, neither. All the guys just gather round them and want to talk."

Cheryl's eyes widen at this diatribe. I turn to the fellow's buddy, a handsome man with a dimpled smile, and ask if he agrees. He nods vigorously and answers, "Hunnert and one percent. Ain't but three kinds of women come out here—drunks, prostitutes, and divorcées."

"Don't forget your lesbians and your dropouts," Pitface supplies. I ask what a dropout is. "That's your woman who likes partying and guys. Your mouthy kind of hussy."

"I'd say," his partner interjects, "that the majority of women who've come out here, their bodies move 'em up. Every woman out here in this oil field has had an affair."

"I haven't," Cheryl protests.

The man gives her his dimpled smile. "You ain't left yet." He turns back to me. "An oil field ain't good for nobody, but especially not for women. The ideal woman for an oil field is big and strong and ugly as homemade sin and works like the devil. That way she wouldn't have no crowd around her, nobody following her around like a puppy dog."

An older man who's been hanging back, listening, comes forward. "I been working this field since the '50s. We done real well without women for thirty years, and we don't need 'em now. Deep down, most hands feel the way I do. Women just get in the way on a platform."

"Even Cheryl?" I ask.

Pitface leans back and appraises Cheryl, who is still slightly agog at resentments that have never been expressed so directly during her stay here. "Cheryl is very much the exception," comes the judgment. "She works more'n any woman I've ever seen out here. If you sent fifty more women, you wouldn't find another one like her. Most summer hands won't work physically. They won't do the nasty work. Cheryl'll do the whole nine yards."

Dimples decides to put in his personnel evaluation. "Her attitude's changed since she's been out here. At first, someone'd cuss and she'd vanish. Now her eyes just get real big." He gives Cheryl an indulgent, paternal smile. "Cheryl's special. You can credit that to her religious background."

"Cheryl makes you think there's hope for the world." This is the first we've heard from a quiet fellow who's worked most closely with Cheryl throughout the summer.

The others laugh at Shy Guy's comment. "Don't pay no attention to him," they advise me. "He's in love."

The next morning, as I'm heading toward the waiting helicopter, I spy Cheryl saying goodbye to one of the men. She thanks him for all he's taught her that summer, then embraces him. It's probably not the first hug ever exchanged on 45CQ, but there couldn't have been many others. The huggee walks away beaming. In her free hand Cheryl is clutching the cross-stitch sampler she's working on. It reads I AM THE LIGHT OF THE WORLD, the words surrounded by apple blossoms.

Slouching over a nearby railing are several of the hands who'd given me their uncensored opinions the day before. They watch the hug—maybe a little puzzled, probably a little jealous, about a gesture that in their world represents foreplay. Then they turn away—definitely still disgruntled—and stare forlornly down into the water they will soon be able to piss into at will.

Silver Pins and Golden Tresses

THIRD COAST, 1987

T here are many stations on a woman's journey to middle age. One of the more popular stops is called Highlighting Your Hair. I made that little jaunt myself recently. It seems to be particularly favored by women like myself who were once blond but whose hair has faded over the years to a color closer to that of garden mulch.

I knew the dangers going in. We've all seen how a few subtle golden streaks can mutate into a full-blown bleach job. Not only that: I'd heard rumors about the process itself, about an excruciating operation involving a bathing cap and knitting needles.

No, no, frosted friends assured me, that's outmoded technology. There's a new, pain-free method in which the strands to be lightened are "painted," then gently wrapped in tinfoil.

I was still skeptical, but quickly lost all caution with the blinding prospect of recapturing the summery tresses of a lost youth. Plus I spotted a special in the paper, a coupon for half-off for first-time highlighters. That pretty much clinched the deal.

The ad spoke of "subtle shimmers of gold" and "the gilded nuances of a week on a Caribbean isle." In spite of the tantalizing imagery, I made and broke three appointments before I finally ventured in. Neon lights coursed through the salon like a pastel circulatory system pumped by an anonymous rock beat. A low-lying cloud of hair spray fouled my glasses. A tall, clear glass vase with black marbles at its base stood next to the reception desk, holding a bouquet of predatory-looking lilies.

"Angie'll be right with you," I was informed.

I thought my appointment was supposed to be with someone named Terry, but I didn't say anything.

A few minutes later a woman in her very early twenties, possibly even late teens, her hair hennaed to a vivid orange and slashed into an asymmetrical cut, bounced out, said, "Hi! I'm Angie," and handed me a peach-colored smock.

"Highlighting, right?" Angie asked. She had the tightly packed physique of an aerobics instructor, the sort that looks like she'd bounce if dropped from a fifth-story window. Angie produced a board with several dozen tiny swatches of different-colored hair attached, then compared my hair to the Barbie scalps.

"That looks pretty close," I offered as she considered the match with Medium Golden Blond.

"No," Angie disagreed, "yours is a lot more drabby. It's this one here."

She was right. Medium Ash Blond was a perfect match, perfectly "drabby." But I'd already taken the first step; I'd admitted I was sick. Now came the fun part: choosing the highlight shade. I directed Angie's attention back to the Golden Blonds, and we settled on a deliriously sun-kissed hue. Then, clutching the Before-and-After strands, Angie mysteriously disappeared. In the mirror, I watched her consult with another stylist. Angie listened so intently and in such a deferential way that the student-teacher relationship became obvious.

As I let the realization that mine might be the first head of hair that Angie had every highlighted sink in, I picked up snatches of conversation from the chairs around me.

"The doctor told her she'd have to stop eating so much salt. But she just said she couldn't eat food if it didn't have salt on it. She's only in her fifth month now and she's gained eighty pounds. Eighty pounds!"

"You really can't ever go back to the person you left because the reason you left them is still there."

"If you know it's only going to be for a couple of days, you can exist on just a few calories. My problem is when it goes more than a few days."

Angie bounced back, carrying a pile of crinkling plastic. "Okay, let's highlight that hair!" I grinned, trying to get with her *Yay, team!* attitude, but my grin faded when she pulled out something that bore an alarming resemblance to a bathing cap. She popped it on my head and tied it under my chin tight enough to dam up my jugular. The skullcap made me look like Copernicus. Still, I didn't say anything until Angie produced a gigantic knitting needle. As she poised the implement over my head, I finally spoke.

"Uh, isn't there another way of doing this? Something involving tinfoil?"

Angie sighed and let the needle slump to her side, completely deflated and bewildered by my question. "Are you here for highlighting or naturalizing?"

"Highlighting?" I answered hesitantly.

Angie brightened and raised her weapon again. "Okay, this is how you highlight."

I asked if she could use the tinfoil method anyway. Angie sighed, undone again: "Well, sure, I can do that, but it's not on the special. Naturalizing is full price." Unable to overcome the bargain chromosome that is the dominant part of my genetic code, I told Angie to proceed. "It really doesn't hurt much," she promised me.

The knitting needle descended, punched a hole in the plastic cap, snagged a strand of hair, and yanked it out. It hurt like all get out. The scream I strangled came out as a tiny little mouse shriek.

Angie winced sympathetically. "Well, actually," she fessed up, "with hair as long as yours, it does sort of hurt. But I'll go real quick." She then began to peck at my scalp like a chicken on PCP. (If you'd like to recreate this feeling in the privacy of your own home, simply take a steel comb of the sort used to groom unkempt sheepdogs and drive it deeply into your skull.) Not since the last time I'd listened to Andy Rooney on *Sixty Minutes*, when he shared his belief that "vegetarian" is an old Indian word for "lousy hunter," had I willingly endured so much pain.

Finally, Angie had about a hundred strands of hair sprouting from the cap. At that point she slathered a foamy concoction on the exposed wisps with a paintbrush. The smell stunned me the way that only a hefty whiff of ammonia right out of the bottle can, stopping my breath in my chest for a few seconds. After a few minutes, Angie rubbed some of the foam off and inspected the hair underneath. She stared at it for a long time, then called over her instructor, whose name, I learned, was "Terry"—the person my appointment was supposed to have been with.

Terry barely glanced at the foam-covered strand. "It's not ready. *All* the color's got to be stripped."

Stripped? What were they saying? All the color stripped?

Terry fingered the foamy tufts and added, "You're doing good. It's hard starting with hair this long."

Starting? So this was *the first highlight for both of us.*

I imploded into totally contained panic a few minutes later when the foam was rinsed off and the extruded wisps of hair were as white as Andy Warhol's. I gave no outward sign that beneath my plastic bonnet I was quietly coming unglued: I had bleached hair, there was no way around it. The nearly transparent tendrils wafted about my head like fiber-optical cable. Where were the "subtle shimmers of gold"? This had the "gilded nuances" of a week at an atomic testing site.

Angie brought Terry in for another consult, and another concoction was slathered on the abused wisps. This goo was the color and consistency of molten taffy. Another knockout whiff of ammonia assaulted me before the whole mess was wrapped up in plastic and I was shunted off to a dryer.

"You should be done in 45 minutes."

Angie handed me a copy of *American Salon*. With a three-year-old *Prevention* magazine as my only other choice, I accepted. It started right off with a message from publisher Robert Mugnai.

"When we speak of profits in the salon, I instantly think, 'Perms!' And this issue is chock-full of perms—perms for resistant hair, perms for tinted hair, and perms for damaged hair.

"Why so much emphasis on perms?" publisher Mugnai asked. "Because you—America's all-American salon owner readers—tell us perms are one of your most profitable services."

Mr. Mugnai went on to report on a survey which revealed

that half of the stylist's customers were "receiving perm services." I was pretty impressed by that figure. Not so Mr. Mugnai.

"What are you doing about the other 'unpermed' 50 percent?" he demanded to know of slacker stylists. "What steps are you taking to convert those 'straights'?"

Mr. Mugnai promised an issue full of marketing ideas to "get the ball rolling" in those goldbricking salons where inspiration was needed to "capture this ticket-building business!"

He closed with this question: "Shouldn't every client be wearing the perm professionally prescribed for them by you? When you figure that the price of perms is anywhere from a low of $25 to upward of $100, that's good business.

"Salon business.

"Your business."

I wondered how Mr. Mugnai had exhorted his readership last month. Had he started off, "When we speak of profits in the salon, I instantly think 'highlighting'"? Had he gone on to include features with titles like "Using Coupons to Drag the Drabbies In" and "Telling the Client It Won't Hurt"?

I was already unsettled when I came to an article that dealt with "Perming Dimensionally Colored Hair." The first thing I learned was that even as I read, my hair was being "dimensionally colored." It meant highlighting, frosting, naturalizing, and a whole world of "professionally prescribed coloring services." What I found upsetting was this little nugget: "Problem: Our client has medium-length, medium-blond hair that's been bleach highlighted. The highlighted hair is drab and lifeless looking and lacks body and bounce."

Would it surprise you to learn that the solution to this problem was a permanent? I feared that Angie had written the letter, already knowing the fate that awaited me, her medium-length, medium-blond client, after this bleach-highlighting. I suspected a sinister plot between Angie and Robert Mugnai which would end up with me looking like Rod Stewart.

A kitchen timer went off, and Angie bounced over, flipped the dryer up, and poked at my hair. She summoned Terry and they both poked. Finally Terry gave her nod of approval. The taffy goo was rinsed off and the cap removed. Fully expecting a hundred shafts of crispy straw to poke out, I was pleasantly surprised to see that my hair was still obeying the laws of gravity.

For far too long, Angie blew-dry, combed, and sprayed. Finally she presented her debut effort. Staring at the results, I realized then that there is a special color which, while not precisely blond, is distinctly *highlighted* blond. It's really more of a grizzling than anything else.

"It turned out good, didn't it?" Angie asked expectantly, fluffing my streaky mane.

"Oh, I love it!" I lied. I could have looked like Pepe LePew and I still wouldn't have criticized such a well-intentioned effort.

Angie continued fluffing, drawing my hair out, then studying the way it fell. "Have you ever thought about a perm?" she wondered with apparent idleness. "You know, just something to give it some fullness—a body wave. Just to add some texture. It'd look really good with the highlights."

I promised Anj I'd think about it.

Take a Strutting, Stomping Twelve-Day Vacation from Your Life

OPRAH, NOVEMBER 2002

As a woman, you almost always want to dance more than the men around you do. At a certain age, those few men who might have danced with you have all achieved the only dance objective they ever had—acquisition of a steady sex partner. You might even be that partner. You might even have a child, a mortgage, a dog, two—God help you, two!—Volvos. In any case, the man in your life doesn't want to dance anymore. And why should he? You have no desire to scream at television sets broadcasting football games. We must all answer to our own passions.

Desperate, you turn to partnerless dance mutations—Salsacize, sweating to oldies, Cardio Hip-Hop, Yo! Yo! Yoga!, and the saddest of all dance substitutes, tap. You even consider belly dancing, but immediately think better of it.

And then you discover "it": you discover flamenco.

What a revelation this passionate, fiery, aerobically enriching dance form is! You don't need a partner, and it absolutely doesn't matter how young or old or fat or thin you are. In fact you learn, to your immense delight, that some of the biggest stars of flamenco are extremely well-upholstered and very suitably seasoned. You feel this might be your last chance to grab at a life-changing soul-body experience.

Well, okay, maybe you don't, but I did—which is why I was delirious to discover that my alma mater, the University of New Mexico, hosts the International Flamenco Festival every summer. For those glorious dozen or so days, the cream of *el mundo* flamenco descends on Albuquerque to perform and teach complete novices like myself in marathon workshops that compress years of weekly classes.

Is it possible, I wondered, in that amount of time for a middle-aged woman to cut loose, shake off inhibitions and a potentially atrophied sense of rhythm, and get her flamenco groove on? I'm encouraged to learn that much emphasis is placed on hand movements and that several all-time legends went by the nickname El Cojo—"the Cripple." Still the doubts descend. I try to recall if I own anything with polka dots. And then, with a go-to-hell shrug that might be the first stirrings of my very own personal flamenco soul, I decide I have to do it. Husband and son will just have to boil their own hot dogs for twelve days. Adiós, muchachos, mamacita is going to dance! ¡Olé!

Let us pretend now that there are no husbands to convince, no boy child to pack off to camp, no dog to board, no mail to stop, no bags to pack, and no panic attacks to medicate because of this utterly insane thing I am doing. Let me be transported magically to the sun-drenched campus where I was a hip-shaking, totally happening coed.

The heart of the festival is Carlisle Gym, an adobe building the color of a baby fawn where I once fumbled through the one other dance class I've ever taken. Modern, I believe it was. I rush in, intoxicated by breathing once again the weightless, piñon-scented desert air of my youth and by being so close to the Frontier Restaurant, home to that staple of my undergraduate diet—cinnamon rolls the size of catcher's mitts. We are greeted by flamenco goddess Eva Encinias-Sandoval, program director and a radiant, unpretentious advertisement for her art.

On the first day, almost two hundred students from England, Canada, China, Mexico, Argentina, and Ukraine, and states from New Hampshire to Texas, crowd the main hallway, changing into practice skirts, putting on makeup, and taping their gnarled, wrecked feet. I hurry to my beginners' class, expecting it to be filled with other goofball novices like myself. Instead I find an ominously large number of the two dozen supposed newbies hooking pointed feet over the barre and folding themselves into the sort of stretches favored by Hindu yogis and professional dancers. I comfort myself by noting two young girls who look to be about ten. How much experience could they have?

Our instructor, renowned Santa Fe performer Ramona Garduño, sweeps in and, after a brief warm-up, introduces us to *la postura*, flamenco's powerful, chest-high, shoulders-back posture that conveys boundless female strength and speaks of the art's deep roots in the Gypsy culture. Next is *brazeo*, arm work. We start with a basic move, *la paloma*, the white dove. Imitating Ramona's sinuous hands, my doves twine heavenward. As my fingers cut delicate arabesques, *floreos*, I feel like an odalisque performing for a sultan, like a temple dancer in Bali.

Then on to the footwork. *Golpe, golpe, tacón.* Stamp, stamp, heel. *Planta, tacón, tacón, planta.* Ball, heel, heel, ball. My wondrous new flamenco skirt bounces and sways to my stomping, and I exalt in being part of this tribe of wild, clacking girls. Even if my footwork leaves something to be desired, the ballet swans have nothing on me. I was born to dance flamenco.

This delightful illusion lasts for, oh, fifteen more seconds, at which point, Ramona gives a diabolical directive: Add the hands. Hands and feet? Together? The instant I attempt to move my hands, my white doves fly the coop. I execute a series of jerky movements that look as if I'm being electrocuted. The rest of the class stamps and twines fluidly. I position myself strategically behind one of the ballet swans and attempt to imitate her. It's a lost cause.

The next day, Ramona throws increasingly difficult combinations at us. Again, my white doves take wing—until they crash and burn at that crucial moment when hands and feet are politely requested to work together. With a wild, feral grace that I covet deeply, Ramona demonstrates some steps set to a puzzling twelve-count beat called the compás. "The most important thing is to start hearing this rhythm," she says. In the crowded class, I turn the wrong way and smash into a girl who is executing combinations in perfect time to a beat I can't hear, much less dance to.

I am far and away the worst student in the class. I cement this position definitively two days later when my new best friend, Leah Powell, an archeologist working for the university, sidles over and whispers, "Do you mean to have your skirt tucked up like that?" All the cool students tuck their long skirts into their waistbands in snazzy ways—on the sides, wrapped over in front, with the ruffles cascading down in back—that each have a Spanish name. The name of my special tuck is "Showing Your Big Fat White Butt." Yes, I turn and see that I have accidentally caught the entire back of my skirt in my waistband.

I slink out of class and head to my old friend, the Frontier. Over one of the catcher-mitt-size cinnamon rolls, I toy with the idea of spending the rest of the festival right here, in this booth, setting a record for most rolls of dough and fat consumed and created. Instead I remind myself: Guess what, self? You're not—never were—planning a career on-stage. You're doing this entirely for yourself. I get a grip and do what I always do when I'm confused and demoralized: I talk to some great women and a few great men.

I start with my classmates the next day and am deeply comforted to learn that at least one of the "beginning" students teaches flamenco back home in Laredo, and that everyone except me has had at least enough dance training to know their plantas from their tacóns.

Once I start getting to know my fellow students, flamenco's true riches begin spilling out. In rapid succession, I meet a former concert guitarist, a probation and parole officer working with sex offenders, several high school kids who worship heavy metal, an English teacher from New Hampshire, a 69-year-old Argentinean, an army research psychologist, and Karen Richmond, who drives in every day from Gallup, New Mexico, where she is the business manager at a facility for the indigent elderly run by Little Sisters of the Poor.

I ask Karen what compels her to make that dusty 270-mile round-trip every day. "Pride," Karen answers without hesitation. "You don't have to be good to get that feeling of pride, and at 51 I want that for myself."

This is more addictive than the Frontier's rolls. Holding out my reporter's notebook like a passport, I quiz everyone who crosses my path.

"In flamenco, your dark side can come out," Fenny Kuo—who teaches trapeze and aerial dance to kids in San Francisco—says. "No other dance form lets you express anger, sorrow, very strong emotions."

"The only emotion you don't talk about in flamenco is timidity," says Heléna Melone, from New Hampshire, as she ices a bunion. "Western dance is a lot of smiling and being sexy for the audience. When I dance flamenco, it is for me, the singer, and the guitar player. The audience is secondary."

Local maestra Lili del Castillo sums up the essence of flamenco in two words, Yo soy—"I am." Lili stands tall and proud as she repeats the words, underscoring the profound importance of a form of self-expression that, like our own Delta blues, was given to us by outcast people whose only other possession might have been the clothes they stood in.

Then I encounter two students—a family-practice physician and a prep school student—who have each lost thirty pounds since taking up flamenco. They both emphasize that weight loss is a pleasant yet secondary by-product of their passion. This reminds me of my initial silliness in believing flamenco might be little more than the latest route to cardiovascular fitness.

For the rest of the weekend I hear the compás everywhere: in a car's transmission, in debris tossed around by a windstorm. Bit by bit, I begin to see the fiend compás as the most beneficent of forms, like haiku. Instead of seventeen syllables, the artist—dancer, singer, guitarist—is given twelve beats to express what is in her heart and to create beauty.

By Monday my muscles and brain have had two days to encode all these strange new signals, and I trample over fewer children. Tuesday is even a bit better.

On Wednesday, the last day of class, I manage to get my white doves twining heavenward while my feet move in rough time. As if applauding my tiny triumph, a mighty counter-rhythm pounds down. "It's hailing!" someone yells, and we all rush to the window, clacking in time to the staccato hammering that strips trees down to bare branches, their leaves mulch on the ground. And then, too soon, it is over. The class gives Ramona a giant bouquet of yellow roses, and we have a hard time saying goodbye—so we settle on hasta la vista, already making plans for next year.

I march off to a new beat, inhaling the glorious fragrance of desperately needed rain and battered greenery—cottonwood, piñon, spruce. And in just those moments, while I create my own twelve-beat haiku, the world seems as wondrously fresh and new-made as it did when I was a coed so long ago.

P.S. Even though it has come to seem incidental, in the interest of full disclosure I must note that, in spite of a diet heavy on the Frontier's cinnamon rolls, carne adovada burritos, and green chile enchiladas, I lost three pounds during the festival. Olé.

Buy, Buy, Birdie

TEXAS MONTHLY, APRIL 2006

Hello, my name is Sarah, and I'm a binge-purge shopper. Don't clap. I know that you, my fellow sufferers, are out there. I know because I'm behind you in line when you check out with that cart loaded as if you're fleeing the Cossacks. And I'm there behind you a week later when the clerk has to call a manager because you're returning most of the stuff and it's all been sacked, plundered, and pillaged. Oh, yeah, I'm watching while you try to convince them that the giant sweat stain in the armpit of that blouse was there when you bought it.

I understand. Believe me, I understand. I have made that round-trip more times than I care to recall and many more times than El Hubbo, the Hub of My Universe, can believe. Men don't return. Their feeling about the black-and-yellow windowpane-plaid suit the salesman at Men's Wearhouse talked them into buying is "Hey, dude, you skunked me. Good one. Couple more sixers and it won't fit anyway."

For women, it's another story. A story of hope and heartbreak. Of new beginnings and gaucho pants that make our butts look as if we need a couple of years on the pampas.

It is a story that almost always involves the bane, and something else that is the opposite of bane and starts with a *b*, of our existence: clothes. Fortunately, within my own personal retail triangle—Ross ("Dress for Less"), Target ("Expect More, Pay Less"), T. J. Maxx ("One More X and You Could Buy Pasties Here!")—returns are easy, frequently bilingual ("Regresar o cambiar?"), and can sometimes even be Biggie Sized.

Thankfully, most stores no longer ask that most humiliating of all questions: "Reason for return?" I guess they got tired of hearing: "It didn't match the shoes I bought it to go with"; "My husband didn't like it"; "The mirrors in your dressing room exist in a parallel universe called Slimbovia"; "The cruel depravity of the merchandising monolith forces me to hate myself and my life and to believe that only a fifty-five-hundred-dollar Hermès Birkin bag will redeem my pathetic sham of an existence. Yet, even after purchase of said bag, I continue to wallow in a mire of self-loathing."

Ladies' fashion is nothing if not a fantasy inside an illusion wrapped in a thong. Every season, there is a new "look," a new "trend," a new "paranoid schizophrenic thought disorder." One of the longest-running delusions foisted upon a gullible public is this: You, vulnerable shopper, are a member of the preppy elite. You must immediately purchase clothing appropriate for playing polo, attending a clambake on Cape Cod, yachting in the Hamptons, and having illicit assignations in someone's boathouse. Ralph Lauren built an empire and sold a lot of navy crewneck sweaters on this very premise.

Touch football at Hyannisport not doing it for you? Try this current fashion fantasy: You are a heroin-addicted New York supermodel. All your clothes have shrunk. Now, get into those tiny togs and hit the runway!

Then there were the dress-for-success years, when everyone thought it a swell idea to dress up in little man suits. I fell for this one during a particularly deluded and vulnerable period. I actually bought a handsome three-piece business suit in spite of the fact that I worked at home, had a colicky baby, and the only "business meetings" I conducted were with a lactation consultant. That three-piece number was my sad defense against the reality that all I really needed in my closet at that point was one urp-resistant sweat suit. So back the delusional purchases went. Buyer's remorse? It's my middle name.

Why do I, do any of us, give in to these ridiculous fantasies? Because something happens in that dressing room. Something that causes my soul to cry out for a wee, tiny jacket that looks as if it came off an organ-grinder's monkey. Something that convinces me that sometime in my immediate future I will need a neohippie outfit with more gauzy, flowing bits than Stevie Nicks in concert. Something that makes me believe I will actually be able to sit down in a pair of low-rise jeans without joining the plumbers' union. Then the gas wears off and I wake up back at home wondering what the hell I'm doing with a pair of harem pants. Why harem pants? The sultan is not going to be summoning me anytime soon. And this long khaki skirt? Do I think I'm going on safari?

Again, I have used fashion as a defense against reality, which is that I'm a suburban mom and 99 percent of my fashion needs can be filled by a couple of sturdy pairs of relaxed-fit (i.e., capacious in the can) Dockers. That's why my mantra is "Don't take the tags off." There are those craven few who would exploit the returns line, bringing back bridal gowns pelted with rice, prom dresses marinated in Bacardi Breezers and K-Y jelly. A friend who owns a store even told me about a returner so notorious she was banned from shops around town. After the ban, the repeat returner forced her nanny (yes, nanny!) to attempt to take back flip-flops with dirt ground into them, skirts with the hems ripped out, and Earth Shoes from the '70s. Me, I'm just looking to trade in a few dressing room delusions.

Because can anything compare to that moment when a pair of shoes Torquemada could have used in the Spanish Inquisition and a denim blouse that makes you look like a fugitive from a chain gang are transformed back into pure potential? You've hit the fashion reset button. It's one of life's few do-overs. It feels as if the retail gods just gave you a gift certificate, a pat on the back, and an encouraging "Nix on the Stevie Nicks, but try again." And so you do, until the pattern of "try on, take home, return" becomes a Möbius strip, an endless repeating loop. In fact, I'm still working through a credit voucher on an ill-considered culottes purchase back in junior high.

Is there any way to stop this insidious gorge-disgorge cycle? Yes. Women, henceforth we must vow to purchase only sensible clothing that fits well and is totally functional. We must stop wasting time and money being slaves to fashion fantasies that don't match the reality of our lives. Chairman Mao had the right idea. We'll each have two pajama-looking outfits. One for summer. One for winter. In black. With a little cap. And our hair in braids. Or maybe a bowl cut.

Who am I kidding? I'm taking this idea back. Reason for return? None of your damn business.

Neck and Neck

TEXAS MONTHLY, NOVEMBER 2006

G rowing up, the high points of my month were the "Can This Marriage Be Saved?" feature in my mother's *Ladies' Home Journal* and Nora Ephron's column in my father's *Esquire*. LHJ generally advised women to "make it work" at any cost—to hang on like a barnacle no matter what kind of low-life, cheating dog he was. Nora, on the other hand, pointed the way to a world so large, so filled with possibilities, that marriage might or might not even be part of it.

Which is why I was cheering when her new collection of essays, *I Feel Bad About My Neck: And Other Thoughts on Being a Woman*, hit number one on the *New York Times* bestseller list. I eagerly helped her out with my own purchase, even though, page for page, the slender volume was the most expensive book I've ever bought. (Twenty-two dollars with tax for 137 pages? State secrets have sold for less.) I hoarded my delicacy until I had time to savor what the reviews were hailing as a triumph of wit and honesty. Nora said the collection was her antidote to those "happy face" tracts that claimed we weren't getting older, we were getting better, and that if we'd just embrace our inner crone, we'd all be having more sex than a boar mink as we rolled into our sixties and seventies.

When I finally dived into the book, I was eager for Nora to work her magic the way she had with her early-seventies essays (the famous one about breasts, for instance; in that piece, you started off reading about mammaries and ended up watching Nora hammerlock the culture with an A cup). As the possessor of a fine turkey-gobbler wattle, I couldn't wait to see how she'd wring the neck of neck wrinkles and iron them out into a metaphor that revealed the larger picture.

I read the whole collection in two hours, and guess what? Neck wrinkles are a giant metaphor for . . . neck wrinkles. Really. Nora doesn't like 'em. And the larger picture? She doesn't think she's a good candidate for plastic surgery, so she wears black turtlenecks—a lot—as do all her friends within the few micrometers of Manhattan she fetishistically details. At least they do when they're not hiding what God has furrowed with chokers and Hermès scarves. On the front cover of the book is a jar of wrinkle cream. On the back is a photo of Nora wearing one of her black turtlenecks, pulled up so that only a chadorlike slice of her eyes shows. In between, she kvetches about purses, fading eyesight, unwanted body hair, Botox, and the disappearance of her favorite cabbage strudel.

The black turtlenecks, though, were what really stuck in my wattled craw—but why? After all, I love me some enhancements: hair dye, nail polish, exfoliants, lip plumper, makeup (hand me my trowel). Even plastic surgery; the day they take out pain, expense, and risk of death and put a face-lift in handy pill form, sign me up.

I was still puzzling over this question when the news

came that Ann Richards had died. Like the rest of the state and the nation, I could not stop staring at those piercing turquoise eyes, that white tornado of hair, the blinding grin. But mostly I studied her glorious and gloriously exposed collection of shar-pei-quality neck wrinkles. And then it hit me: Real Texas Women don't wear black turtlenecks. If neck wrinkles bothered a Real Texas Woman as much as they bother Nora and her bescarfed friends, she'd go out and find the best plastic surgeon around, have the damn lift, and throw a party to show it off. Or she'd get herself something a lot bigger to worry about, like taming a frontier or being governor or becoming one of the greatest female singers in the history of rock and roll. (Janis Joplin, you freed more women from undergarments and hair straightener than you will ever know.)

I don't think a Real Texas Woman would do quite so much of what Nora herself calls "dancing around the D word" (that would be "death"). She'd take the wrinkles and the sags, the wattles and the bags, for the extremely useful reminders they are—that at this great banquet of life, those of us wondering where we put our reading glasses are a lot closer to the dessert cart than we are to the pupu platter. If that woman is Ann Richards, she would probably get up, go back for seconds and thirds, then bring a bunch of the best stuff back to the table for everyone to share. And if—in spite of being born in (shudder!) California—she's one of the Realest Texas Women Ever, if she's Molly Ivins, and she's lost her hair to chemotherapy, she would appear in a magazine beaming, beautiful, and magnificently bald.

I found myself wishing I'd had a chance to ask Ann how she felt about her neck wrinkles. Then, bobbing on the ocean of ink that poured out to celebrate and mourn her passing, an answer to my question appeared. Rena

Pederson, formerly the editorial page editor at the *Dallas Morning News*, recalled the last time she saw the governor: "She was complimented about her appearances as a political commentator and asked why she didn't have a TV program. Without hesitation, she grabbed the folds of skin under her chin and flapped them with her hand. 'They don't want you on TV with this,' she said." Pederson writes that when Ann was asked why she didn't just have plastic surgery, she replied, "I don't think that's the kind of example I want to set for my granddaughter."

A few nights after she died, I had to give a speech not far from the Capitol, where Ann W. Richards gave the state of Texas four of the most inspiring years of its life. Knowing how merciless the speaker's podium is, I had reason to flirt with thoughts of wattle camouflage: the jaunty scarf, a little ascot action, that black turtleneck. Instead, I took inspiration from Ann and made such a howling fool out of myself that everyone worried more about my precarious mental health than my neck wrinkles.

Besides, it's just too damn hot in Texas for turtlenecks.

Is This Really What Meemaw Had in Mind?

SPEECH AT ANNIE'S LIST/
TEXAS TRIBUNE LUNCHEON, APRIL 26, 2017

Well, hey, look at us here today just breaking records, helping Annie's List raise money for progressive female candidates all over Texas.

Now, being the insecure egomaniac that I am, I would love nothing more than to believe that this overwhelming turnout is . . . all for me!

But we know the real reason why our beloved Annie's List had to move us to a larger venue.

It is the same reason that we now have to have defibrillator paddles handy every time we check the news.

It is the same reason we now have our representatives, most of them conveniently gerrymandered up to south Wichita Falls, on speed dial.

It is the same reason that we are maxing out our credit cards giving to the ACLU, Planned Parenthood, Mother Jones, the Sierra Club, and most importantly, most immediately, giving to Annie's List.

And that reason is November 8. November 8, when the will of the people was subverted, the cornerstone of democracy undermined, and the second election in recent memory was stolen.

On November 8, the country reeled in shock to discover that we would now be governed by a cabal of race-baiting, woman-hating bullies. And we Texas women, we shed a few tears, too, but we had a slightly different reaction to the Tangerine Apocalypse, and that was, "Hey, all y'all! Welcome to our world, America."

It was a response that echoed even more strongly through our African-American and Latino communities with their even longer histories of betrayal and dreams denied.

Women across the nation went into mourning when they learned that we would have an administration bent upon turning Margaret Atwood's novel *A Handmaid's Tale* into a documentary. But we Texas women, well, we just shrugged and said, "Been there. Done that. Got the T-shirt and the intravaginal ultrasound to prove it."

The reason we are here today is because, as Texas women, we have a special obligation to turn this nightmare around. Since this is not our first time at this particular rodeo, we have already had many cruel decades to learn that empowering bullies does not make them nicer and awarding power to the power-hungry does not make them less greedy for power. And that is why we know with an even greater urgency than most that the need to get *more progressive women* into office as quickly as possible has reached a crisis level.

On January 21, between 3.3 and 4.6 million progressives marched in solidarity with all those threatened by this administration. Here in Austin, at least fifty thousand of us took to the streets. Even the lowest estimates make the Women's March the largest protest in United States history.

Before that epic event was even over, though, those

on the other side were saying that we were just "a bunch of sore losers throwing a tantrum." That the march was "self-indulgent" and "didn't prove a thing."

They said that our opposition had no momentum. That, once our little feel-good moment was over, we'd all just pack up our kitty-cat hats and pink Wendy Davis butt-kicking tennies and go back to our hot yoga and pumpkin spice lattes. Never to be heard from again.

Hmmm? How was that for fake news?

Because the real story is that we are here today breaking records and more committed than ever to saving democracy and turning Texas a bright, beautiful blue by finding, training, funding, and electing progressive women candidates to every level of government.

For me, the truth is that, until the unimaginable happened, I was snoozing happily in my post-racial Blue Bubble, where children had been given the outrageous freedom to use whichever bathroom fit their gender identity and millions had health insurance for the first time. Though my home state still had a long way to go, nationally, the arc of justice did seem to be bending in the right direction.

On the evening of November 8th, I put on the closest thing I could assemble at Goodwill to a Hillary pantsuit and went to a party ready to celebrate the fact that a woman was about to be elected president. I could not have been happier. I whacked at the crotch of a Donald Trump piñata and candy rained down on me. Fun-size Snickers and M&Ms. Both peanut and plain. All that and a lady president in my lifetime. What could be better? What could possibly go wrong?

The Tangerine Apocalypse was a wake-up call so horrifying that it left me in a state of permanently adrenalized anxiety, wondering how I could speak out as, day by day, the outrages and the impeachable offenses mounted. Like most of you here today, I responded by frantically writing checks, going to meetings, and helping to fill up my MoCs' voicemail. In the midst of this undirected frenzy, I was contacted by an aide for a state lawmaker who informed me that the Texas State Legislature wanted to honor me as an esteemed author and role model for girls.

Me! A Yankee carpetbagger.

I got a bit weepy reflecting upon the magnitude of my own magnificence. Was I flattered? Oh, you bet I was.

But what really impressed me was that, in the invitation, they had cited the wee tiny book slash pamphlet slash fat greeting card that you all have in front of you today. Because in that book I had lovingly burnished the stars in my own personal constellation of Texas Women heroes: Molly Ivins, Ann Richards, Lady Bird Johnson, Barbara Jordan.

As if sent by the heavens, this then was the answer to the question of how I could make my woman's voice heard in the halls of power.

Determined to speak as my progressive heroines would have spoken, I set about writing the speech I assumed I would be asked to deliver. Because, really, when you honor someone who spends his or her life torturing the alphabet, isn't a speech expected?

Halfway through writing said speech—which I was taking pains to make extremely diplomatic and white-gloves polite—a dark suspicion entered my mind, and I realized that I should probably check in with the organizer.

"Dear Genuinely Courteous Organizer," I emailed.

"I am writing to confirm that I will be allowed to speak. I'm afraid that simply accepting an honor from the Texas

Legislature will seem like I support them without question. And I have many, many questions which I would welcome the opportunity to share.

"Since you mentioned my small book, *A Love Letter to Texas Women*, I would especially like to plead with this august group to stop Using the Bodies of Texas women as a political battlefield.

"I would also like to bear witness to the fact that I, absolutely, would never have become a writer or even the person I was meant to be without access to safe, affordable, women's health care.

"If I will be allowed to do what I am being honored for, to truly be the role model for girls you refer to me as, and speak out, then I wholeheartedly accept. If not, then I'm afraid I cannot accept.

"I eagerly await your reply."—Sarah Bird.

Within minutes, I received a genuinely courteous response from the genuinely well-intentioned organizer that started off by informing me, quote, "I regret that you will not be attending . . ."

The instant I read that I had been disinvited, the white gloves came off and I wrote the non-diplomatic, IM-polite screed that instantly boiled up in me and was, eventually, published in the *Texas Tribune*.

In it, I demanded that the Texas State Legislature stop "getting all up in our lady business via the gnat swarm of bullshit laws you all keep inflicting upon us."

I asked if our Texas lawmakers were also OB/GYN researchers since they had so much secret knowledge about the dangers of abortion: inside information that was utterly unknown to the rest of the medical community, which continues to hail the procedure as one of the great lifesaving breakthroughs of the twentieth century.

I pleaded with these dipshits in the Capitol to face the fact that their cruel suppression of Texas women is done for one reason and one reason only: it gets votes and accomplishes the goal that they center their lives around— the sacred business of keeping their jobs.

I never heard a word from my intended audience, and the reality is that if I had delivered even the polite, toned-down version of that speech, my words would have fallen on deaf ears. And why should they listen when far too many of our legislators have used our ovaries, our uteruses, and our right to control our own bodies as a tenure track to job security?

There is a saying: "If you can't change their minds, change their faces." I would add, "And, most definitively, change their reproductive organs as well."

And that is why we are here today and why Annie's List has been fighting for Texas women since 2003.

It has not gotten easier.

Not with the individual installed in the White House, who has admitted, in the most graphic and most demeaning of terms, his belief that the ultimate expression of male power is the power to control women's bodies.

Not when he has surrounded himself with a Taliban-worthy administration of misogynists that has emboldened women-haters around the country and given rise to charming headlines in alt-right publications that ask the question, "Would You Rather Your Daughter Have Feminism or Cancer?"

Not when we are faced with the horrifying sight of a pack of Republican mullahs, with not a female face to be found, sitting around a table deciding that maternity care is not an essential health benefit.

Not when this new gang has empowered the Biblebanging nutbars who have run Texas politics for far too long to ramp up their own brand of Lone Star misogyny to a weapons-grade level of toxicity.

We are here today because we have now learned the bitter lesson that Annie's List has been preaching since 2003: it is not all about the White House. In the last eight years, more than nine hundred seats in state legislatures around the country went from Democrat to Republican. And, as you know, since it's mostly the legislatures that draw the congressional districts, they have been gerrymandering us into extinction.

Annie's List knew this. They knew that the takeover of state politics by those who would oppose a progressive agenda didn't happen overnight. It's been part of a methodical push that has allowed the GOP to outpunch its weight in Congress for far too long.

We are here today because we know that this abomination of an administration will come down. We have already seen it splintering in the special elections in Kansas and Georgia. We are seeing it in the figures released three days ago by Emily's List, reporting that a tsunami of eleven thousand women have already reached out to them about running for office.

We know that this administration will be defeated and that, with your support, here in Texas, Annie's List will have candidates ready to fill every seat from the proverbial dogcatcher to governor.

In the midst of the Darwinian hellscape that those currently in power would have us substitute for the shared dream of a common good that guided America through her darkest hours, through the Great Depression and two world wars, there are some bright spots.

First, of course, is that this past election has torn down

one of the greatest obstacles that used to stop women from running for office. Yes, believe it or not, before this election, women were hesitant to run because they felt they weren't qualified. Well, I think we can safely say that that hesitation has been laid to rest.

Another bright spot from the last election is that Texas saw the biggest Democratic shift in the country, from a crushing sixteen-point defeat in 2012 to a survivable nine-point defeat in 2016. The Dems picked up five seats in the state house. And with your support Annie's List helped elect or re-elect thirty-seven women statewide.

Two Annie's List–endorsed candidates have already made national waves by speaking our truth in the halls of power. First was Sheriff Sally Hernandez, who resisted the other side's cynically manufactured immigration hysteria with these ringing words: "I will not allow fear and misinformation to be my guiding principles."

And now we have Jessica Farrar. This eleven-term representative illustrates why we need humans with female bodies making our laws. Only a woman could have pointed out the sadistic absurdity of legislation that restricts women's access to healthcare by proposing to fine men $100 when they masturbate. Alongside the penalty for wasting semen not resulting in a pregnancy, Farrar's bill would require that before any vasectomy or Viagra prescription a man must undergo a "medically unnecessary digital rectal exam."

Representative Farrar's brilliantly satirical bill would almost be funny except that, according to a Population Research Study, in the years since the state's drastic 2011 reduction in funding for Planned Parenthood and the institution of bizarre rules leading to the closure of many clinics, the number and rate of pregnancy-related deaths in Texas have nearly doubled.

We have to elect more progressive women to speak our truth in the halls of power.

We are Texas women. We deserve better.

The current catastrophe in our state house is not what your great-great-great-grandmothers survived months in a covered wagon for. They did not cross the Rio Grande into an unknown and often hostile country for this. They did not endure enslavement on the vast sugar and cotton plantations that the Texas economy was built upon for this. They did not triumph over crazy German husbands, over screwworm infestations, over the Texas Rangers and over the Ku Kux Klan to see their great-great-great granddaughters saddled up to a pair of stirrups so that some pinhead lawmaker could ride herd on her ovaries. This was never in your meemaws' plans.

We have all suffered a terrible, a shocking setback. But we have been here before and we know what to do. We are Texas Women. We are not going to agonize. We are going to organize, and donate to our sisters in the trenches.

We are Texas Women. We are not going to get mad. We are going to get on our school boards, by supporting Annie's List.

We are Texas Women, we have this mission in our DNA. Our state's history is filled with models.

We have the paragon of grit and graciousness, Lady Bird Johnson.

We have fearless activist Emma Tenayuca, who fought the Ku Klux Klan and triggered the largest riot in San Antonio history in her fight for fair wages for Mexican American women.

We have Ann Richards, our last governor to truly let the people in. Ann Richards, one of only thirty women, out of a total of well over two thousand governors, ever elected in her own right in the entire history of the United States.

We have the hero of my life, the woman who spoke truth to power and left both sides in stitches . . . we had, we will always have, Molly Ivins.

And, finally, in closing, we Texas women are so blessed to have the enduring legacy of that undimmed moral beacon, Barbara Jordan, and the magnificent obligation that she left for us to fulfill. In simple words spoken with the force of an Old Testament prophet, Barbara Jordan laid out our mission as only a Texas woman could have.

What the people want is very simple, Jordan told us. *They want an America as good as its promise.*

Yes, we are Texas women. But first and foremost, we are American women and, working through Annie's List, we can build an America that will make good on its promise.

TEXAS

—

So Many Ways for a Girl
to Lose Her Virginity

Clouds

FROM *BETWEEN HEAVEN AND TEXAS*
BY WYMAN MEINZER, 2006

Clouds, those giant Rorschach tests in the sky, inspiration to dreamers and songwriters like Joni Mitchell who looked up and saw "Rows and flows of angel's hair. . . And feathered canyons everywhere," haven to poets such as Elizabeth Barrett Browning who, when not counting the ways in which she loved thee, yearned to "build a cloudy House for my thoughts to live in."

Me, I just wanted to eat them.

It was my father's fault that I developed such a visceral relationship to these, the most ethereal of elements. The Air Force had just landed my family in Japan, though not the Japan of oxygen tanks on gridlocked corners and white-gloved "pushers" cramming riders into bullet trains. This was the fairy-tale Japan of geishas and cherry blossoms that still existed at the tail end of the Occupation when we were there.

We were stationed at Yokota Air Base for three years, and it would be decades before I learned the dangerous truth about the Cold War reconnaissance missions my navigator father flew over what we once called the Soviet

Union and Red China while we were there. All I knew as a small child was that a crackling static of anxiety accompanied those missions, whose destination and duration we were never allowed to inquire into any more than we were allowed to ask about the daddies of our friends who never came home.

Then, one day, as my father packed for another mission—balling up socks, tossing in the Gillette Blue Blade, the bottle of Aqua Velva—I asked where he was going. Perhaps because of my "high-strung" temperament I got away with breaking our rule of silence. My father answered that he was going "up there," into the clouds. More than a decade away from my own first plane ride, I wondered what they were like, the clouds.

"They're made of marshmallow cream," my father told his jittery daughter. Already well-acquainted with my sugar obsession, he added the one thing guaranteed to ensure that I'd be delighted for him to leave: "And I'm going to bring some home for you. I'll throw a bucket on a rope out the window and scoop up a great big mound."

A bucket of marshmallow cream? I couldn't fling the socks in fast enough.

Though I had already signed on to the concept that rain, not marshmallow cream, came from clouds, I assumed that this meteorological detail only applied in "The States," the "Big PX," the great and wondrous mother ship we had left behind. Here in this magical country where walls were made of paper and shoes of wood, where you could eat the paper that candy was wrapped in and gods answered prayer notes tied to trees, different cloud rules apparently were in force.

The sky came alive for me as I inventoried each day's stock of marshmallow cream and found that new delights had appeared on the menu: Mountains of ice cream, tundras of nougat, drifts of meringue, rippled waves of whipped cream. Those weeks of waiting for the bucket to be delivered were delectable ones in my increasingly candy-centric view of the universe. The field behind our house tended by a farmer in a conical hat and rubber shoes with a pocket for his big toe came to resemble an Andes Mint, the chocolate dark soil topped by a furze of minty green shoots. Rising above those acres of after-dinner mint was a miraculously unimpeded view of Mount Fuji. For some, a holy national symbol. For me, an upended coconut sno-cone. Of greater interest were the clouds that wreathed the perfect cone. The setting sun turned the halo to a pinkish rose likened in haiku to a crown of cherry blossoms. I knew better. Those clouds were cotton candy and I hoped my father would toss the bucket out above the sacred mount.

The summer afternoon several weeks later when we, my ravening brothers and sisters and I, waited at the Flight Line for our father's return was hot enough to turn the landing planes into shimmering wobbles of silver. The heat didn't bother me. All I was concerned about was how I was going to neutralize the competition. I was considering some equitable split with my siblings along the lines of "you get to lick the empty bucket," when my father emerged in his olive green flight suit with its magician's array of zippered pockets. I searched for a bucket on a rope dripping billows of sugary fluff, but all he carried was a white box containing the leftovers from that day's flight lunch. Even on a day hot enough to make airplanes shimmy, the tiny packets of mayonnaise, the cue ball–hard apple, the half of a Snickers bar, were wondrously cold. I had no heart, though, to be amazed by or even to compete for these offerings from a frigid world high above our heads. Who cared about a fraction of a frozen Snickers bar when you'd just lost a bucket of marshmallow cream?

The awful truth about clouds came clear in second grade when a steamy terrarium dripping beads of moisture demonstrated their extraordinary ordinariness. Just like American clouds, Japanese clouds were nothing but water. We'd even walked through them. Fog? Nothing but a cloud too lazy to stay up high. Disappointing though this revelation was, the little terrarium held its own sweet dollop of mystery. Through spelling list words like "condensation" and "precipitation," I discovered that not a single drop of water was ever lost. Every trickle sprinkled across the Slip 'n' Slide, every pitcher transformed into cherry Kool-Aid, every bathtubful that cycloned down the drain, all were reclaimed by the clouds, purified, and returned to us as rain.

An astonishing extrapolation followed: Cleopatra might very well have bathed in one of the molecules I used to brush my teeth. There could be—probably was!—a dinosaur tear in the ice cube in my Shirley Temple. As befits a country brought forth by the two divine beings, Izanagi and Izanami, from a "sea of filmy fog floating to and fro in the air," clouds hugged Japan tightly in a misty embrace. These foggy days gave me, new devotee to the meteorological sciences, ample opportunity to stroll through what I now knew to be a distillate of history.

I could have remained on this fog-feathered island forever, but the United States Air Force decreed otherwise. Our new assignment was someplace called Harlingen, Texas. We were, in GI parlance, "short"; we were going back to "The World." Three years of garrison life had turned me into a super patriot, citizen of an idealized America. I had no state identity. I wasn't a Michigander, though I'd been born there and spent one fairly unformative month in the state. Arizona, Texas, Idaho, California, all places we had lived, had left equally negligible impressions. To a child formed overseas, states were arbitrary outlines on a map. States were fifty fingers of a hand that had clenched into a fist to smite undeniable evil in war, then opened in victory as, possibly, the most magnanimous conquerors the world had ever seen. I was an American and I was going home.

Decades later, I would write about a troop of macaque monkeys that had overrun the piney forests outside of Kyoto where they were regarded as sacred animals, beloved of the imperial family, and enshrined as the resourceful trickster stars of many fairy tales. They were demoted to public nuisance status when they took to raiding farmers' crops, menacing housewives, and defecating in temples. An international effort saved the half of the troop marked for extermination and the monkeys with the watermelon-colored faces and behinds were shipped from their snowy, mist-shrouded sanctuary to the sun-stricken mesquite and prickly pear plains of south Texas. I recognized in the shell-shocked faces of those transplants my own stunned and panting initial reaction to Texas.

Via the same steamship line that had delivered my family and me, the air force returned us to the other side of the earth. We docked in San Francisco and the seven, soon to be eight, of us packed into an exceptionally snazzy, two-tone Bel Air station wagon with a circus troupe's supply of suitcases strapped to the roof. And we drove. And we drove. Through a hole cut in a giant Sequoia we traveled south from redwood country to grapefruit country. Unfortunately, all those suitcases rattling against the roof of the car were filled with the wooly jackets, earmuffs, gloves, and boots that had kept us warm and dry in Japan. Even though we stripped off as many layers as decency would allow, we still arrived in Texas gasping from the heat.

Other shocks followed. The food. Apparently, it was not going to be enough to torture Bird children with temperatures we hadn't experienced since our last trip to the *furo*, the communal bath. No, internal searing would be added. Chips? With hot sauce? What hellish world was this where pieces of cardboard dunked in a caustic, burning solution were considered a treat?

But the major problem was that this country was simply too big. I desperately missed the claustrophobic embrace of a small island, populated by small people, who had created a small world perfectly scaled for children. Someone had taken the dome off of this Texas terrarium, exposing it to an enormity of sky that was frighteningly beyond my comprehension. Someone had let the clouds that cuddled the earth into hospitality escape. Fog? Not a chance. Clouds here were not friendly visitors brushing your cheek with molecules of Cleopatra's bathwater and ringing small mountains in pink cotton candy; here they were titans. They were hectic monsters churned up from the Gulf of Mexico that flayed the earth with hurricanes. Or they were bullies called blue northers that muscled their way down from the Arctic Circle and forced the temperature to drop more in a few hours than it would have during an entire year back in Japan.

The other cloud creatures who entered my life around this time were nuns since my parents had enrolled their children in St. Anthony's Catholic School so as to avoid the eternal damnation the Church guaranteed any parent who failed to do so. Clad in cumulus-white habits originally issued by the Mother House for nursing African pagans with leprosy and repurposed for teaching American ignorami with ringworm, the nuns floated among us with a dangerous unpredictability. Like the cruel clouds outside, Sister Immaculata was just as apt to strike out with a ruler whack of lightning across the palm as to rain down gentle learning.

Given that Latin was the official team language, it was natural that, in our Weather Unit, Sister Immaculata should teach us what the Latinate names of the clouds meant. They all derived from three shapes. Anything wispy was a *cirrus*, a curl of hair. *Stratus* meant layer and was for those lazy, blanketing fog clouds without enough energy to get airborne though they could cover vast swaths of sky. The ice cream clouds, scoops, balls, puffs, were *cumulus*, meaning heap. Like Mr. Potato Head just a few additions here and there could completely change the designations of these configurations. Compound clouds were cobbled together by adding *nimbus*, rain, *humilis,* small, and *incus,* anvil. The prefixes *cirro* and *alto* made any of the basics into either high- or middle-altitude models. Latin suffixes as lovely as the clouds they described trailed after, explaining themselves as they went: *undulatus, fibratus, radiatus, translucidus, opacus, congestus.*

The association between clouds and Catholicism was cemented on our first-ever, full-on, official Good Friday. Unlike previous, carefree Good Fridays which we had given over to dying shredded coconut green for decorating bunny cakes and eggs in a rainbow of pastel hues for hunting and other such pagan activities, this one was spent in church observing the Stations of the Cross. The hours we passed meditating upon Christ's suffering—crowning with thorns, whipping, crucifixion—left me in a more-than-usually-high-strung, susceptible state of mind. Which is why I took it very personally when I marched out of the church that

Good Friday and beheld wildly theatrical clouds performing their own Passion Play. Wispy black ones that had to
be *cirrus* feathered high across the dark sky like ink spilled
into water. Billowing up in front of these bit players was
a brute spectacularly bruised in lurid greens and purples,
shaped like, yes!, an anvil. I beheld a magnificent *cumu-
lonimbus incus*. Sunlight found its way between him and
the layer of high cirrus and golden rays streamed out from
behind in an effect not seen since Cecil B. DeMille.

These Texas clouds meant business. I figured it was only
prudent to get on better terms with them .

That summer, when the real hammer of Texas heat
dropped on our house, where the air was "conditioned" by
several fans whose major purpose seemed to be to speed
up the time it took the superheated air molecules to reach
me, I escaped outside. I climbed the only tree of any size in
our yard, a tall hackberry, and took refuge in what breezes
passed by. When not occupied spying upon my family (the
favorite activity of many a "sensitive" type of child destined to torture the alphabet for a living), I found myself
lost in cloud reveries, finding odd fauna revealed in their
puffs and pouches. A bunny licking its paw, a two-headed
dog, an elephant in pajamas, Sister Immaculata's beaky
profile, but mostly, didn't that sheep's flock of fluffy white
cumulus humilis look like sopaipillas? Especially as the sun
set, turning the underdone delights into the golden puffs I
had recently discovered? Yes, though still homesick in Harlingen, I was beginning to make my peace with Texas. Any
state that put doughnuts with honey right up front there on
the main menu couldn't be all bad.

That sweet thought was followed by another astonishing extrapolation from the lessons of the terrarium about

the essential nature of clouds. If clouds were no respecters of history, they were even less likely to be observers of borders. If they contained molecules from every moment in time, they certainly mixed in ones from every point in space as well. The moisture that escaped when we boiled eggs to be dyed for Easter could slip through customs up in Cloud Land and mingle with droplets from pots bubbling in Idaho or England or, best of all, Japan. These sopaipilla clouds I was staring at could very well contain the chlorinated essence of the swimming pool we'd left behind at Yokota or vapor from the *furos* or steam from the small brass pot of green tea the farmer boiled every day in the Andes Mint field in front of Mt. Fuji. Though the hackberry might be rooted in Texas soil, Texas clouds, vaporous amalgamations of the distilled essences of every country on earth, were international.

I gave up spying and took to watching the sky. Like my first, most necessary form of escape, books, they transported me. Though I still yearned for mist-hugged Japan, I noticed how my thoughts had a way of soaring to new heights and unexpected places in this land with no lid. Forced to reach out to distant clouds, the range of my dreams increased as well until these Texas clouds became conduits to a world of imagination.

And then we went to the beach. Yes, clouds scudding across a high Texas sky are revelatory, transporting, but stick a palm tree into this picture and wow, there's the umbrella in your cocktail. A photo from that time, deckled along the edges, curled with age, shows a Padre Island shoreline devoid of anything except well-fed Bird children getting sand into the crevices likely to chafe most. There is not a single hotel, condominium, or parasail rental shop.

The gas station where we always stopped to rinse the salt off the car isn't even visible. The only things crowding the empty beach besides us are clouds.

Beach clouds spoke Latin all day long. The first lesson commenced at dawn when the sun bobbed like a pink jellyfish through the morning haze I knew to be a *stratus* cloud. Its translucent opalescence suggested Latin modifiers. *Translucidus? Opacus?* I wondered as I bounced on gentle rose-colored swells, but the sun was already burning the haze away. Later in the day undulant rows of clouds appeared that mirrored in white the rippled footprints waves left in the sand. They all but whispered their name, *altocumulus undulatus*. I watched for exciting developments among the cumuli. A *congestus*, perhaps. Or even the titillating *mammatus*, the pouch-like cloud named for their resemblance to pendent breasts. I even learned I had the power to make clouds appear and come to me. With one Cheeto, I could command a beady-eyed, white and gray cloud of seagulls squawking their fretful cries, orange beaks aimed at orange Cheeto. That evening, as we crossed the long Port Isabel Causeway, droopy-gulleted pelicans cut through a tangerine sunset that reflected on the water below. Above that long link to Padre Island, unnamed clouds, floated, golden in the waning light.

From Harlingen, the air force decreed that we should move to San Antonio. Then, a few years later, to Albuquerque. Again the station wagon was packed. Suitcases lashed to the roof. My heart was broken. I had made friends. I loved Texas. The air force did not care. My father headed up to Interstate 10, the highway that cruise control was invented for, turned left, and punched the pedal to the metal. As we barreled along, I slumped against the window, searching the sky for clouds. The farther west we went, the fewer I spotted. Like trees, grass, and water in liquid form, they had up and blown away from this increasingly flat, increasingly barren country. The vertiginous, exposed feeling I had when we'd first moved from Japan returned in full force.

West Texas was a land that truly had no lid. Flat as a gym floor, it rolled out in either direction to horizons too distant to see, although, somehow, the farther west we went the greater the distances I was able to see. It was as if I'd gone to the ophthalmologist and updated the prescription on my glasses. I suspected that the novena I'd offered up to ease the world's suffering, stop the Soviets from destroying Holy Mother Church, and be granted super powers was being answered in the form of super vision. Though I would have preferred the ability to fly, super vision was good. Then my father, the navigator, began marveling about "visibility" and "low humidity," and I went back to searching the sky. In this treeless land, clouds were precious, casting what little shade might fall on the parched land.

"Is Alvin Turkey going to be like this?" my youngest brother asked, watching a vulture riding thermals overhead.

"Yeah, only not so green," my father answered. "Maybe a little dryer."

"He's kidding," my mother added.

I was dubious and dismissed an unimpressive stratus formation off in the distance that was trailing a veil of gray shadow across the land. We drove straight into it and, sudden as flipping a switch, we went from dusty, desiccating sunshine into a deluge.

"Just a little shower," my father, who'd ridden out typhoons and enemy fire said, pressing on.

The "little shower" streamed down in blinding sheets that turned the windshield into a wobbly porthole. Water surged across the highway. When a semi engulfed us in a wave that soaked the suitcases on top and made the station wagon shimmy across the saturated road, my father pulled over. We watched water rise all around us as steadily as a swimming pool filling. And, then, just as suddenly as it had started, the clouds swept past, leaving behind a world renewed, dazzling in its freshness. The endless sky emerged, scoured to a cobalt blue so intense and saturated it hurt to look at it. Fragrances unlocked by the rain—moist earth, sage, creosote—filled the car. The cleansed air was even clearer than before. Mountains in the distance sharpened into crisp focus. Momentarily stunned by the tumult of weather and its magic aftermath, all of us squabbling children fell silent as we motored on.

The sunset that evening was so spectacular that we couldn't take our eyes from the sky even to look out for the signs we found indispensable during these migrations: "Swimming Pool." The blue intensified to the heart-stopping hue of a Vermeer canvas as the mountains darkened into a saw-toothed silhouette. Streaks of salmon, vermilion, lilac crept higher into the blue then tinted the underbellies of clouds in blazing slashes of copper. The show that night was a double feature. Behind us, to the east, swirling above the Apache Mountains was a formation I'd never hoped to see, *altocumulus lenticularis*. The lentil-shaped cloud pulsed an iridescent violet as it whirled over the ridge, its flying saucer shape and eerie glow enough to make my two youngest brothers poke each other and demand in robot voices, "Take me to your leader."

Night ended the alien invasion. We fell asleep in the car and woke in Albuquerque beneath a periwinkle sunrise feathered with vermilion cirrus. Four years later, I flew back over those mountains on my first airplane ride.

Nineteen hours to Okinawa where my family had been transferred. Nineteen hours to get over a faithless boy-friend and a broken heart. I spent them chasing a sun that never stopped setting, glued to the window, mesmerized by the sensation of staring *down* on clouds. I was a spy soaring above empires I'd only guessed at from glimpses of their undersides. There beneath me was the kingdom of the heavens plotted out on a vast crenelated topographical map. I flew over domed cathedrals. Mosques with mina-rets. Turreted castles. Disneylands of cloud with streams of vapor blew through the streets. Vast knobbly plains like an endless field of cauliflower rose up to be followed by polar ice caps of snow, mountainous drifts that went on forever. Unlike love. Sniff-sniff. I imagined my tears evaporating in the cabin and being sprinkled by the exhaust system directly onto the clouds which would pass those molecules around until they fell on Albuquerque. On him. Sigh.

Clouds on the semi-tropical island of Okinawa were closer to utilities than weather. Like clockwork, every afternoon, the sky would clot with gray rain clouds and release a precisely timed torrent. So reliable was the daily downpour that I took to standing beneath the rain spout that drained our flat roof, bottle of Herbal Essence sham-poo in hand, to wash my hair in the unchlorinated runoff. The locks never looked better.

Other parts of the world, other clouds:

A fantastic orange haze blanketing Frankfurt, Germany. Stratus? I wondered. No, a local corrected, pollution.

A chair lift strung up the side of the French Alps sway-ing ominously beneath the unblinking eye of a feeble sun pearlized and haloed by the nacreous haze of a *cirrostratus fibratus*.

On the White River Apache reservation, a *cumulus con-*

gestus as brilliantly white and high as Marie Antoinette's wig surging up above a red canyon dotted with yellow asters.

A cartoon sky in Maxfield Parrish pastels over Palo Duro Canyon, rows of blobby clouds, pink and rose against a background of Prussian blue. "That's what we used to call a buttermilk sky," the old rodeo contractor I was visiting informed me. His wife said, "No, it ain't."

A male orangutan hooting from the branches of a magnificent ironwood tree beside a river dark as coffee in Kalimantan, Borneo. Above his head, black squiggles of cirrus brush distress signals into a sky obscured by the smoke from agricultural fires raging out of control.

The turning point in my relationship with clouds occurred long before Borneo. I was in England, another small, wet island. This one on intimate enough terms with clouds to call their foggy weather "soft." A few winter months in Leeds, England and the "softness" had dissolved all my lingering affection for low-lying clouds. I came to feel I was living inside an oyster. The day *The Last Picture Show* opened, I was at the theater, ready to endure sugar in the popcorn, ice cream bars at the concession stand, and any number of other British oddities. Some might say that Larry and Peter's classic was filmed in black and white, but to me it was in pure living color. I took one look at the sky above Anarene, Texas, with the clouds way up high where they belonged, started crying, and stopped only long enough to buy a ticket home. My love affair with clouds that hug was over.

As I write, it is almost Valentine's Day. Outside my window, a high scrim of stratus diffuses the light into an opalescent haze that flatters the greens we are lucky to have at a time when ice and snow cover less-fortunate landscapes. The haze makes a perfect rice-paper canvas for elegant crepe myrtle branches, bare and ivory pale in the somber light, to fork their frozen lightning into, for banzai kinks of live oak limbs to brush their elegant calligraphy across.

What else is written there, it appears, is my life in clouds. Having recorded far more of a shared history than I had imagined existed, I glance up from my computer at my son, 15, hypnotized in front of his computer, and wonder what cloud memories he will one day look back on. Will they mostly derive from screen savers? I worry. Cloud memories, clearly another area I've failed in as a mother.

We take the dog for a walk. The haze has lifted, revealing high patches of rolled and tucked clouds that remind me of the sky above Palo Duro Canyon that the old-timer had called "buttermilk."

"So," I ask, with the nonchalance mothers posing fraught questions learn to imitate so well. "Do you have any cloud memories?"

"Like, do I remember clouds?" His tone implies that the total mental collapse he'd long anticipated has occurred.

I explain, fearing his recollections will linger lovingly over the exquisite resolution of his new computer game.

Instead, this: "Remember when you took me on that insane walk during that storm? You were all, 'It's fine. Don't worry. This is great walking weather,' and there were, like, lightning bolts striking. So I ran ahead and got to the top of the hill at the end of the short loop and all of a sudden there's this monster cloud that goes from a couple of feet off the ground to miles into the sky and it's this brown that no cloud has ever been before. Sort of like a giant dust devil, but it didn't touch the ground. The trees on either side of the street made a channel with the cloud and this enormous gust of wind came from the cloud and shot all these leaves at me."

"Pretty vivid memory. Do you ever just look up into the sky and see things in the clouds?"

"No. Most people will look up at the clouds and say, 'That kind of looks like a rabbit. Or a dog smoking a pipe.' When I look in the clouds, I go, 'I think I'll try to find a guy with a monocle. I'll find Mr. Peanut.' And he'll be there. If you look the right way, you can find anything you want in the clouds."

"Do they ever look like something good to eat?"

"No, mom, not really."

Unlike a Virgin

THIRD COAST, 1985

I n this world, there are a couple of recondite pleasures known to writers and to members of no other profession. The first is, of course, the freedom to work in your pajamas. The second is the license to peer down the untraveled byways of one's life, the roads not taken.

For me, one of those untaken roads is North St. Mary's, a street in San Antonio that passes by Providence High School. Providence is the Catholic girls' school I would have gone to if the air force had not intervened. Decreeing that my family had many miles to go (770, to be exact) and my father much peace to keep, the military transferred us to Albuquerque, New Mexico, and I was thenceforth cast into the secular void of public school.

How different, I wondered, would my life have been if I'd attended Providence? And did authentic Catholic girls still exist in 1985? The answers waited for me there on North St. Mary's. I arranged to visit my almost–alma mater.

What to wear? I want to blend in. A costume isn't hard to pull together, given that not too many seasons back, the non-parochial fashion of America happened to coincide with that of every Catholic schoolgirl: blazers, knee socks, a navy-blue skirt. The only items I am missing are saddle oxfords, a scapular, and a beanie. Of course, I can always bobby-pin a Kleenex to my head if we go to Mass.

My memories of Providence are based on the one trip my parochial-school friends and I made there to take an admissions test. As I pull off I-35, I am remembering the gracious institution we'd visited, with its manicured grounds sprawling in the cool shadows of towering pecans. I head for North St. Mary's and wind my way through a neighborhood that realtors would describe as "iffy." As soon as I spot the nondescript beige building behind the sign ("Providence High School, Grades 8 to 12"), I am forced to conclude that either the years have not been kind to PHS or that I was awfully easy to impress in my youth. Gone are the pecans, the grounds, the graciousness. I wonder what else has changed—or was never there to begin with.

Will it be like the Catholic schools of my youth? At St. Anthony's in Harlingen, Texas, where I attended fifth and sixth grades, there had been long, dark, polished corridors with statues of saints holding up bleeding stigmata and Christs offering a flaming sacred heart at every turn. Once inside Providence, it doesn't take me long to see that things are incalculably different.

Inside the front door, visitors are greeted by a bulletin board with a red satin banner, of the sort beauty contestants wear, pinned on it. Written in gold glitter across the sash is the last word I expected to see: "Sexiest."

A few girls drift past. They are wearing shorts. One has on a Duran Duran foreign-legion cap, and the other has half a dozen pairs of knee socks in neon colors stairstepping up her legs. I want to stand up and show them how a Catholic schoolgirl is *supposed* to dress, but Sister Margaret appears. She is not wearing a habit.

"The silly hats and socks aren't part of the regular uniform," she explains with a weary smile. "It's Spirit Week." Even in her fatigue-green polyester civilian clothes, Sister Margaret is an immediate link to the past. Back then, there were only two types of nuns ruling our world: bad ones—the mean, cranky, sour ones who seemed to have signed on exclusively for the pleasure of beating the shit out of kids' palms with rulers—and the good ones. I try to figure out what it is Sister Margaret, clearly a good one, has in common with those kind, black-habited women of yesteryear.

She welcomes me to Providence and asks if I have any questions about the school. She has plenty of answers: Tuition is about a hundred a month. The school receives no money from any source except parents. It tries to keep tuition low so that the predominantly Mexican American, working-class families the school serves can afford to send their daughters. Some classes are now co-ed with the boys from Central Catholic next door. Out of a faculty of about forty, there are only ten nuns—Sisters of Divine Providence, the order that founded and still runs the school.

What about problems? I wonder. Drugs, for example? Oh, yes, they've had problems with drugs. There was one girl year before last—or was it the year before that? Anyway, Sister Margaret had to speak to her. And that was the sum of Providence's drug problem. If she had to name her major discipline problem, it would be boyfriends. "Girls fussing at each other about boyfriends," Sister Margaret laughs.

When my questions are all answered, Sister Margaret bustles off to locate classes for me to observe. As I wait for her, I wonder what would have happened if I'd stayed and gone to Providence. Perhaps I wouldn't have lost my faith.

Much was made in parochial schools of "losing your faith." A certain Father Motz was particularly gripping on the subject. A hulking, bearish man who had the cumin odor of an enchilada dinner, he would lumber regularly into class to deliver dire warnings on the subject. "Look to your right," he would order, and thirty little heads would swivel in that direction. "Now to your left. Okay, don't expect to see one of those people in heaven because half of you are going to *lose your faith*!"

It was a horrifying thought, and we all vowed (none louder than I, an overachiever in religious zeal as in all other areas) that we would not become the apostate, the fallaway, the backslider.

But I did, and I wish I could claim a crisis of faith as the reason I became one of Father Motz's casualties. Or even that I never believed any of it to start with. But my problem wasn't that. If anything, I believed too much. What did me in was French kissing.

Pre–Vatican II Catholics lived in a world of crisp moral delineations. From birth to death, you knew exactly where you stood on the big Parcheesi board of life. Sins were mortal or venial. You could chug along with quite a load of venials—talking back to your parents, fighting with your brother, not cleaning your room—but one mortal would retire your marker.

Not many markers were taken out of the game, though, until about the time our teacher, Sister Mary Tabernacula, sent the boys out of the room for their own special chat with Father Motz while she showed the girls a filmstrip on the joys of "Becoming a Woman." It was less than specific. The film had me looking forward to a new phase in life when I, a desperately uncoordinated bookworm, would play tennis, swim, ride bikes, and generally "stay active all during that time of the month." It promised to be a time when Kotex would help keep me fresh and dainty through the frenzy of athletic rigors that were intended to signal my passage into womanhood.

When the lights came up, Sister Tabernacula, a grumpy nun of the old school, segued into what constituted the entirety of my sex education in Catholic school. Sister Tab informed us that our bodies were temples of the Holy Ghost, and that we could expect some major renovations in the temple to begin shortly. She finished up with the stirring tale of St. Basilissa, an early Christian martyr who chose to be boiled in oil rather than put out for the centurions. Or renounce her faith. The moral was that a Catholic girl's faith and her chastity are the two treasures she must guard with her life.

Some of my classmates comprehended the message a bit more clearly than I, even divining that tennis and boiling oil had something to do with boys. My friend Annie Garcia, a vivacious girl with an unconscious boldness that rankled Sister Tab fiercely, was especially astute in this area. Annie raised her hand and asked how long you could kiss a boy before it was a sin.

Sister answered immediately and unequivocally: ten seconds.

"What about—" Annie started off, then paused and looked up as if trying to formulate a purely hypothetical question. "What about Frenching?"

Sister Tabernacula's little mustache twitched a few times before she passed sentence on Annie. "Anytime you kiss a boy with any more feeling than you would kiss your brother, it is a mortal sin."

So there was never any question in my mind that French kissing was a mortal. When I finally discovered that this activity had substantially more to do with Becoming a Woman than any urges to wax athletic, that there were at least a couple of boys I might want to break the ten-second limit with, the faith was lost.

I think about Annie as I wait for Sister Margaret to return with my class schedule. How had her life turned out? Like most of my friends from grade school, she'd gone to Providence. Would I have continued on as a religious overachiever and ended up in the convent? Or married to a boy from Central Catholic with a station-wagonful of little papists, teaching Christian confraternity classes in the evenings and blowing my household allowance on bingo? Would I have kept my faith?

Sister Margaret strides back in, chuckling to herself. One of the teachers says her girls have prepared some questions for their class today. Questions about sex. "I asked if she'd be embarrassed having you sit in," Sister Margaret says, still bemused. "She said, if she wasn't embarrassed talking about sex in front of thirty freshman girls, one adult wouldn't do it."

Watching Sister Margaret practically sparkle with amusement, I figure out what she and the other good nuns I'd known have in common. They always seemed to be having a much better time with their lives than almost anyone else.

The bell rings, and Sister Margaret points me down the hall to my first class, Classics II. An odd giddiness bubbles through me as I walk down the corridor, alive now with girls in plaid skirts and knee socks; I'm about to start my first day at Providence High School twenty years too late.

The classics teacher is a round, red-haired woman who proves to be exceptional. She begins talking the instant the bell stops ringing. "Are there any final questions on *The Od-yssey*? Good. Today we start on *Gulliver's Travels*."

As the students dutifully scribble down that Jonathan Swift was born in 1667 and, starting in his teens, had a long-lasting relationship with Esther Johnson, I glance around the room. Of course, there is a crucifix above the blackboard. But that is the only Catholic-school set dressing. No bleeding stigmata. No heart on a hand. It could have been any sunny classroom anywhere. Except that the lecture is unusually literate and the students unusually attentive.

"Anytime you see Lilliput," the teacher explains, cracking Swift's code for her students, "the author is really referring to England. Blefuscu is France. Flimnap is Sir Robert Walpole, the English prime minister. The Lowheels and the Highheels are the Whigs and the Tories. LaPuta"—here the teacher stops for the obligatory chuckles from the Spanish speakers—"is Parliament. Lagado is London. The Little Endians are the Protestants, and the Big Endians are the Catholics."

I think back to my reading of *Gulliver's Travels* in public high school. It had come after years of history as taught by the nuns, which, at that time, was essentially a study of famous Catholics and the ceaseless struggles of Holy Mother Church against the benighted forces nipping at Her heels. Only in public school did I learn that Martin Luther might have actually had a few things to complain about and that the Crusades really had more to do with trade routes than redemption of the infidels.

Still, choosing up sides early did have the advantage of making the ancient quarrels that Swift parodied come alive for me in ways that, say, a Unitarian would never emotionally understand. In my public-school English class, packed as it was with Protestants, I had the thrilling feeling of being a Big Endian who'd infiltrated the Little Endians, and I secretly rooted for my team.

Freshman English is next. On the chalkboard is a list of "1985 Providence Words." This year's words are "awesome," "massive," "getting into trouble bigtime," "spare me," "kroger," "radical," and "sike."

Many of the girls sport Spirit Week bows, knee socks, hats. Nearly half the class is stationed at the back windows watching the boys in the Central Catholic band practice in the field next door. The bell doesn't bring them to their seats.

The teacher—prettier and more stylish than the others I've met—asks them to sit down. The girls keep hanging out the windows until the teacher orders them to their seats in a thunderingly resonant voice. Once they're seated, she passes out mimeographed sheets with the lyrics to "Dancin' in the Dark" typed on them. The day's lecture is on poetry. I try to scan the sheet, but find that the words remain tethered to their familiar beat:

You can't start a fire
You can't start a fire without a spark

"Is Bruce Springsteen really talking about starting a fire?" the teacher asks. A few hesitant voices answer, half in the negative, half in the affirmative.

"Is he a pyromaniac? What is he talking about?"

A cute girl in the desk next to mine wearing a red bow tied Madonna-style around her head raises a hand. "Yes, Lydia," the teacher calls on her.

"Well, is he talking about arguments, because you can start arguments with anyone, and sometimes they end up with guns?"

The teacher is only momentarily nonplussed. "Okay, Lydia, that's true. But what else is he talking about here?"

No one is quite sure.

The teacher presses on. "When you start a fire, what else do you think about? Heat? Light? Getting burned? Would fire be a good symbol for love?"

A few heads nod. It might be, if Bruce wanted to go that far out on a metaphorical limb.

After the textual analysis of The Boss's latest, we turn to other sources, and I have only a moment to wonder what ever happened to "Tantum Ergo," to "Ave Maria."

"Lydia, would you share your book with Miss Sarah?" the teacher asks the girl next to me. "We don't have any extra books." Lydia smiles at me. She's as bright-eyed and appealing as a gerbil in a bow and braces. Lydia scoots her desk over next to mine so that I can follow along as the teacher performs a reading of John Updike's "Lament, for Cocoa" that rings with stage training.

The scum has come,
My cocoa's cold.
The cup is numb,
And I grow old.

. . . .

How wearisome!
In likelihood,
The scum, once come,
Is come for good.

"Is the author talking about anything else besides his cocoa getting cold?"

No response. For these girls, Updike's dilemma can be solved with a microwave.

The next question is easier. "Did you like this poem?"

"Ugh, no," Lydia, my book partner, bursts out. I'm surprised she heard the poem, as she had seemed absorbed in the particularly rococo rendition of the name FRANK she was executing in her notebook in fluorescent marker.

"Why not?"

The answer comes from various places in the room. "Scum. Gross."

"All right," the teacher moves on quickly. "The assignment for today was to write a poem that doesn't rhyme but does have rhythm. Six lines. Two figures of speech. Priscilla, you want to start us off by reading your poem?"

Priscilla slides out from behind her desk. A perky bow perches on top of her head. A Van Halen button is pinned to her blouse. She is barely able to suppress a giggle as she takes the podium and starts reading. "Loneliness. Loneliness is when you cry and no one hears you. When it is dark like the bottom of the sea. A tunnel that goes round and round and comes out nowhere."

Next up is Tammy. She's a chubby dumpling, also giggling, whose neon-striped knee socks are sliding down around her dimpled ankles. She rests her paper on the podium, composes herself while her friends keep trying to make her laugh, and reads: "Death. Death is a nap that lasts forever. Death is a big headache. Death, why don't you leave me alone? I'm not ready for you yet."

Tara, Yvette, Angie, Juanita, Millie, Gina, Eunice, and Minerva follow with more despairing laments: "Where have all my dreams gone to. Sorrow fills all the days of the year." "Love is for everybody but not for me." "Death. Death is so ugly. Death is like a night without a moon."

"Lydia, would you read yours?"

Lydia seems as happy about this as she is about everything else. "Love," she begins. "Love is like two beautiful, twinkling stars in the sky that meet and stay together. Forever." She looks up, pleased with her poem, pleased with herself, and pleased with love. Back at her desk she continues work on her FRANK piece.

When everyone has read, the teacher looks at the clock. "The period *still* isn't over?" she asks incredulously. I, too, am incredulous. We cannot believe where the time is *not* going. Not since, well, high school has an hour seemed so interminable. I wonder if the legislators mandating longer school days remember how one classroom hour can be like a day in the Gobi Desert. The teacher calls for a break and tells the class they can talk quietly until the end of the period. She comes back and sits beside me. I ask her where she learned to project so admirably.

"I used to do some acting. That's all teaching is, isn't it? Acting." She explains that she just transferred from the public-school system and has taken a $4,000 pay cut to do so. "Why?" I ask.

"You don't *teach* in public school, at least not where I was. Half the kids couldn't even understand English. You just try to keep order. I got tired of it."

What does she see as the reason for the difference between the two systems?

"The parents. Here the parents care. That makes all the difference."

The bell rings for lunch and I ask where the cafeteria is. Lydia, who is tenderly closing her notebook over the illuminated name of FRANK, volunteers to take me.

Lunch is classic cafeteria fare: chicken barbecued in old motor oil, canned green beans the color of olives, yeast rolls the density of antimatter, and, of course, lime jello with fruit cocktail embedded in it. Lydia gets the ladies in hairnets and plastic gloves to swap out the entire selection for one drumstick and four rolls.

We take places at an empty table, and half a dozen girls quickly join us. Aurelia, Lydia's best friend of the moment, sits across the table. She is a brown-skinned Kewpie doll with her dark curls and heart-shaped face. The only Anglo in the group, Brenda, a bony girl with white-blond hair, sits beside Lydia. Lydia introduces me to them all as "Miss Sarah." The girls' conversation is the perfect complement to lime jello.

"Ew, Lydia, who are you going to the dance with?"

"Frank."

"Frank Sosa? You're just going with him so that you'll have a boyfriend at Valentine's. You think you have to have a boyfriend at Valentine's. Just like at Christmas when you were going, 'Oh, it's Christmas. I've got to have a boyfriend.'"

Lydia covers her braces and laughs at being found out. She touches my wrist. "Don't listen to Aurelia, Miss Sarah. She's coo-coo in the cabeza." She turns to Aurelia. "Ew, I just remembered. I had this dream in third period . . ."

"You had a dream in third period?!" Aurelia gives me a look that makes us co-foils for the zaftig Lydia.

"Yeah, I fell asleep. But this dream was about that real fat girl, Marta . . ."

"Lydi-a-a-a," Aurelia hisses, jerking her thumb to the right. Lydia follows the gesture toward a chubby girl eating at the end of the line of tables.

Lydia ducks her head down and touches a finger to her lips. "Oops, sorry. Okay, what if I say I had a dream about this sort of *panzon* girl?"

"Guy, Lydia, we still know what you mean," Aurelia admonishes primly. "Maybe she can't help it."

Lydia is peeved now. "Okay, there's no panzon. No

dream. No nothing." She balls up her napkin and drops it onto her tray.

"Don't be that way, Lydia," Aurelia whines.

Lydia turns away and starts talking to Brenda, who doesn't have a lunch tray. "Aren't you going to eat?" Lydia asks her.

"No, I'm on a diet. I'm just eating these." She holds up a package of chocolate cookies.

"Why? I'm the one who should lose weight."

"Oh, Lydia, you always say that. You just want me to be panzon like—" Brenda stops and jabs a finger toward the hapless Marta, grazing contentedly with her own crowd.

"You guys," Aurelia wails, "quit being so mean."

Brenda and Lydia exchange mock-chastised looks. "But she's got friends," Brenda offers in their defense. She leans around Lydia to catch my attention. "That's what's different about here and public school," she tells me, answering a question I'd asked earlier. "In public school I'd always see a lot of girls eating alone. Especially the, you know...." Brenda glances at Aurelia and stops herself before she says "fat." Instead she holds her hands out in front to indicate unrestrained girth. "But here everyone is in a big group. No one's alone. It's like a big family. It's better here."

"No, it's not," Lydia disagrees. "It's better in public. It's too strict here."

What about not having guys around? Does that make any difference?

The girls look at each other for a minute. Lydia is gnawing on a drumstick. "Yeah," she answers. "A lot. If there were guys around I wouldn't be eating like a savage!" Grinning, she bites a hunk off the drumstick. The table laughs.

How would you be eating?

"I wouldn't be eating at all if there were guys around,"

Aurelia answers. "Or else I'd be eating like this . . ." She waves her fork delicately over her tray. "Pick, pick, pick."

Throughout lunch a steady stream of girls flows by the table, stopping to banter with Lydia or one of her cronies. To pay court. It slowly dawns on me that Lydia and her crowd are popular, probably somewhere in the exalted range of most popular.

As the girls chatter, I tune in on Brenda, the Anglo in their midst. She speaks in the same chirpy, singsong way that her buddies do, making her "ch's" hard where they should be soft and soft where they should be hard. Speaking exactly the same way they are, just the way Brenda is, I might have been a Brenda at Providence because, for me, it was true: there were no outcasts in Catholic school. I had the best friends of my life in seventh and eighth grade, and I might have have ridden the coattails to popularity instead of being exiled to the social limbo I endured in public school.

Lunch ends, and the next class is religion. The teacher has an enormous cold sore blossoming on her upper lip. A couple of girls doze off before the bell stops ringing. In the old days, when you weren't memorizing excruciatingly tedious catechism Qs and As about why God made you, religion could be pretty gripping. Nothing could beat the Catholic Church back then for gore. There was always a new dimension in sadomasochism to explore, with martyrs who died disemboweling themselves or having all their more-tender bodily parts yanked out with red-hot pliers.

And if that wasn't enough to catch the attention of a sleepy eighth grader, there were always tales of eternity. Eternities where Catholic boys and girls who had defiled their temples burned, then froze, then burned, then froze for millennia, at which point the eternity they were doomed to suffer through had only just begun. In short, the grue never stopped.

But five minutes into this religion class, I have to agree with the sleeping critics—the Church has really become a snooze. The room is decorated with a poster bearing the title "My Declaration of Self-Esteem." It proclaims: "I Am Me. In all the world there is no one else exactly like me. I own me and therefore I can engineer me. I Am Me and I AM OKAY." Sacks of aluminum cans sit around waiting for recycling. On the shelves are books like *Jonathan Livingston Seagull* and *God Is for Real, Man.*

The text for the class, *A Journey in Faith*, is filled with pictures of longhaired young men sitting cross-legged on the grass, playing guitar for smiling ethnic children; close-ups of dewdrops glistening on leaves dappled with sunlight; shots taken from the back of black and white arms linked in friendship. No question, the grue was gone.

The last class of the day, Sacraments, is the one where an unembarrassed teacher will be discussing sex. As I walk into the room, I spot Lydia, Aurelia, and Brenda. Lydia waves violently for me, calling out "Miss Sarah." She makes the girl sitting next to her move over so I can sit down. In with the In Crowd.

"Okay, girls," the teacher, Miss Connie, a sweet-faced woman wearing Spirit Week socks and a Peter Pan hat, quiets her class. "Yesterday we discussed the sacrament of reconciliation."

I recall that "reconciliation" is the new name for confession, the House of Horrors sacrament that haunted my girlhood, riddling it with guilt and anxiety about impure thoughts; accidental nibbles on the communion host, meant to be swallowed whole; and the possibility that my intense love of the Beatles might be idol-worship.

Miss Connie continues, "And there were some questions about what was right and what was wrong about sex. So, what I want you to do today is write down your concerns, pass them in, and we'll put them in this little basket and shake them up so no one will know whose question we're reading and no one will be embarrassed."

The room falls silent, interrupted only by whispers and giggles, as the girls write their questions.

"Oh, I know what I want to ask," Lydia blurts out, seized by inspiration. Turning to Aurelia, she lowers her voice and asks, "Do you know what a semiannual erection is?" Aurelia shrugs. Lydia writes the question on a scrap of paper and passes it in. "I always wanted to know what that was," she mutters.

Miss Connie shakes up all the scraps of paper in the basket and plucks one out. "Is it bad if you're going with a guy but you keep wanting to mess around with your old boyfriend?"

"Oh, Lydia," someone on the other side of the room catcalls.

Lydia drops her jaw in a pantomime of amazement. "That's not my question!" she protests.

"Girls, girls, we don't care whose questions these are. Okay, first of all, feelings are never good or bad, they just are. Also I think that the writer's feelings are confused, and she needs to reevaluate her current relationship in light of her feelings for her old boyfriend."

What?! What about protecting the temple with your life? What about burning, then freezing, for all eternity? What about sin? This is Catholic school, not *The Phil Donahue Show*.

The teacher pulls out another question. Lydia is busy coloring in all the names of the gods in her pantheon.

Duran Duran, INXS, Billy Idol, The Fixx, Madonna, and U2 all dance around FRANK.

Miss Connie reads, "I get confused when people say you have to be on your period to get pregnant. Do you?"

Lydia puts aside her markers and listens, suddenly rapt. The news is bad: "A woman can get pregnant at any time of the month." Lydia sighs and pulls out a makeup kit as other questions are read and answered. "Can sperm go through your clothes if you have a really bad orgasm?" "What's an orgasm?" "My boyfriend tells me if I don't do stuff with him it means I don't love him."

Miss Connie dips into the basket again as Lydia scrunches down in her seat, holds up a hand mirror, and begins to line her eyes with a lapis lazuli–colored pencil. "This question is a joke," the teacher says, wadding up the bit of paper. The class demands to be in on it. Exasperated, she reads, "Okay, what's a semiannual erection?" Lydia stops circling, one eye iridescent blue, the other naked.

"Semiannual means twice a year," Miss Connie explains to her befuddled class. "So it's a joke."

Aurelia covers her mouth and points to Lydia. Lydia slaps her hand away and hisses at her to shut up.

Last question: "How far can you go before it's a sin?" Miss Connie looks up and asks, "Anyone want to help me with this one?"

I yearn to raise my hand and blurt out the answer: Any kiss over ten seconds delivered with more passion than you can work up for your brother is a mortal. But I fight the urge. It wouldn't be fair; I've already had the course. No one else volunteers, so the teacher tackles the question herself.

"Sex is a beautiful gift from God. For a very long time the church has downplayed the beauty of this gift. But it *is* beautiful when used in the best of circumstances—when two people who love each other are open to new life. The main thing is that it's a matter of personal choice."

It is clear now that the road I didn't take no longer exists. It's been paved over, the curves straightened, and the dark, shadowy trees chopped down. My untaken road has been transformed into a broad and sunny avenue that even Annie Garcia could have skipped gaily along, bopping to The Boss and making her own sweet personal choices about whose tongue she allowed into her mouth. I despair of ever again catching even a glimpse of the twisted path I once trod.

And then Lydia asks, just to get everything straight, "So kissing and stuff is okay?"

Miss Connie, a woman about my own age, who surely grew up with the All Eternity penalty for infractions against the ten-second rule, pauses a moment before answering. "Now, that's not what I said," she answers with a little laugh. "There are different degrees of kissing. A friendly peck on the cheek, no problem. A short goodnight kiss—again, no problem. But once you start getting to French kissing—"

I hold my breath, Sister Tabernacula's mustache twitching in my mind.

"—you start to have a problem."

Lydia swabs on a third coating of lip gloss just as the bell rings, hops out of her chair, and rushes from the room. Stopping briefly at the door, she yells back, "Bye, Miss Sarah, it was very nice to meet you. I hope you can come back to Providence again someday." Then she is gone, her face a neon rainbow waiting to blink on for FRANK.

From the Archives of the Heartbroken and Spiritually Bereft

MOTH RADIO HOUR, RECORDED DECEMBER 12, 2012,
PARAMOUNT THEATER, AUSTIN, TEXAS

I like to tell people that I came to Austin for graduate school. But that's a lie. The truth is that I moved here in 1973 for love. Crazy, stupid, young love. The object of my mad obsession was a guy who could make me laugh until I wet my pants and was hotter than lava in bed. So, naturally, when he told me that he had to move to Austin, Texas, to take "some courses," I could not pack fast enough.

My Albuquerque friends had a going-away party and gave me what they thought I'd need for my new life in Texas: three cans of hair spray and a toy six-shooter. Once in Austin, Mad Obsession and I set up a sweet little love nest in Travis Heights and he went off to what I assumed were graduate courses at the university. Very quickly, he became so deeply, scarily immersed in these courses, that he barely even came home. Not knowing a soul in this strange place or speaking the language in which Guadalupe became Gwadaloop, I became painfully homesick and more than a little clingy.

Watching myself slide into pathetic loserhood, I realized that what I needed was a job. A good job. Not one of the crap jobs I'd always had working my way through college. So I held out for that really good job and finally the perfect one came my way: temporary archivist technician at the Lyndon Baines Johnson Presidential Library. This was it. I could see myself discovering secret correspondence from Ho Chi Minh and never-before-seen briefs about civil rights initiatives. I imagined how proud my beloved would be if I could only get that job. And so, motivated by love and armed with a canny combination of lying and making shit up, I replaced my degree in Anthropology with a major in American Studies and a minor in Achievements of the Great Society. I got that job.

I raced home to give my beloved the wonderful news. I felt warm simply imagining how I would once again be basking in his admiration. He wasn't home. This was not unusual. But that night as the hours rolled by I had time to reflect and I started thinking about how much my sweetheart had changed since we'd arrived. How aloof and distracted he'd become. Why, it almost seemed as if he were keeping something from me. I had to face some very grim suspicions. When he finally dragged in around two in the morning, I confronted him. There followed a soul-searing, gut-wrenching showdown in which I forced him to tell me the truth. That's when I found out that, yes, he was in love with someone else. And that someone else was L. Ron Hubbard, the founder of Scientology.

My darling explained to me that Scientology is a religion dedicated to spiritual enlightenment through the pursuit of self-knowledge. He hadn't told me about it because he was scared I wouldn't understand. "Not understand?" I bleated. "We're both fall-away Catholics. Of course I understand. I understand the hunger for certainty, for black and white, for answers, that being a Catholic leaves you with for the rest of your life. Tell me. Tell me all about Scientology."

There followed a period of bliss in which we explored Scientology together. I learned about e-meters and engrams. About Operating Thetans and going Clear. I even took an introductory course. It was like a cross between an assertiveness training class and a toddler's birthday party. We had staring contests and the first person to blink lost. We played Simon Says. We played it the way it would have been played in the Prussian army.

The really sad thing was that as much as I wanted to believe, and no heretic on the rack wanted to believe more than I did, I just couldn't. In fact, the more I learned about this religion, the less plausible it seemed. In the end, I had to conclude that Scientology was a sci-fi pyramid scheme. When I shared this opinion with my darling, a wall like the Gaza Strip went up between us and overnight we became an interfaith couple.

Things at work weren't any better. I spent my days unpacking giant brown boxes and filing their contents into handsome red buckram boxes emblazoned with a gold presidential seal. Instead of civil rights initiatives and secret correspondence from Ho Chi Minh, though, the big brown boxes contained copies of Lady Bird's recipe for Bunkhouse Chili and reams and reams of letters from outraged schoolchildren telling LBJ that he was the most meanest president they ever knowed and ordering him to stop lifting his beagles, Him and Her, up by their ears.

The heaviest of the brown boxes were filled with photos. Photos of LBJ hiking up his shirt and showing that famous gall bladder surgery scar. Portraits of Lady Bird in a swoopy hat standing in a field of bluebonnets. And lots and lots of pictures of LBJ's beautiful daughters Lucy and Lynda.

I remember one in particular of Lynda's fairy-tale wedding. In it, she's standing next to her handsome new husband, a Marine captain, and they're cutting their gigantic, fruit-cake wedding cake with his sword.

I remember another beautiful photo. This one captured Lynda on her dream date with George Hamilton. They're dancing together, the magnolia-pale Lynda and the mahogany-brown George Hamilton.

But what really riveted me were the makeover photos before the date that showed Lynda having her widow's peak hairline plucked away, then her face being spackled in geisha white makeup, and finally having Big Bird eyelashes glued on. A makeover? I wondered. Is this what I needed?

Then I realized, no, it wasn't a cosmetic makeover I needed. It was a spiritual makeover. If it was spiritual enlightenment that gunned my baby's motor, then I decided that I would give him the kind of sweet, hot, smoking spiritual enlightenment that would curl his toes and clear his sinuses.

I set to work. I speed-dated all the isms. Taoism, Buddhism, Shintoism, and Hinduism. I signed up for Transcendental Meditation and brought my guru the items he required of me. Three clean, folded white handkerchiefs, four marigolds, and a check for thirty-five dollars. In return my guru gave me my own personal super-secret mantra, never to be revealed to anyone—inda—and then he taught me how to meditate.

Again, I raced home to the love nest. When my darling returned late that night, I very ostentatiously plunked myself down on the floor of the living room, and began to meditate. Being the grade-grubbing, overachiever that I was, I had no doubt that I would zoom to the head of the enlightenment class and start levitating. I imagined that my beloved would be so dazzled that he'd fall on his knees in front of my hovering form. When I opened my eyes, however, he was on the couch. Asleep with his back turned to me.

I gave up on all the theologies and philosophers except one, my boy Edgar Cayce. The Sleeping Prophet of Kentucky. I read Edgar on my lunch break on the days when I didn't spend the hour crying. I liked to sit in the shade of a live oak to thaw myself out from the cryogenic temperature the library was kept at and consume my invariable lunch of pimiento cheese sandwich, vanilla wafers, and the one, single, solitary thing I liked about Texas at that point, Diet Dr Pepper.

Then, one fateful day, just as I was starting in on my nilla wafers, I came upon Edgar Cayce's thoughts about soul mates. Edgar believed that some couples were so meant to be together that their love would transcend death and they would find each other again and again through many lifetimes. I put the book down and blinked up at a warm sun. Edgar was writing about me. Me and my soulmate. I brought my last cookie toward my mouth, and almost gulped it down, but in the second before I did, its artificial vanilla scent brought back a flood of childhood memories. That Proustian moment combined with the wisdom of the Sleeping Prophet showed me clearly what I had to do.

Back on the fifth floor, I started in eagerly cataloguing the very next acid-free, archival box that I would place on the shelves of the LBJ Presidential Library. To stay there forever. Through many, many lifetimes. When the red box was filled, I sniffed that vanilla wafer one last time, embedded its scent in the limbic chambers of my brain, dropped it in, and shut the lid. I put the box on the shelf certain that in some future existence, reincarnated Sarah would find it. Perhaps she would be researching Lady Bird's recipe for Bunkhouse Chili or Dream Dates of the Presidential Daughters. All I know is that Future Sarah would open the box, the scent of fake vanilla would overwhelm her, and she would remember that she had been here before. And that she had to find her soul mate. How she was going to do this I didn't know. I couldn't figure everything out for Future Sarah.

Hope was born again. Sure, there were problems, a few wrinkles to be ironed out in the here and now, but I had figured out the big one. I had figured out eternity. My beloved and I would be together. Forever. When I got home he was packing his car to leave.

"What are you doing?" I asked.

"I've been called to LA to work at the Celebrity Centre," he informed me.

"No," I pleaded, "you can't leave. We're soul mates. We're meant to be together in this life and in all future lives."

He stopped packing, riveted me with the patented Scientology laser stare, and said, "That can never happen, Sarah. You're an SP."

An SP is a Suppressive Person, the worst thing you can be in Scientology. SP means: you are dead to me. When he drove away, I was so shocked and heartbroken that I couldn't even cry.

Along with my grand affair, my temporary job was also coming to an end. Finally, there was only one big brown box left to break down, a huge one on the top shelf that I'd saved for last. When that box was emptied, my life in Austin would be over and there would not be one single reason I shouldn't pack up and head back to Albuquerque.

I braced myself as I reached up to heave that last box off the shelf. But when I hefted it up, the box was so light that it threw me off balance, and I went clanging backwards into the empty shelf behind me. The box felt empty. Puzzled, I rushed it over to my work area and there under the bare bulb, I opened up the big brown box. Inside the big brown box I found dozens and dozens and dozens of little heart-shaped boxes covered in white satin with red curlicue writing on the top. I plucked out one of the boxes and opened it. Inside the little white heart was a tiny packet covered in a red foil doily. I unwrapped the doily and inside was what appeared to be a piece of jerky. Gradually, I realized what it was. This was Lynda Bird's fruitcake wedding cake. The instant I realized that it was or had once been edible, I popped the withered nugget into my mouth and bit down. This little piece of fruitcake jerky had been sitting on the tinfoil for such a long time that it was thoroughly metallicized, and when I bit down, it was exactly like biting into a piece of tin foil. I got a giant shock in my back molars.

At that literally electric moment, I started to sob. Because I knew, finally knew, that it was over. If this, this fruitcake, the only truly eternal baked good there is, had turned into such a tasteless metallic puck, what chance did the vanilla wafers whose scent was supposed to rekindle my lost love have?

That was it. I didn't have a soul mate in this life and I would not be sending any messages to a future soul mate in the next.

My sweetheart did end up going to Los Angeles and at the Celebrity Centre, he met an actress named Mimi who took his last name, Rogers, when they married. Mimi ditched my old flame for Tom Cruise. Tom dumped her for Nicole. And then there was Katie. And then there was Tom jumping up and down on Oprah's sofa.

As for me, I stayed in Austin. I went to graduate school.

I became a writer and grew to know and love all of the university's libraries. And just last week my super-cute husband and I celebrated the thirty-fourth anniversary of our first date.

I don't think much anymore about eternity and reincarnation. I'm a fallaway Catholic who's gotten comfortable with uncertainty. But the one thing I am certain of is, my life, my real life, the life in Austin I was meant to have, began on the day that I found Lynda Bird's wedding cake in the LBJ Library.

Road Coma

SOUTHERN MAGAZINE, JULY 1987

T here is really only one way to cruise the infinite flatness of west Texas that is bisected by Interstate 10: you must be tucked cozily into one of the classic American living rooms on wheels. A Lincoln Continental, a Chrysler New Yorker, a Buick Electra—any automobile that makes you feel as if the landscape whizzing past is simply an especially boring movie will do nicely. And you must have your windows sealed tightly against the flatland's two major features: heat and dust. Air-conditioning must be present and switched to Polar Blast. You must have cruise control, and it must be set at the highest legal limit. When all these conditions are met, you can pretty much snooze from Austin to El Paso. Oh, you might bump off the black-top every now and again, but road and terrain are so similar that going from one to the other will barely ruffle an eyelid.

This is the way to do I-10 right. Unfortunately, the way I normally traversed this noble strip of asphalt was in a 1973 Vega. No AC. No cruise to control. An engine that melted down if you drove too fast, too long, or too hot. Since the 583 miles between Austin, where I lived, and El Paso, where I was often bound, are chiefly defined by speed, length, and heat, a 1973 Vega was not the vehicle of choice. Still, the cigarette lighter worked, which would have been a great comfort if I'd smoked. Anything other than the aluminum engine I had to replace twice, that is.

During the seasons I followed the rodeo circuit, I spent untold hours babying the "Vegematic," as I termed it, along I-10. I saw wondrous things on that stretch of highway. I saw a pack of millipedes a half-foot long squiggling across the highway, which unsettled me so much that I had to pull off on the shoulder; I thought the road was full of cracks and they were coming alive in my mind. I saw a man, naked as a newt, in an open-sided jeep who stood up and drove alongside me for several miles. I saw a flash flood that turned the alkaline flatlands into the bottom of a swimming pool, one filling with a speed so frightening it had me searching for a higher ground that wasn't to be found for one hundred miles. Luckily the rain stopped, the sun came out, and fifteen minutes later the land was again as dry as a ballroom floor. I saw Ali Baba's Baghdad complete with flying carpets in mirages that shimmered forever just ahead.

If you've got the rhythm right, though, you won't even slow down for a flash flood, let alone a Middle Eastern mirage. The idea along I-10 is not so much to drive as it is to point, aim, and fire. To make your car a bullet headed straight for the heart of Ozona, Fort Stockton, Balmorhea, El Paso. After countless hours of observation, I concluded that nobody did ballistics driving better than the rodeo's madman, The Bullrider.

Out on I-10, The Bullrider, not Roger Miller, is King of the Road. The Bullrider is cleared for takeoff on 1-10.

Of course he drives a Cadillac. The Bullrider buys more Cadillacs than underwear and wears them out even more quickly, barreling down roads such as I-10 to get from one rodeo to the next. It was an exciting moment when one would hove into sight in my rearview mirror. I could see him coming up on me for twenty miles or so, unmistakably The Bullrider. I could spot him on sight because he held the patent on the I-10 look, a look that consists mostly of a cowboy hat with a monstrous wingspan, and shoulders only slightly less wide, filling most of the windshield. And, if that wasn't identifiable enough, he had the posture. The posture is a trademark lean that draws The Bullrider toward the center of the car so that his head lines up squarely with the hood ornament. I can only guess that cozying up to a long succession of female partners leaves The Bullrider with a strange kind of tropism that pulls him to the right whether the passenger seat is occupied or not.

Still ten miles behind me, The Bullrider would start easing into the other lane to pass. It would seem to take him forever to swoop down on me. Then, in an instant, he'd blow by. The Vegematic's fragile, fiberglass body rattled and shimmied like it'd been sideswiped by a semi. For the next half hour, I'd watch as The Bullrider gradually veered back into the right lane. This long, sweeping pass is the true mark of I-10 royalty, for it demonstrates absolute mastery of the I-10 road coma. Only a certified road coma adept can burn up an entire tank of gas without once easing off the accelerator or moving his hand more than a fraction of an inch away from high noon on the steering wheel.

I didn't need that demonstration, however, to remind me that The Bullrider in his Caddie was king and I in my Vega a serf. Where his majesty charged past on his sleek steed, I tooled along in my Vegematic, a peasant inching her way across the beet field. I putted, I crept, I crawled across that monumental stretch of real estate. Most of the time I was tensely anticipating the moment the engine light would blink on and signal that it was time to buy, not oil, but another engine. If it wasn't that, I was anxiously searching for the rest-stop-suitable hill or grove of trees that never materialized. If it teaches the female motorist nothing else, I-10 will teach her just how far it is between Dairy Queens.

Still, there were moments when even I achieved road coma. They came after a long day on the road when, dehydrated and bored with waiting for the Vega to signal that she required another engine transplant, I would give myself over to west Texas. Instead of emptiness, I'd see mesquite trees with tiny green leaves, Spanish dagger plants presenting arms to the sky, prickly pear bright with radish-red "tunas." I'd see how the chartreuse creosote bushes, with their roots that repelled invaders, each occupied its own evenly spaced square, creating a strict checkerboard that marched all the way to the far horizon. Along fence lines, patient cows plodded home. At those times the black V's of the turkey vultures hovering overhead seemed the only thing between me and a blue eternity beyond. Perhaps these moments transcended road coma. Perhaps the majestic expanses caused my spirit to soar. I can't say. All I know is that I'd come to seventy miles later and find myself pulling into Van Horn with no recollection of how the previous hour had vanished.

Thinking about it now makes me want to saddle up and hit the trail again, to ride I-10 one more time. Thankfully, the Vegematic has long since gone to its reward in that big lemon grove in the sky, so this time I could do I-10 the right way, the way that would pay homage to both the grandeur of the land and the massive tax support accorded the Texas Highway Department. I'm thinking of a Winnebago. Fully loaded. In-cabin sanitary facilities. An air conditioner that

could lay a chill on the Astrodome. Cruise controlled well
into triple digits. Once I had my extra capacity reserve tank
topped off and my clip-on sunglasses in place, I would hit
the trail like a cow patty. I would get out there, a sure strike
on God's own bowling alley, and show The Bullrider just
what road coma is all about on I-10.

Bumfuzzled

TEXAS CO-OP POWER MAGAZINE, 1998

My introduction to rodeo came in the person of Dakota Prewitt, whose real name is even more cowboy than Dakota Prewitt. Dakota, with his Walmart sex appeal, physical courage, and stiff-necked disdain for all social fripperies from toothbrushing to functional literacy, became emblematic for me of the hardest of hardscrabble worlds.

I first laid eyes on Dakota at the Duke City Truckstop off University Avenue in Albuquerque, New Mexico. I was "on assignment" working as an eager, endlessly exploitable young freelance photojournalist of the sort that editors of soon-to-be-defunct city magazines with no intention whatsoever of paying said freelancer would give assignments to—such as the venerable old chestnut "How Much Do You Make?"—and send off to stick a camera in strangers' faces and ask them what their take-home pay was.

It didn't matter. I was fresh out of grad school, and like most who'd tarried too long in the groves of academe, I wanted only what the Velveteen Rabbit had thrown it all away for: the chance to be real. Since this was 1977, let's add one other ingredient to the fantasy cocktail, "Urban Cowboy." Yes, along with the rest of the nation, John Travolta had convinced me that every tile salesman, carpet layer, and cable installer who owned a pair of boots and a big hat was—Hai Karate men's cologne and leather-look vinyl jacket notwithstanding—a mythical American figure of deep and enduring glamour.

This then is what criminal psychologists would have called my "mind set."

I did not, however, sashay into the Duke City Truck Stop specifically trolling for cowboys. I was actually looking for a lady truck driver. As I entered the truckstop through a cloud of cigarette smoke, old grease, and bitter coffee that shrouded the truck stop, the place didn't fall as silent as, say, the Dairy Queen in Snyder, Texas, would have if a five-foot-eleven, unaccompanied female draped in cameras had sauntered in, but a shift in attention, like a drop in barometric pressure, was instantly detectable. It came with a particular acuteness from the far corner booth, where Dakota and three of his running buddies were caffing up. Their gazes stalked me as I shuffled from table to table stalking my own prey.

As it turned out, the only female truck driver in attendance that night at the Duke City wore her hair like Rudolph Valentino, carried her wallet on a logging chain and weighed only slightly less than a banker's desk. In answer to my perky-polite invitation to say cheese and share her salary with the world, my subject allowed as how she did not care to have her "*^%*&^% picture made." Though I backed off as quickly as I could, it became immediately clear that, in the parallel universe of 350-pound female truck drivers, inquiries about average annual earnings were tantamount to death threats that had to be answered with much high-volume cursing. Being condemned to hell by the equivalent of one-and-a-half Roseannes brought the attention level up even more sharply.

The mother trucker stopped screaming for a second, and the place fell silent. Then, from that booth in the far corner: "Hey, darlin', make my picture."

Was it being rescued? Was it being called darlin' for the first time in a life of punctiliously complete suffixes? Was it that smile? Teeth mottled brown and white from the well water like caramel cremes, like a water spaniel, like a spotted fawn. Whatever, I smiled back and turned away from the disgruntled trucker like she had never existed. Dakota shoved the crony next to him out of his seat, and I slid in, sheltering beneath the pterodactylian wingspan of his black Resistol, ready to begin the lesson that would last for the next five years and take me fifty thousand miles across five states and northern Mexico. The lesson that the suburbs flow right through a person, but rural soaks in to the bone.

Dakota Prewitt smelled like Dinty Moore Beef Stew. His eyes were blue as the faded Wranglers he wore stuffed into his boot tops. His nose had been resculpted several times by fist and horn, the same forces that had silvered his lips, chin, and forehead with scars pale as the underside of cottonwood leaves. He and his posse were driving back to Clovis from a rodeo in Farmington where Dakota had won the bullriding competition. They were celebrating with shots of Wild Turkey bootlegged into their truck-stop coffee. Did I want one? Dakota asked, smiling that smile. I decided that participatory journalism had to be the way to go. Two cups later, Dakota agreed to answer the annual income question.

"Fifty thousand dollars." It was a lie. But it would be some time before I figured out that a bull rider on the amateur circuit could win every competition at every rodeo held within the continental United States for an entire year and not make that kind of money. This didn't matter, either. Dakota's buddies laughed while I wrote the figure down, then they all tried to crowd into the photo I took of him. Then I drank enough cups of Wild Turkey coffee to make me feel like it was even money whether I'd pass out or jump up and kickbox the lardy lady driver who was still glowering with hair-trigger paranoia at me.

Around the sixth mug, Dakota tilted the saucer-sized buckle holding his jeans up at me, so I could see that he was the Roswell Pioneer Days Bullriding Champion of 1975. The light from the fluorescent fixture sizzling above our heads caught on the silver plating of the buckle and reflected back into my eyes, dazzling me. In that instant, with caffeine and alcohol duking it out for possession of my brain, I fell a little in love with both Dakota Prewitt and with rodeo.

At three in the morning, the posse was ready to leave. While the other three piled into the double cab to wait, Dakota started to say goodbye. At 3:30, the guys in the truck began honking the horn. At 3:45, without a word, they picked Dakota up and carried him away.

"Darlin', come see me in Clovis," he yelled back at me. "Livestock auction. Any Wednesday afternoon."

I finished my assignment. It was printed. The magazine went out of business. I was never paid. A few months later, having finally realized that freelance journalism was a hobby I could not afford, I accepted a job in Austin, Texas. Now, there are two ways to get from Albuquerque, New Mexico, to Austin, Texas. There is the southern route: go out the back door, turn left at El Paso, aim for Austin, put on cruise control, and catch up on your reading. The other way, the northern route, would take a cowgirl newly in possession of a pair of Wrangler jeans die-rectly through Clovis, New Mexico.

I took the northern route. And I left before dawn on a Wednesday. Auction day in Clovis.

I saw Dakota off and on over the next couple of years whenever a rodeo brought him within striking distance of Austin. I found out a lot of things about Dakota Prewitt. I found out that his real name was Marlin, but that he'd have to hurt anyone who dared to use it. I found out where each of the silvery scars that sprinkled his body had come from. I found out that, although he frequently worked like a coolie from can see to can't see, his greatest fear in life was "the nine to five." Mostly I found out the truth of the bumper sticker wisdom that decreed: "Only a cowgirl is tough enough to love a cowboy," and that no matter how many pairs of Wranglers I bought, or g's I dropped from the endings of my present participles, or DQ Hungerbusters I ate, I would never be tough enough because, yes, it is true, the suburbs do flow right through a person, but rural sinks in to the bone.

The last time I saw Dakota, he was packing up and leaving Clovis for parts unknown. There was a possibility in Montana, a buddy up there had a spread. Needed some help. 'Course, another friend was running contraband steers across the border, might look into that. He wasn't sure.

"How can I get in touch with you?" I asked. Dakota tilted his head from side to side like a cat when you pull two pieces of string apart in front of it. It was from Dakota himself that I'd learned the words to describe this expression of utter puzzlement: bumfuzzled. Dakota was bumfuzzled by my question. "Whudda ya mean?"

"You know, your address. What's your address?"

Dakota thought about it, the idea of addresses, of staying in touch. Then he smiled his mottled smile—and it was radiant in that Midas western light that gold plates everything it touches, from a cloud of blossoms on a redbud tree to a rusted-out hay baler—and answered, "Address? Just write me in care of wherever night overtakes me."

So Dakota, wherever night may be overtaking you these days, this one is for you.

Talkin' Trash

THIRD COAST, AUGUST 1982

The tennis-tanned matron, trim in her madras bermudas, kneels on her manicured piece of the Milwood subdivision savaging a patch of crabgrass. She glances up, hearing the unmistakable bass rumble, the groan of air brakes, the clank of metal against metal, the whistles, the men's cries. Her husband, retired now, comes around from the back yard drawn by the sounds which mean that the show is about to begin.

It's a thirty-second spectacle where East meets West Austin. It's a raucous two-man Mardi Gras parading through Tarrytown. It's garbage day in west Austin.

The humpbacked white truck weaves up the hill in a series of crazy parabolas. James Wingwood and Robert Cleveland hit the pavement running before the truck stops and hustle over to the clutch of some sixty Hefty bags the lawn-care couple has spawned. The woman's trowel freezes in midair as she reads the message on Wingwood's cap: Sex Instructor, First Lesson Free.

Wingwood and Cleveland are a team, friends on and off the job, a job they've been at since graduating high school, three, four years ago. They attack Mt. Hefty and start tossing the plump green bundles into the truck's hopper. All easy baskets. Wingwood goes for a tougher shot and slings a bag from behind his back. It's a little wide of the mark, but Cleveland snags it in midair and taps it into the hopper. Finally just a lone can remains. Wingwood pops off the lid, grabs the handles, and kicks the can with his imitation, zip-up army boot, launching the container into a controlled arc. Not so much as a Polident wrapper spills out until the can is over the hopper. Wingwood dumps it in and spins the can back into place on the sidewalk in one fluid motion.

Cleveland punches the button that works the truck's mouth, making it chew and swallow the green-bagged load. The hopper blade scrapes the whole mess back into the truck's belly and packs it down while the two men sprint to the other side of the street as the truck lurches forward.

"Ho!" Wingwood yells and the truck takes off. The pair scrambles to their perches at the back. Cleveland hangs off to the side to grab a few lungfuls of fresh air and to dry the sweat soaking his shirt. Wingwood cocks his hips jauntily and rests a foot on the hopper lid.

The retired couple watch warily, fascinated, until the truck disappears over the hill, then they go back to creating Thursday's deposit.

If you had to have either no doctors or no garbageman in your city, which would you choose? It's a silly question, sort of like having to decide whether you'd drive over the side of a cliff or mow your mother down, but it does, for a brief moment, make you think about this most basic of subjects. Garbage, refuse, solid waste, trash, whatever you call it, Austinites don't devote nearly as much time to thinking about it as we do to creating it.

Last year the city handled 148,000 tons of the stuff (for

those of you who like visual aids, that's enough rubble to fill a twenty-one-story Memorial Stadium), and that was only 40 percent of Austin's total offal output. The rest is carted away from large apartment complexes, shopping centers, industries, and the like by private haulers. It will cost us, the city's 95,000 residential customers, $7.8 million this year to disencumber ourselves of stuff we don't want. We cover that sum with the $4.80 on our electric bill designated for residential sanitation. That we *don't* have to spend more money and time thinking about the accomplishment of this massive chore attests to the quality of our refuse (the officially preferred term) collection force.

Our garbagemen haven't gone out on strike since 1966. They voluntarily put in a lot of extra cleanup time for six weeks after last year's flood. We have two-day-a-week service while many cities have cut back to one. Austin's trashmen will haul off just about anything you can lug out to the curb, though other cities have banned yard debris and mandated that everything else must be plastic-bagged. And most remarkably, while Austin has lengthened her garbage pickup roster by 26,000 customers, only one three-man crew has been added in the last ten years to the fifty already in service, with no further additions predicted for the next couple of years.

A garbageman's day starts early. Before seven in the morning, they're heading down East 12th past the Soul Train Record Shop, the Groovy Bar, King Tears Mortuary, and the Untouchables Lounge, across Pleasant Valley Road and over the railroad tracks to "the yard"—Sanitation Division headquarters. The Boss Hog, Wheat, Stick Shift, the Reverend, and the Dean of the Can Throwers are already there. They're veterans, and it's a Monday; they know Mondays are heavy days. The men range from boys barely finished with high school up to Matthew Simms. Sixty-two years old and a deacon in his church, Simms has seen more than twenty years of sanitation service.

Simms is one of fifty-seven drivers, one third of the three-man crew on every truck. The other two men in the crew are what the city calls "public service helpers." There are 113 helpers, the can tossers, the Hefty hefters. The men themselves refer to public service helping as "working the ground." In an average day on the ground each man will lift six or seven tons of garbage. A fifteen-ton day is not unheard of. The median salary for can tossers is $5.81 an hour. The median for drivers is $7.30.

Among the 170 men are carpenters, ex-cooks, former long-haul truckers, farmers, deacons, ordained ministers, and men you wouldn't want to meet in a dark alley: the congenial and the convicted. The large majority of the men on the ground are black—72 percent—10 percent are white, and 16 percent are Hispanic. The figures shift a bit for drivers: 47 percent are black, 22 white, and 25 Hispanic.

What makes a good helper? "We look for an attitude towards the public," says Freddie Verrell, superintendent. Verrell, like the six supervisors under him, has worked the ground. He started in 1952 pitching brown paper bags onto the back of a flatbed truck for sixty-seven cents an hour. "We don't want someone who's going to rip and run, breaking cans. Out of every ten we hire in the winter, nine stay. Last summer we hired fifteen and only seven of them made it. It takes a strong-minded person to stay with it."

It doesn't hurt, either, to have a stomach to match. "You can be here twenty years," says Jesse Morales, a husky family man who favors dangling earrings and is chairperson of the first Employee Task Force, "and never get used to that smell. You've never smelled anything until you've smelled fish or shrimp that's been left out over the weekend in August." Stench also has a way of corporealizing into something those who know refer to as "crawling rice."

"My first summer here," recalls Morales, "just when it started warming up, I popped the lid off this can and there they were just crawling all over everything. Maggots. Man, they flew up or jumped up and were all over me. I quit eating rice that summer." Morales dropped 50 of his 240 pounds during the first strenuous six months. "I would of quit if I'd been a single man."

Edward "Wheat" Anderson, 36, like many of the men, covers his hair in plastic, "so that I don't have to wash my head every night." Anderson started thirteen years ago and went from 218 to 195 pounds in his first two weeks. When asked how he keeps in shape for the work, he glances at Morales and the two men smile. "Don't have to," he laughs. "The cans'll keep you in shape."

There are times, though, when even being in shape isn't enough. Three years ago Morales pulled up beside a long, goose-neck trailer blocking a row of plastic cans. He and his partner had to scurry around the obstacle to collect the trash. When they'd dumped the plastic cans, they tossed them back over the trailer. The owner of the cans and trailer stormed out spewing insults. Morales advised him that collecting verbal filth wasn't part of his job. The man left and reappeared a few seconds later with a .357 Magnum which he fired off. The driver hit the floorboard of the truck, the other helper became a shirttail flapping down the street, and Morales faked catatonia until the police showed up.

Then there was the time some gentle soul mined a plastic bag with shards of broken glass. When Morales's partner lifted the bag, the shards popped right through plastic, pants leg, and a major artery. Another favorite trick is dumping hot coals in the trash. Morales recounts stories of unwitting pyromaniacs who've set entire trucks packed with seven tons of trash on fire.

The stories go on: The can that three men couldn't budge. The couches people expect them to feed into the back of the truck. The burns from battery acid, solvents, and dangerous chemicals all mixed in with the eggshells and coffee grounds. The bag records—110 at one house. And the complaints. Complaints about missed trash logged by late sleepers. Complaints about garbagemen strewing trash. (Trash that usually turns out to be heavily pocked with canine tooth marks.) Complaints about service that is too early or too late, too loud, too fast, or too slow. People expect a lot for their $4.80 a month.

But flaming trucks and .357 debate tactics, as dramatic as they are, are only the occasional catastrophes that add spice to life on the ground. To find out what garbagemen despise most on a day-to-day basis, let's head back up to far, far northwest Austin, back to Milwood.

Mr. and Mrs. Garden Trowel undoubtedly consider themselves models of neatness, with tiny moats edging their lawns and their incessant yard work filling dozens of twist-tied bags. Well, folks, the truth of the matter is, they are a garbageman's nightmare. Their route, number 49, is one of the most hated in the city. Why? All that flora they mow and clip and rake is, as we learned in Bio 101, mostly liquid. Then they stuff it into a thirty-gallon bag. Consider for a moment how heavy one gallon of milk is. Now think of lifting thirty gallons. A few thousand times. On a 100-degree day, when the bag has disintegrated in the sun and falls apart when you pick it up.

Oh yes, lawnatics: they hate you down at Solid Waste Services.

But bulging bags of cow chow aren't the only explanation for Route 49's infamy. While the average route has a maximum of 850 houses, the growth in this remote tentacle of Austin has so far outstripped the city's ability to manage it that the feared 49 has a staggering 1,600 stops. If that weren't enough, it is twenty-seven miles from the municipal landfill. On heavy days the trucks may reach their twenty-five-cubic-yard capacity three times. That means three fifty-four-mile round-trips out to the fill. On one monumental Monday last April, after the first burst of spring cleaning, crews worked until midnight hauling away six truckloads apiece of Route 49 cast-offs. Even on a fairly average day, like the Monday I rode Route 49, you quickly learn just how revealing those castoffs can be.

Garbagemen see it all. They see the lawn clippings, the ceiling fan boxes, the jugs of dirty motor oil, the empty charcoal bags, the beer cans, and they know how you spent your weekend. They see the mildewed roll of lime-green carpet, the brown and brittle pine with a few strands of Christmas tinsel put out five months after Christmas, the battered Jimmy Carter for Reelection sign, the rusty set of weights, and they know your follies and dashed dreams. But mostly, they know your wastefulness

"Anything you can imagine, they'll put it out," affirms Wheat Anderson. In his thirteen years with Solid Waste Services, Anderson has toted home a veritable yard sale of goods—telephones, blankets, radios, toasters, pictures. "Those high-priced pictures with those good frames. Took them home and put them right up on the wall."

Kerry Lee, 27, has been on the force only one week, working in Balcones Hills, and has already seen brand-new stereo speakers, turntables, clothing, sterling silver, and "anything else you can think of" heaped by the curb for collection. "Yeah," Jesse Morales chimes in. "For two years I didn't have to buy boots, work clothes, nothing. That was before the ordinance."

The "ordinance" is actually a combination of a state law that says no employee shall benefit personally from his job, and a department policy that hasn't been enforced until recently. The dormant policy came to life two years ago after a man lost three fingers while attempting to snatch a cowboy hat away from a hopper blade. Needless to say, the newly enforced policy against what's called "junking" is not popular with the men, many of whom used to count on the deposits from the soda bottles they retrieved for lunch money and the castoff clothes and boots to round out their wardrobes.

Junking is not much of an issue on the second-most-hated route in the city. Here the garbage can is not the horn of plenty it is in northwest Austin. They call this the Tenth Ward, that area between Pleasant Valley Road and IH-35 bordering Town Lake where imagination and passion show themselves in electric blue and hot pink houses guarded by live roosters and plaster madonnas. Here the problem isn't bags of dead vegetation, but the live stuff.

About three years ago the city cut funds for the maintenance of alleys, which is where most of the trash on the Tenth Ward is collected. The alleys are a trash hauler's own little Vietnam—tropically overgrown and booby-trapped with tree limbs that whip the unwary in the face. Our men get precious little support from the local populace: residents were supposed to take over alley maintenance but few have. Clearance for the big trucks in most alleys is nonexistent, so the men in back can't hang off to the side to grab a breath of untainted air. They have to cling to the back, usually ducking down to avoid the big branches that come whipping over the top or bobbing to absorb the shock of potholes that sink the trucks down to their bumpers.

The day I rode along on the alleys I watched two rare specimens in action: a pair of white helpers, Bill Dzenowski, 52, and David Whitley, 25. Dzenowski has been working the ground since 1958 and shows every minute of it. He's got forearms like Popeye and his chest, shoulders, and belly strain his T-shirt, the one with a picture of his favorite beverage on the front—a Lone Star Longneck. To watch Dzenowski is to see a consummate pro in action. With those massive Popeye forearms cocked to the side just like the Sailorman himself, he approaches two metal—metal, mind you—cans. Dzenowski grabs one in each hand, carries them over to the truck, and upends them both as easily as if they were giant meringues filled with cotton candy. They aren't.

Here in the Tenth Ward you get right down to basic nutritional debris—cereal boxes, banana peels, milk cartons. No stereos and framed pictures. Not even many aluminum cans. Most of those are sitting in a box in the backyard next to the sack of newspapers bound to be sold by the pound. Such frugality, it seems, would make the garbageman's load lighter. Apparently it doesn't.

Jesse Morales asks the question: "Where do they get all that trash? You pick up on Tuesday and by Friday they've got just as much. Do they go out to the dump and get it?"

"I don't know where they get it," says Superintendent Verrell. "Just eating good, I guess. Us poor folks believe in eating first," he laughs. "That's why those folks out in Balcones Hills are rich—they don't eat. They can afford to throw away radios, pocket watches, wristwatches. Even found a 30-30 Winchester once. Shot many a deer with it. But no, I don't know where all that garbage comes from."

Whatever its source, the combination of three-day-old food scraps and an airless alley is a real stomach-turner. Whitley and Dzenowski rush through the route hurrying to pack in a load. When the truck is full they head out to the Municipal Landfill.

If it's been used or wasted in Austin, this is where it's likely to end up, the Municipal Landfill off US 183 south of Bergstrom, 126 acres of what once was gullies, ravines, and washouts owned by Buck Steiner. Since it was leased to the city fifteen years ago, almost all of those natural excavations have been deepened and then filled.

A steady stream of white trucks lumbers off of US 183 and onto Elroy Road like wounded elephants headed for the burial grounds. "Leaches," says one of the men, pointing toward a couple of trucks emblazoned with the university's orange and white seal. For a moment I think they are passing judgment on the ultimate social relevance of our universities. Then I notice, in gleaming chrome on the side of the truck, the trademark, Leach. "Worst garbage truck ever made," they continue. "Not worth a plug nickel."

Garbagemen relate to their trucks the way cowboys do to horses, washing them down at the end of a hard day, making sure they're tended to with the right diesel fuel and oil, arguing the merits of one over another. I learned that "the best garbage truck ever built" is a twenty-five-yard Heil Easy-Pack bed mounted behind the Mark V International Harvester cab. "All the action's in the blade. It drops down and scoops everything up. Nothing else moves."

Outside the landfill are clumps of stray bags bumped off the end of a truck. They rustle in the wind like lost souls in purgatory waiting for admission to their final resting place. A lot of garbage has found eternal repose here. We drive out to the edge of the ravine and dump our load. Compactors, giant, metal-treaded affairs, push the unending deposits into the abyss, then tamp them down. We sit on fifteen years' worth of garbage, seventy-two feet of it.

The smell is not what you'd expect. Instead of rot, the odor is a cross between that of a bunch of week-old bananas and a transmission repair shop, a sort of overripe industrialism. It helps that there's a steady wind blowing off all the landing strips at Bergstrom and that they cover each day's mashed-down accumulation with six inches of dirt. When an area has been packed to capacity it's covered with two to three final feet of soil. Maize is growing on some of the closed-out sections. In a farmed-out area where one cutting a year is all that's hoped for, the rubble-rich ground is yielding two to three.

Most of the fill has been closed out. In less than a year it will be full. The city has filed a permit application to site another dump at Pearce Lane off of FM 973 east of Bergstrom. The 647 acres the city is applying for have a projected life span of forty years. The city has already taken steps to ensure that the new fill's life expectancy is not cut short.

Most garbagemen are not given to waxing philosophical on their place in a grander scheme. It's just a job, one they can perform without a college or sometimes even a high school diploma. One that keeps them in shape and looking good for the women who appreciate a fine body. And it's fairly secure work. It's a job that has to be done and they do it in rain and sleet and gloom of night without any epic poems or chiseled monuments to celebrate their perseverance. They know that streets can be potholed, burglaries unsolved, and parks untrimmed for months and no one will complain, but let them slip up on their jobs for even one day and the telephone wires will burn up.

Through it all, Austin's garbagemen display a surprising amount of dedication. "It's our job," says Wheat Anderson, "we got to get it. If they put it out, we got to get it. Just have to get it the next day if we don't. It's our job."

Clifton E. Dukes has spent thirteen of his thirty-one years with Solid Waste Services, ten of them on the ground. When he started out he was still in high school, working nights. During the days his buddies would ask, "How can you *do* that?" He was six foot one and weighed 137 pounds. The old hands told him he'd never make it. At the end of his first day his only comment was, "Is this all?"

Dukes made it; he is now a supervisor with thirty-six men under him, a few of them those same high school buddies who scoffed at his career choice. You get the feeling that he'd trade his desk in for the cab, or even better, the bumper, of a twenty-five-yarder in a second if the management job didn't pay so well. "Some people get a thrill out of sailing or flying. I get that thrill on the back of a truck. It's like riding a motorcycle. There's a freedom about it. I loved every minute of those ten years. There's something about the back of a garbage truck that just makes you feel good all over."

Jesse Morales picks up the theme. "We have our sweet days and we have our bitter," he muses. "The bitters are Monday and Tuesday, the sweets are Thursday and Friday."

Unless, of course, they've been fishing down in the Tenth Ward or that couple up in Milwood has been out mowing and clipping again.

Knocking on Heaven's Door

THIRD COAST, JULY 1983

We were three women in low-heeled shoes and belted dresses going door to door to tell complete strangers that they were living in the Last Days as foretold by the Bible. My companions, Jenny Turner, 33, and Georgeanna Matthews, 67, are two of Austin's twelve hundred Jehovah's Witnesses and they were doing what their church calls "pioneer" work. I was tagging along as an interested observer, sort of witnessing the Witnesses.

It was early Saturday morning and the neighborhood we were driving through was working-class with aspirations. The lawns were neatly clipped and edged. Many of the simple frame houses had been spiffed up with masonry work. But the vehicles told the tale. Trans Am–type autos ripped up and down the street. Vans wore magnetic signs touting "Red's TV Repair" and "Insta-grow Lawn Service." Three, count 'em, three jeeps were parked outside one house.

Georgeanna checked her House-to-House Record as we pulled to a stop. We would be visiting houses where no one had been home on earlier calls. "Okay, pick up a number,"

Georgeanna said. Jenny obliged and we zeroed in on our first target.

I'd met the two women a couple of months earlier when they'd appeared at my door to "share a thought from the Bible." Since I usually greet strangers bearing Bibles with all the cordiality one reserves for, well, strangers bearing Bibles, I can't explain why I didn't employ my typical response and hide behind the sofa until they left. All I can say is that Jenny, with her sparkling brown eyes, round cheeks, and close-cropped curly hair, begs to be described as "baby-faced." And Georgeanna? Imagine, if you will, your favorite, most grandmotherly grade school teacher. The pair was irresistible.

So for $2.50 I bought the red book they were offering that day, *You Can Live Forever in Paradise on Earth*, and spoke at length with them about the pitiful shape the world is in Suddenly, as I made expressions of polite interest, I began to wonder what it would be like to stand on a strange porch and attempt to interest someone behind a screen door in your worldview.

Although Georgeanna and Jenny were surprisingly receptive to my request to accompany them on their visitations, it still took about a month for my mission to be approved. The delay was due to the fact that the Witnesses have no paid clergy, so I had to wait until the circuit supervisor, Steve Misterfeld, came to town to meet me and okay my request.

Misterfeld supervises the twenty-congregation circuit that includes Austin's eight English and two Spanish Jehovah's Witnesses congregations. His circuit runs from Temple to Lampasas and he and his wife travel it in a mobile home, staying for a week with each congregation to "give spiritual encouragement through public talks, to take the lead in door-to-door missionary work, and to help the congregation with personal problems." There's a circuit assembly of all the congregations every six months, then Mr. Misterfeld turns around and starts all over again.

He explained how each congregation is directed by a Body of Elders approved by the governing board in the group's Brooklyn headquarters, site of their massive publishing operation. Elders are all men who meet standards the Witnesses have drawn from the Bible. Women, though they comprise a majority of most congregations and shoulder the bulk of the pioneering responsibilities—the door-to-door visitations that the Witnesses consider their most important work—are not allowed to serve as clergy.

Misterfeld okayed my request to accompany Georgeanna and Jenny on the conditions that I wear a dress, not smoke, and observe silently. I agreed. Now, on this sultry, sleepy Saturday morning I was about to find out what it was like on the other side of the screen door.

I was nervous as we approached the first house. After all, it was just after nine in the morning in a neighborhood that clearly took its Friday nights seriously. As we passed an engineless Mustang propped up on blocks in the front yard, I was on the verge of suggesting that we go for coffee and give everyone a chance to wake up. But Jenny strode purposefully up to the door and knocked. We waited. Jenny picked up the newspaper. She knocked again. Just as we were about to leave, the door opened the barest crack. A doughy woman in a baby-doll nightie stood behind it. Her body was upright, but her mind was clearly waiting for her back in bed.

"Oh, gosh, I hope we didn't wake you up," Jenny apologized, handing over the newspaper.

The woman answered sweetly that she was not feeling

well and the only reason she'd answered the door was that she had mistaken Jenny for her sister-in-law. Jenny promised to call back another time and we left.

On the sidewalk, Jenny noted the woman's response and marked her down for a return visit. Witnesses believe that angels guide their pioneering work. Georgeanna remarked on the "coincidence" of Jenny's resemblance to the woman's sister-in-law and they exchanged a look that said, "Chalk one up for the angels."

Georgeanna took the next house. Her rap was more forceful than Jenny's and it was opened immediately by a mid-thirtyish man in a western shirt.

"Hello," Georgeanna started off, "we're sharing a few thoughts from the Bible with you and your neighbors today." Her firm tone and authority testified to her years as a junior high school English teacher. "Do you believe we're living in the last days?"

The man's mouth creased into a thin, hard line that spelled trouble to me, but didn't even slow Georgeanna down. She dived right into the Witnesses' scriptural keystone: "It says in Luke 21:32 that 'this generation will by no means pass away until all things occur.'"

The man's lips tightened even more. Georgeanna continued outlining some of the other telltale Last Day symptoms—disease, crime, food shortages—then stopped to ask the man if he had ever talked with a Jehovah's Witness before.

The seamed mouth ripped open. "Yes, as a matter of fact. I talked with you all about two weeks ago for five minutes. And frankly, that was four minutes too long."

Whew.

On the street, Georgeanna allowed as how it might be a good idea to cross him off her list of return visits.

Had the man been more receptive and allowed his visitors into his home as I had done, he'd have learned a number of things about how Witnesses look at the world. First and foremost, it's doomed—not to destruction, but to transmutation into a fitting habitat for the righteous. According to the Witnesses, we are living in the Last Days. Through a series of labyrinthine calculations that involve working the Bible like a double-crostic, they arrived at 1914 as the year the big countdown began. Those living in that year are the generation that Luke refers to. Since members of that generation have all nearly checked out, the red book I purchased assures us that, "Shortly now there will be a sudden end to all wickedness and wicked people at Armageddon."

After Armageddon, in which the wicked are destroyed, the righteous will inherit a paradise on earth. Only a few of the ultra-righteous—144,000 to be very, very precise—will go to heaven. The other survivors will live on earth in "paradise conditions." The red book features a few illustrated scenes from this paradise. Looks like those of us who make it will spend the rest of eternity gardening, woodworking, clipping hedges, throwing pots, frolicking with friendly wolves and lions, and mingling at interracial barbecues. Everyone appears to be dressed by Montgomery Ward except the Laplanders, Nigerians, Hawaiians, and Hindis, who will wear their colorful native garb.

Another illustration pictures a few of the unsavory types who probably won't be woodworking away for eternity. Slated for destruction if they don't wise up are a skinny Asian man crashed out with an opium pipe; a swarthy sort shooting up; a man hanging onto a bottle; another man smoking a filtered cigarette; a scantily clad couple boogalooing their hearts out; and two bare-chested Michael Caine lookalikes embracing.

Even the cartoon colors of the red book illustrations pale when compared to some of the Witnesses' more controversial beliefs. As outlined in their publication *Jehovah's Witnesses in the Twentieth Century*, they are:

- God's name is Jehovah.
- Christ is God's son and is inferior to him.
- Christ died on a stake, not a cross.
- Earth will never be destroyed or depopulated.
- Wicked will be eternally destroyed.
- There is only one road to life.
- Satan is invisible ruler of world.
- A Christian must have no part in interfaith movements.
- Man did not evolve but was created.
- Taking blood into body through mouth or veins violates God's laws.

Their injunction against transfusions has won the Witnesses a goodly share of notoriety. In contrast to the Christian Scientists, who forbid any kind of medical intervention, Witnesses heed only the biblical advice to "keep abstaining from things sacrificed to idols and from blood and from things strangled and from fornication."

But we didn't get the chance to go into any of that with the tight-lipped man in the western shirt. The next few houses were equally unproductive. A couple of no-answers. Then a blind man with a pot belly swelling over his jeans who said he couldn't talk right then, followed by a man in a wheelchair who said he was leaving with his wife to celebrate her birthday.

As we trudged on down the street, I asked Georgeanna which neighborhoods were the most fertile fields for pioneering. She answered that you couldn't stereotype them, except for Northwest Hills where she lives. "They have their own kingdom," she says, by way of explaining why her neighbors aren't receptive to the message about Jehovah's Kingdom. "They're not concerned with other people."

Asked what is the most common reaction she's experienced in her thirty-three years as a door-to-door proselytizer, she answers, "Apathy." What about irritation? Hostility? Georgeanna and Jenny search their memories. Only one time, they note with pride, has anyone ever threatened to come after them with a gun.

I ask Jenny if, given the increase in sex crimes that the Witnesses point to as one of the signs that we are living in the Last Days, she's ever frightened about approaching strangers. She smiles and answers that Witness women always travel in pairs and "just use common sense." Beyond that, apparently, they trust their safety to the angels. So far, that strategy has worked for Jenny, who has been pioneering for twelve years.

Jenny turned away the first Witness who came to her door with the offer of a Bible discussion, saying she was "happy with what she had," which was the Baptist religion. "But Jesus must have seen something in me that was worth saving," she reasons, because shortly afterward, her husband brought home a Jehovah's Witness friend from work. Pretty soon they were studying the Bible with him. Jenny was baptized before her husband was. He had to give up smoking to be accepted into the congregation as a "sheep," which is how the Witnesses differentiate themselves from the "goats" outside their flock. Since that time, they've both quit their former jobs and now own a janitorial service which keeps their days free for pioneering.

As we approached the next house, we heard a woman yelling out the back door, "You leave your brother be or

I'll tear your behind up." Georgeanna's brisk knock was answered by a skinny teenager in a droopy T-shirt that stopped just above her cut-offs. As she lounged sleepily against the door frame, she called to mind a Dorothea Lange Dust Bowl photo.

"Is your mother or father home?" Georgeanna, the retired schoolteacher, asked.

The girl straightened up and bristled, "I *am* the mother of this house."

Georgeanna smiled. "Well, I hope you're old enough to be flattered by my mistake."

The girl, whose name turned out to be Tammy, was appeased and listened attentively as Georgeanna asked her if she was concerned about conditions in the world today.

She was. She tilted her head and listened as Georgeanna filled her in on what famine, the arms race, increasing lawlessness, and rampant disease really mean. She explained that they were all signs that the Last Days were upon us and that they'd started in 1914, the year World War I broke out. "And do you know why they called it a *world* war?" Georgeanna asked.

I could almost feel my hand going up, but Tammy just shrugged. "Got me."

"Because it was the first war in which nation fought nation. That was one of the signs foretold in the Bible. Would you like to see a righteous government unite the world?"

Tammy allowed as how that "would probably be a lot better than what we've got now."

That was a strike. Georgeanna tried reeling her in. "We've been coming into homes talking to people about the signs of the Last Days. Many like to have us come regularly." Would Tammy care to be one of them?

"Well . . ."

Before she could slip away, Georgeanna held out her two copies of the *Watch Tower* magazine and offered to leave them with her. "Do you have thirty cents to cover printing?"

Tammy brightened. "Sure."

On the street, Georgeanna marked her victory in "placing literature" and the fact that Tammy was "interested in Last Days" in her notebook.

Next door, a little boy answered when Jenny knocked and reported that his mother was "still getting her clothes on." We pressed on.

At the next door, Jenny stepped back to let Georgeanna take over. "This is yours," Jenny said, stepping back even farther. "You didn't get anyone back there." A boy afflicted with the catatonia of pubescence answered. Jenny left some *Watch Towers* with him.

A couple more no-answers, then we were walking up a driveway in which a Cadillac Coup de Ville, vintage early '70s, was parked. A Mr. Brown, of approximately the same vintage, answered. He quickly informed Jenny that he was a Catholic. She asked if he didn't agree that all of us, no matter what our religion, need to go to our Bibles and identify what Jehovah God wants from us. Mr. Brown replied that, well, he didn't know, but that he tried to live the Bible day by day.

Georgeanna held up her Bible and told him that the proof was right in there that those days were numbered. That was when Mr. Brown unleashed his bête noire. "If it's going to happen, men are going to destroy themselves with this new-clar stuff," declared the old man, beginning to rev up.

Georgeanna thumbed through her Bible for a passage prophesying annihilation.

Mr. Brown could barely wait for her to finish. "I'm a

pretty good authority on this new-clar stuff," he continued. "I've put thirty-three years in with the government. Saw tests at Edwards Air Force Base. Nobody knows how to control this new-clar stuff. Just one error on the part of one personnel and that's all she wrote. I don't know who talked Austin into this new-clar stuff but . . ."

"I think you'll be interested in this," Georgeanna interrupted. She'd found an item in the *Watch Tower* about the Catholic bishop's condemnation of nuclear war. The *Watch Tower* has interpreted it as tacit approval by the Catholic Church of all *other* forms of warfare. (The Witnesses miss few opportunities to get in their licks against Holy Mother Church which they characterize as the "whore of Babylon.") Georgeanna concludes by asking if Mr. Brown doesn't think it's comforting to know that Jesus will be bringing all this strife to an end soon when the righteous triumph.

Mr. Brown adds an intriguing twist to his argument. "This new-clar thing could happen any time. These people here in these United States don't know how to treat atomic burns."

"Yes," Georgeanna agrees, trying again to get back in control of the conversation, "but isn't it a comfort that Jesus has promised to protect us? The Bible is warning us that we're living in the generation of which he spoke."

"Yeah, but I'll tell you, this younger generation doesn't take anything serious."

Jenny leaps through that opening to share something from another *Watch Tower* article about young people who are so devoid of hope that they commit suicide.

"Yeah," Mr. Brown continues, "a lot of these young folks, they go into credit, then there ain't no way they can meet their obligations."

"Isn't the whole government that way?" Georgeanna inquires.

Mr. Brown ignores her question. "Take rental property for example. It's just unreal. This house right down there. Five hundred a month they're getting for it. It's unreal."

Georgeanna seizes the opportunity to point out the folly of putting our trust in things of this world.

"I remember that Depression," Mr. Brown says. "If we have one now, that 1929 will be a drop in the bucket. I was raised on a farm. Sold oats for ten cents a bushel. Now they's plenty money, but they's a shortage of other stuff. It's all created by the manufacturers. Just like when the gas companies come up with that gas shortage deal."

Georgeanna leaves Mr. Brown, who still has a great deal to say on a number of topics, with a *Watch Tower* article "that points out what man alone cannot do, but what we can do with God." Mr. Brown gives her a dollar for the magazines and won't take his seventy cents change.

But he'll still get it back. Georgeanna notes the seventy cents excess which she'll be repaying in literature on future visits. Witnesses are scrupulously honest. At their meetings at the Kingdom Hall they listen to testimonials written by motel owners about Witnesses who mail back washcloths they accidentally packed into their suitcases. Their reputation for honesty is so widespread that Kingdom Halls (all Witness gathering places are called Kingdom Halls) receive frequent calls asking if any of the "sheep" are interested in maid or janitorial work. Employers rest easy having someone dusting their valuables who believes thieves will be slated for destruction.

I got a glimpse into how this scrupulousness is inculcated when Jenny stopped by one day with her twelve-year-old daughter, Tess. Like many Witness children, Tess frequently accompanies her mother on her pioneering work. Though the day was hot and the Bible passages long, Tess sat through the visit with a minimum of fidgeting. Jenny confided to me that the secret of successful child-rearing was strict adherence to Bible principles. She told of the time she was grocery shopping and discovered that Tess had taken a peanut from the produce department. She marched Tess back into the store to return the pilfered peanut.

So there's no doubt Mr. Brown will get his change back with seventy cents worth of literature, which is also Georgeanna's ticket to future return visits. "I haven't been having good conversations like that," she said as we walked away.

It turned out to be the last "good conversation" of a day that was becoming increasingly hot and muggy. Georgeanna, tan and fit from her unending pioneering treks, was still fresh and peppy. "I have an 8103," she said looking for the address. "A Mrs. Paul. She took a *Watch Tower*." We locate the house. A woman in her late twenties, with a bleached mustache and wearing lime-green terry shorts and matching top, answers.

Georgeanna tells her about the twenty-first chapter of Luke. The bleached moustache twitches in silent irritation. Georgeanna either doesn't notice or chooses to ignore the hostility. "We just talked to one of your neighbors who was concerned about nuclear war," she goes on doggedly.

The woman, who has barricaded herself behind her arms folded over her chest, starts to speak. But Georgeanna is already expanding on her message of sweet doom. She finishes and holds out two *Watch Tower* magazines. "I'd like for you to have these."

Again the woman starts to protest, but instead takes the magazines and hands over the thirty cents.

Pleased at having reached that step, Georgeanna stretches for the next one: "May we come back?"

"I'd rather you didn't," the woman answers curtly.

"Will you read the articles I mentioned?" Georgeanna asks.

"I may or may not."

Georgeanna is downcast. On the street, she asks why people even take her literature when they have no intention of reading it.

I start to tell her about how hard such brutal frankness is for most people, but how especially difficult it is for women. Even when someone intrudes on your time and privacy to take potshots at your life and beliefs by implying that, without a major overhaul, you're doomed. That it's simply a lot easier to fork over the thirty cents and take the magazines. But I don't say any of that because it *is* difficult.

And because, for a surprising reason that has nothing to do with Armageddon, Jehovah's Witnesses deserve courtesy. When they appear on your doorstep, you should remember they represent a group that, in the opinion of the American Civil Liberties Union, has won more victories for civil liberties than any other. I'll explain why, but a little history is in order first.

The Watch Tower Bible and Tract Society was founded in 1881 by Charles Taze Russell. It was one of a number of millenarian groups that were flourishing in America at that time. This was some three years after a Pittsburgh paper reported that Russell had been found on a downtown bridge dressed in a white robe, waiting to be wafted to heaven. Throughout the group's history, it has been embarrassed by over-specificity. At least five different times, Russell's followers have published apocalyptic dates, but the world has gone on.

By 1931, the Russellites were calling themselves Jehovah's Witnesses and had developed a stiff-necked disdain for things of this world and critics of their religion, comforting themselves with the knowledge that both were slated for destruction.

They seemed to inspire persecution. In the 1930s and '40s, members of the church were tarred and feathered, molested, jailed, and victimized by mob violence. In 150 state supreme court cases and thirty precedent-setting US Supreme Court cases, they tested the law and, according to the ACLU, ultimately broadened the meaning of the First and Fourteenth Amendments. At issue were their refusals to salute the flag, which they regarded as idolatry; to sell religious tracts without being taxed; and to refuse military service. Their obstinate perseverance on these and other points forced the courts to recognize the rights of minority groups under the Bill of Rights.

Parked outside the next house were three motorcycles, two cars, and a Jeep. Georgeanna was excited about this call because she'd talked to someone named Mike here earlier and had noted that he was receptive. The young woman who answered the door was surprised when Georgeanna asked for "Mike" by name.

Several minutes passed before Mike shuffled to the door. One side of his face was pillow-creased. A big, red hickey festooned his neck. Swaying in the doorway like a rhino who had just taken one from the tranquilizer gun, Mike struggled to get Georgeanna and her mission in focus.

Georgeanna had chosen to examine the question of why, with all our advanced medical knowledge, disease was more rampant than ever. Didn't he think it might be a sign that the Last Days were upon us?

Mike blinked. He looked as if he personally were living

in the last *moments* of his own Last Days. "Uh, yeah," he mumbled.

It was clear even to Georgeanna that she had a comatose one on the line. "I was going to tell," she paused, "the young woman who answered the door not to wake you if you were asleep, but she left too quickly."

"Uh, yeah."

Georgeanna asks if he'd like to have the *Watch Towers* for thirty cents, "just to cover the cost of printing."

Mike pats his pockets. "Uh, yeah."

Back on the street Georgeanna whispers that "people are weird." Explaining her earlier pause, she says, "You hesitate to even refer to someone as 'your wife' nowadays."

Indeed, if the young woman who answered the door was *not* Mike's wife, they are both fornicators and, according to the Witnesses' beliefs, doomed. They take matrimony very seriously. "The Bible encourages you to stick together and work things out," Jenny explains. She confides that she and her husband were having "marital problems" around the time they started their Witness-guided Bible studies. Entering into The Truth—as the process of becoming a Witness is called—helped them overcome those problems.

The solution was subjagation. "The Bible gives instructions to husbands on being the head of the household," Jenny reports, "and to wives on being subject." Georgeanna admits that some women have "a real problem" with subjagation. "They want to be matriarchs."

The red book, "You Can Live Forever in Paradise on Earth"—a sort of Jehovah's Witnesses primer—is quite explicit on this point: "A marriage or a family needs leadership. The man was created with a greater measure of the qualities and strengths required to provide such leadership. . . . As the Bible says, the woman was made as a helper to her husband."

Several inconclusive visits follow our discussion of feminine frailty. It is nearly noon and I am wilting visibly. Georgeanna designates the next house as the last of the day. A chic, slim, middle-aged woman answers.

"How do you feel about the future?" Georgeanna plunges in.

The woman smiles. "Let me put it this way, I don't have any children and I don't plan to have any. Look," she continues, affably heading Georgeanna off. "I have a lunch date that I'm already late for. I go to the Crestview Baptist Church, but I have a lot of friends who are Jehovah's Witnesses and I think it's a fine thing you're doing." With that she hands over a dollar and bids them a friendly goodbye. All in all, it's the best encounter of the day.

I remark that it seems a cordial relationship must exist between Baptists and Witnesses. Georgeanna gives me a mildly horrified look. "Other religions are trying to keep The World afloat. They promote looking to men for solutions. (When Witnesses refer to "The World"—always capitalized, in their literature—they mean everything and everyone outside the Kingdom Hall.) Only the Creator can solve our problems. Fixing up The World," she concludes, "is like shining up the brass on a sinking ship."

This attitude is one of the keys to understanding the Witnesses: while they are thoroughly *of* the American mainstream, they remain steadfastly *outside* it. Their theology counsels them to be honest, hard-working, upright, sober, and respectful, observing a morality that embodies American middle-class ideals. Their dream of paradise is an Americanized Eden as rendered by Norman Rockwell. It is a dream that guides the devout through all their days.

They hold themselves apart from The World, a big, decaying lump that they are happy to let rot.

In its place they substitute visions of glory and a system of utter certainty. The World is a place of unbearable chaos, of frightening ambiguity, until they "enter The Truth." Once truth, all truth, is limited by a definitive article into a singular entity, answers to life's questions come in two colors—black and white. All those annoying grays drop out.

Having corrected me on where the Witnesses stand vis-à-vis Baptists and The World, we pack up and head for home. On the drive back, I ask once more the question I'd been posing in different guises since I had first met the two women: why do they do it? Why do they push themselves into strangers' lives, lingering on doorsteps, risking—no, courting—rejection? They respond with variations on the answers I'd already gotten—that they simply want to share the good news, that the Bible enjoins them to spread their message. They reiterate that there is no church to join and since they change territories frequently, they aren't spiritual headhunters out to fill any specific quota.

We ride along in silence for a few minutes. Georgeanna observes that it's been a pretty good day as far as placing literature goes. Then, like the P.S. on a letter that tells the real story, she adds, "Follow-through is a different story, though. Only one out of every twelve who gets into Bible studies becomes a disciple."

A disciple? I ask.

"That's our purpose," Georgeanna answers. "To get them to go out and spread the word."

I remembered having read that there are 2.2 million Witnesses around the world. But Jenny had told me that over six million people attended the Memorial of Christ's Death, the one "holiday" on the Witnesses' gloomy calendar.

Georgeanna explained that if you aren't canvassing for Jehovah, you aren't counted as one of his witnesses.

It finally clicked: they don't care about your thirty cents, your hangover, your membership in another church. What the Witnesses really want is the rest of us—the goats—out there on the street with them. They want *us* on *their* side of the screen door.

The Furs Were Flying

TEXAS MONTHLY, MAY 2006

There is a world where the kings of small African countries send cases of Dom Pérignon as hostess gifts, where Marc Anthony entertains at your parties, where former presidents are "darling," where visits to Buckingham Palace number in the double digits, where museums ask to borrow your clothes, and where the glass is always half-full. Of Dom Pérignon. Welcome to Planet Thrash, the world of über–Houston socialite Becca Cason Thrash.

So how the h-e-double-hockey-sticks did the Bargain Queen, Empress of Target/Ross/T. J. Maxx, land on this planet for a couple of days? Just how did the über-socialite meet the über-goober?

It started with a chance encounter. I was part of a delighted group listening to the irrepressible BCT bubble on about how, though she'd been to Buckingham Palace ten times, she'd only recently visited Balmorhea. *Quelle surprise* to learn that the glitterati and I vacationed at the same state park! I was about to ask if her party had selected the deluxe trailer hookup or if they'd splurged on a room at the cute motel right there on the park grounds when Becca mentioned that Charles had brought Camilla along for the weekend. When I couldn't recall seeing a certain jug-eared heir to the throne and his horse-faced consort splashing around the public pool, I realized that she was talking about Balmor-*al*, Queen Victoria's "dear paradise in the Highlands," not Balmor-*ay*, "the only cold, wet one in West Texas not in a six-pack."

When I was introduced to Becca, I blurted out the one fact I then knew about her: she lives in a house with thirteen powder rooms and two bedrooms. Before I could ask if she ran a potty-training academy, the effervescent Harlingen girl, proud of her working-class roots, who devoured *Vogue* while her mother shopped because they couldn't afford the 95 cents it cost back then, burst out, "You *must* come and see them!"

I must, indeed.

Now, you might expect a glamorous socialite to be downright adorable, but you wouldn't necessarily think she'd immediately feel like a best girlfriend. BCT was both. Still, I was certain that the impulsively generous invitation would be rescinded once Texas's queen of haute couture, voted one of Houston's best dressed and such a clotheshorse that *Harper's Bazaar* featured her in an article called "Couture's Big Spenders," realized that I was a known wearer of shoes the shape and style of pinto beans. (Women are divided into two distinct, frequently hostile camps: those who wear sensible, comfortable, blunt-nosed shoes and those who wedge their feet into shoes so lethally pointed that cockroaches flee in fright.)

So I'm surprised when, a few days later, an email arrives from Becca detailing the "costume change requirements" for my visit. Among them are a "luncheon suit," "casual cocktail," and "cocktail or festive." Hmmm. I know that women are issued luncheon suits when they join the Republican Party, but I don't have time for that. As for the rest, I just hope that enough cocktails will be involved that the glitterati won't notice my Targetwear. The one item I'm certain I must acquire, though, is a pair of those needle-nosed cockroach killers.

Which is why I'm hobbling when I follow the house manager into Becca's guest house a week later. Once he leaves, I investigate. I discover two toilets, side by side. "How companionable," I think. "The rich really are different." Then I think, "Whoa, I'm no rube. I lived in France for almost a year. I know a bidet when I see one." What I don't know is not to lean over and turn the damn thing on. After spritzing myself in the face, I remember that I was *une domestique* in France and the only waterworks I ever dealt with belonged to *le bébé* I diapered.

This moment dampens my enthusiasm in ways both literal and figurative. The luncheon suit event is coming up, the needle noses have crippled me, and static electricity is making every fiber of my polyester Targ garb cling to me like kudzu. Worst of all, I find out that the lunch is officially the annual Grand Gala Ball Fashion Show at the Museum of Fine Arts, Houston.

So I am feeling like the Little Match Girl when Becca makes a fairy godmother appearance holding two furs. "Do you need something for the chill?" The gray-and-white-striped chinchilla or the violet beaver shearling poncho? "You'd think I lived in Fairbanks, I love fur so much." Hoping that shearling is a Locks of Love sort of deal where benevolent beavers voluntarily surrender their pelts for chilly city girls, I choose the poncho. It settles on me like a cloud. I could be wearing a muumuu under it and look smashing.

This is better than the moment when the kindhearted mice stitched up a ball gown for Cinderella.

Thanks to Becca's shearling, I blend right in at the museum, where there are more furs than at a Mountain Man reenactment. Also Chanel suits, pearls, diamonds, nothing but pointy shoes, and lots of "work." Faces filled and Botoxed until they have that quilted, Donatella Versace look, upper lips placid and puffed as a llama's. "Why do they do that?" Becca whispers as one duck-billed dazzler passes. "The lips walk into the room, then the rest of their body catches up."

The fashion show starts with a dancer who undulates as if she's fighting ingestion by a giant, ruffled python. Models walk down the runway with their pelvises tilted forward in the standard "may I offer you an ovary" posture. They all seem to be leaning so far backward to keep their tiny breasts from rolling off their tiny, sunken chests. Their defiant sneers announce to those of us nibbling chicken salad at their feet: "You can buy the clothes off my body, but you will never break my spirit."

One model strides out in a dress so short that Becca observes, quite accurately, "You can see her tortilla!" To say nothing of the whole enchilada.

After lunch we zip over to the office where she organizes her charity fundraisers. It is just down the hall from "41's." ("Clinton is here all the time. They're darling together.") As we drive, I ask what would happen if all the money disappeared tomorrow. "Having money calms your nerves. It buys toys. It doesn't buy health or love. I do have a charmed life. The money is just a big ol' bonus. I'm married to a man I love. If we lost it all tomorrow, we'd be fine. If I had to move to a trailer, it would be the cutest, chicest trailer you ever saw!"

And I can help her decorate it with bargains from my shopping venues! What a gay time we'll have scouring Target. She's going to love walking a mile in *my* pinto beans. They're a lot more comfortable.

Step Lively

TEXAS MONTHLY, JUNE 2006

I t's long past time that I thank Texas—that I thank all the Czechs and Germans and Mexicans and cowboys, both real and urban, who made this the dancingest state in the union. Without them I might never have gotten married. While I'm at it, I should probably thank the heat as well. The hellish, hellish heat.

August. Austin. 1979. AC goes out in bachelorette pad. Roommate suggests vacating premises for Aqua Fest: giant drunk on banks of Colorado River where strangers—many of them members of fraternities—throw up on one another's feet. Could not pay me enough to attend. Then varnish on furniture begins to bubble and linoleum on floors melts. Aqua Fest becomes tempting alternative. Once at Fest, more uncharacteristic behavior follows. Ask cutest boy in all of Aquafestlandia to dance to the polka being played. Boy maintains it's a waltz. Twenty-seven-year argument ensues.

An astute reader recently pointed out that my new novel, *The Flamenco Academy*, and my last one, *The Yokota Officers Club*, both featured introverted heroines transformed and released by dance. Well, duh. As a seriously shy—okay, borderline catatonic—high schooler, dance transformed and released me. Why wouldn't I let it do the same for my heroines? Why not let them discover that simply through the relatively rhythmic flailing of one's limbs, one could make contact with the opposite sex? But for dance I would have been Emily Dickinson. (Except for the part where she does Jell-O shots with Walt Whitman. What? You didn't cover Whitman: The Party Years in your American Poetry class?)

As with Isadora Duncan, the height of my terpsichorean triumphs was a two-week stint as a go-go dancer in Tokyo. (Now you're telling me that Isadora didn't work the cage?) I was the intermission act for a comedian who fantasized that he was Bob Hope entertaining the troops and I was Joey Heatherton. He was, maybe, a third-rate comedian. I was, maybe, a fourth-rate go-go dancer. Together we added up to a thoroughly seventh-rate act.

Sometime after my "tour," I returned to America to discover that the sun had set on the Golden Days of Dance. Long gone were the brand-name dances of my youth: the cool jerk, the funky chicken, the ecstatic tuna. All had devolved into a free-form hippie-esque grooving that consisted of slopping around the floor like amoebas, though not quite that structured. Barefoot girls swayed and waved their arms like seaweed in a slow ocean current. Boys executed maneuvers reminiscent of a tai chi master being electrocuted. Feigning copulation with a speaker was a guaranteed crowd-pleaser.

Fred and Ginger wept.

Imagine my delight, then, at ending up in Texas, which had not only a state flower and a state bird but also state dances: the two-step, the schottische, the cotton-eyed Joe.

Why the runaway success of TV's *Dancing with the Has-beens* surprised anyone is a mystery to me. Women love to dance. The other mystery is why men waste their lives on girl-getting gambits like accumulating vast wealth, fast cars, and astronomical scores on Quake when dancing is right there in plain sight. Guys, do you dream of women falling into your arms? Want to tell them which way to go and how fast or slow to get there? Simple: Learn to dance. Is it an accident that so many wives run off with personal trainers of both sexes? No. And why? Because personal trainers have what dancing gives anyone: permission to touch. (Same deal with husbands and dental hygienists.)

Women almost always love to dance more than men, who endure the activity only long enough to get someone to sleep with them. Far sadder are the guys who never dance at all. Perhaps they fear that dancing will cause them to appear as something less than a towering stud. Not here in the great-state-of. In Texas, not only do men dance, but the absolute manliest of men are the best dancers of all! Back (again) in bachelorette days, I ended up in Stamford for the Texas Cowboy Reunion. I stood on the sidelines at the dance that evening, astonished at how hydraulically smooth the couples gliding past were, when a real, true, calf-castrating, fence-mending, jeans-tucked-into-his-boots cowboy asked me to two-step. Fresh from years of amoebic slopping and sensing that cool jerking to "San Antonio Rose" was not going to work, I admitted that I couldn't "touch dance."

He sluiced his chaw a little deeper over to the side of his mouth and asked, "Can you walk? Cuz if you can walk, you can two-step." Then he taught me just the way his Czech mother had taught him back on the ranch, after she'd cleared the furniture out of the house to make room for her and her many children to quick-quick, slow, quick-quick, slow. I hooked my thumb on his belt loop, and just that easily, I joined the circle of couples waltzing counterclockwise across Texas.

But this doesn't mean that dancing is only for bachelors. Husbands, the words your wives most yearn to hear (aside from "Is anyone else chilly? Can we turn down the AC?" or "Here, baby doll, you control the remote." Or even "Give me that. Women as fine, fine, *fine*-looking as you shouldn't be pushing around a vacuum cleaner!") are "Gosh, I've always dreamed of taking tango lessons." Salsa is also good.

Here's how desperate women are to dance: They pack into classes offering all the partnerless mutations of the real thing—Jazzercize, Zumba, Cardio Hip-Hop, Yo! Yo! Yoga.

All I'm saying is, mamas, don't let your babies grow up to be nondancers. Help them fulfill their Lone Star destiny. Clear out the furniture and teach them to dance. Get them ready for the moment when fate steps in and knocks out the AC in your future daughter-in-law's bachelorette pad.

Oops, gotta go. They're playing our song. El Hubbo, the Hub of My Universe, maintains it's a waltz. I'm pretty sure it's a polka.

Horn 'em, Hookers!

TEXAS MONTHLY, JANUARY 2007

Gosh, how I loved football games when I was a grad student at the University of Texas. I was the biggest football nut going. I *lived* for game day. I and the other supernerdettes residing in a co-op boarding house two blocks from campus counted the minutes until kickoff. Why? Because that's when all the bellowing Burnt-Orange-heads would get the hell out of our neighborhood. Ah, bliss! For those few hours we could study, sing madrigals, and walk outside without being hailed by our football-loving frat neighbors with their signature greeting: "Hey, lesbo-dyke-whore!" (Seemed odd that the brothers would automatically assume that people of the same gender who all lived together and paddled one another and carried out secret nighttime rituals were homosexual. Yet they did. Oh, wait, I forgot. *We* weren't the ones doing the paddling and the rituals.)

I grew up in a house in which men screamed at television sets. Week after week, month after month, football season after football season, this little cult never seemed to grasp that the tiny players in the magic picture box could not hear them, that their rage and insults had no effect whatsoever on the outcome of the game. I did everything I could to ensure that the family psychosis did not strike me, until an article in *Seventeen* advised that in order to "be interesting to boys" I had to "be interested in what boys are interested in." Knowing that I couldn't fake a passion for burning up ants with a magnifying glass, I asked my father to explain the rules of football to me. The words "first down," "turnover," and "end zone" went directly into my brain's spam filter and lodged there forever, right next to "quadratic equation." Boys would just have to be interested in me for my family fortune and smokin' hot body.

And then I watched twenty minutes of football that changed everything—specifically, the final twenty minutes of last year's Rose Bowl. What Vince Young did that confetti-filled evening can stand next to any of the greatest human achievements: Michelangelo's *David*, $E = mc^2$, the appletini. I vowed then and there that I would do what I had never done during the quarter of a century I'd lived in Austin: I would go to a Longhorns football game.

Before you could say "Horn 'em, Hookers!," I was one of 88,972 fans surging toward Royal-Texas Memorial Stadium for the UT–Iowa State game in late September. My trusty guide to all things gridiron was El Hubbo, pride of South Texas's Gregory-Portland Wildcats, a football-playin' fool with the knee surgeries to prove it. His expertise, fine-tuned during years of two-a-days on fields hot enough to smelt pig iron, was immediately brought to bear: "Uh, the kickoff is kind of important." This insight was delivered after the sound of a distant roar reached us in the cafeteria of a mercifully air-conditioned UT dorm where I was having an IV of Diet Coke inserted. Reinvigorated by meth-addict levels of caffeine, we rejoined the Bataan Death March.

Memorial Stadium. Looks big from the outside, right? Optical illusion. They pack those fans in like rush hour on a Tokyo subway. Our neighbors in section 30, row 49, seats 1 through 39 were not amused when we arrived late and forced them to assume positions only recently legalized in the state of Texas as we wedged past on our way to seats 40 and 41. I apologized copiously. One old gent excused me, saying, "At least you don't stink like that bongo-playing hippie who used to sit down there."

As he pointed to a spot nearby, I checked for other signs of heatstroke.

"You know. That Hollywood guy. McCafferty."

Okay! The personal hygiene habits of major stars—now *this* I could get interested in. Unfortunately, our other neighbors seemed to actually be trying to concentrate on the ants dressed in the color bronze that is called burnt orange on the field far below. Hostile glares cut my conversation about Mattie Mac short. I thought I'd better ingratiate myself with those whose feet I'd trodden upon. To show how much of a Hookers fan I was, I held my fingers up in a "Gig 'em" sign and screamed out, "Husk the Cornholers!"

"That's Nebraska," El Hubbo informed me. "And it's Cornhuskers."

"Oh."

"And you just did the 'Hang Loose, Brah' sign from Hawaii."

"Oh."

"Do you want me to explain what's happening?"

Since hellish, unimaginable heat had melted my lips shut, I shook my head no. I feared the words "offensive lineman" might inflict irreversible damage upon my poached brain. I slumped into a listless, torpid state, capable of fixating only on bright, highly animated objects. These would be the cheerleaders. I wondered idly what parallel universe they might exist in. On Planet Earth, I barely had enough energy to wipe away the tsunami of sweat pouring off of me. On frosty cold Planet Pep, the cheerleaders were bouncing around like howler monkeys on PCP.

This was so not like my cathartic Rose Bowl experience. What, besides Vince Young, was missing? Ah, yes, close-ups. El Hubbo called my attention to the Godzillatron, which was in fact providing both CUs and replays. If only I'd had a quart of cookies 'n' cream and my own personal air-conned house, I could have duplicated my special Vince moment.

El Hubbo made a good call: "Let's go to the End Zone Club."

End Zone Club? This sounded promising. With a name like that I was certain I'd witness another sort of athletic perfection: strippers working the pole. But no. The End Zone Club turned out to be just a giant tent with big TV sets. But it did have the one ingredient essential to the enjoyment of football: beer. We found a quiet table as far from the hubbub as possible, and if everyone in the baked-bean-colored garb would have piped down and let me read my novel, I could have really started to enjoy football.

Now, I'm not saying who is right and who is pathologically insane in regard to football. All I will say, though, is on that day many were praying for the Longhorns to win. A few were praying for the Cornholers. Me, I was just praying for the whole hideous ordeal to end. Then, in the third quarter, the heavens hurled bolts of lightning upon Memorial Stadium of such ferocity that, for the first time since 1996, a game was postponed because of weather.

Make of that what you will, but there's no denying that my prayer was answered before 88,971 others.

Goodbye, Mrs. Chips

TEXAS MONTHLY, MARCH 2007

S o many ways for a Texas girl to lose her virginity. My own deflowering was witnessed by 88,971 spectators at Memorial Stadium when I attended my first-ever University of Texas football game last fall. In the time-honored tradition of so many coeds, though, I chose to re-virginize and lose it again. A whole world of Texas First Times still awaited. But which quintessential Lone Star experience had I missed? Visiting Boys Town? Swimming naked in a stock tank? Shooting my daughter's cheerleader competition? Wrong sex, wrong body, bad aim. That left playing Texas Hold 'em.

I had a problem with poker: I worried that too many Slim Jims, pork rinds, and shots of rye whisky would be required. That ritual anointings with Right Guard and Brut might be involved. That, in short, I wasn't man enough. And then: poker with aromatherapy! How could I resist? The Lake Austin Spa Resort was offering a three-day Texas Hold 'em workshop with Susie Isaacs, the first player to win the World Series of Poker ladies' championship two years in a row and the second-highest female finisher in

WSOP history. But isn't the purpose of spas to starve willing dieters? On my way to the spa, I pulled over at an Oh Thank Heaven and loaded up on—well, why not?—Slim Jims, pork rinds, and a sixer of DP, the national drink of Texas. I arrived just in time for lunch, but instead of a vat of cottage cheese or a bale of carrot sticks, the choices were walnut, garlic, and rosemary–encrusted trout or roast apple–stuffed pork tenderloin. I was liking poker more by the minute.

Filling the lull until Poker 101 started, I perused the menu of spa classes. Would it be Kundalini Yoga and Meditation, Nia Dance of Joy, or Pilates Foam Roller? I chose instead some low-impact Channel Surfing and retired to my room. Emerging in time for my first Texas Hold 'em lesson, I felt energized in the manly way that only an hour of viewing an outdoor prison riot, a man falling from a Ferris wheel, and a street luger almost getting his foot severed on Spike TV can make a girl feel.

I should have been watching Martha Stewart commit unspeakable acts with doilies and potpourri, because the convivial group that gathered in the cozily elegant Treehouse Lake Room was ladies only. They included a retired schoolteacher, the assistant to the president of a haircutting franchise, a stock analyst, a former librarian, a pharmacist, and several women whose occupations—full-time volunteer, "aerobics gal," "spa addict"—tended to involve either family money or the acquisition of a wealthy husband. And Susie Isaacs, poker shark? An insanely cute human being. Think "nicest kindergarten teacher ever," a Kewpie doll in a black denim and rhinestone World Series of Poker jacket. On becoming one of the game's female pioneers, the Nashville native said, "My husband retired and wanted to be a poker player, so we moved from the Bible

Belt to Sin City, Las Vegas. Five years later I was a professional poker player and I didn't have a husband anymore."

Susie started us off with a cheat sheet that explained what beats what. ("Royal flush? Bet your family.") We learned some basic etiquette: Don't "splash the pot" (toss chips into the pot), "break the rail" (pick your cards up off the table), or "leak the salty wet ones" (cry like a little girl when you lose). Then we got into Hold 'em lingo: "big blind," "small blind," "the river," and many other schizophrenic terms having nothing to do with the things they describe. Only those, like me, without cable don't know that Hold 'em starts with every player's being dealt two cards. These have colorful names as well that only soon-to-be-bankrupt people with too much time and increasingly less money on their hands can invent: Two kings are "cowboys," a king and a queen are a "marriage," a queen and a jack are "Oedipus Rex," and a queen and a three are a "San Francisco busboy" (that would be a queen with a trey—I guess that's why they call it "poker" and not "sensitivity training").

Susie dealt a practice hand and tossed me two queens: a "Siegfried and Roy." (Again, what poker lacks in cultural awareness, it does seem to make up for with outdated stereotypes.) Confident in my pair of queens, I "pushed all-in," shoving all my chips into the center. Everyone else folded. Susie announced that it was time to talk about "tells." Apparently, my tell—balling my hands into tiny little fists and waving them in front of my face while bouncing up and down—subtle though it was, had tipped the other players off. Too bad this tell thing had not been covered earlier, since I didn't see "paint" (face cards) again for the next two practice sessions.

Wearied by the rigors of the gaming table, I sought to refresh myself, calm the spirit, and clear the mind for the big tournament coming up the next day. I considered the traditional poker approach—opening a Benzedrine inhaler and eating the contents—but opted instead for a French lavender oil massage at the LakeHouse Spa. Only when I was lying naked on a gurney waiting for the masseuse, a young woman so sweet and aromatic and alternative that I'll call her Crunchy Granola, did I remember why I don't get massages: they make me incredibly tense. With my face planted in the little toilet seat thing and my naked backside exposed, I visualized Granola entering the room wearing a hockey mask and holding a meat cleaver. I banished that thought and tried to imagine how a mentally healthy person would be reacting to the sensation of being kneaded like a giant log of Play-Doh in the giant, warm hands of an exceptionally loving and skilled toddler. It almost worked until I noticed the background music: a multiethnic mélange of temple bells, chimes, and a chanter calling for all the oppressed peoples of the world to rise up and massacre the lavender-scented overlords.

Tense was good. Tense players are alert players. I was tense and smelling heavenly when I stepped into the Lake Room for the tournament. Perhaps it all would have ended differently if I'd had those Slim Jims circulating through my system. If I'd been perfumed with Brut instead of French lavender. As it was, I was the first player eliminated. My royal flush was a pretender to the throne.

Hog Wild

TEXAS MONTHLY, JULY 2007

I'd been to a University of Texas football game. I'd learned how to play Hold 'em. What other seminal Texas experience was left? I was wondering if a can of Skoal might be hovering in my future when I came across an article in the *New Yorker* about the debate over whether the Metropolitan Museum of Art should return some of its antiquities to their countries of origin. In the story, we discover that Carlos Picón, the curator of the Greek and Roman department at the Met, spent several years in San Antonio, where he "learned to shoot, in order to participate in weekend house parties dedicated to boar-hunting, a pastime that is to Texas billionaires what golf is to those in the Northeast."

I don't know what lowly *millionaires* hunt—nutria, probably—but I too wanted in with the boar- and antiquity-hunting Texas billionaires. The first step in my social climb would be to worm my way onto a happy hunting ground. After much angling, I cadged an invitation to the legendary Rancho Grigiot. But there were conditions: I had to educate myself about the menace that is the feral hog; I had to acquire necessary supplies; and because my hosts don't want to be besieged by billionaires, I couldn't reveal their true identities.

Turns out Texas has a Hogzilla of a problem. When the offspring of barnyard pigs-gone-wild met the black, bristly Russian boar introduced to Texas in the '30s, the resulting Cold War détente with those commie porkers produced the one and a half million hogs currently rooting up farms and wetlands.

Education covered, my pig-hunting compañero and husband and I picked up supplies at a magic land I never would have set foot in otherwise: Cabela's. As with so many boy-intensive activities, from war to golf, most of the fun is in the gear. Who knew camo could be so complicated? The solicitous clerk wanted to know what I was "going for" and where. Would I be needing the arid tans of their Open Country pattern? Or might a lusher Mossy Oak be in order? I tried on a pair of Open Country pants and asked the clerk if they made my butt look big. "Butt? What butt? All I see is a torso floating in midair." Sold!

Next on my list was boar attractant. I passed Bucker-Up, Stump Likker, and Buck Stop before finding Pig Out, Pig Lickkor, and Hog Heaven. (Apparently hunters are connoisseurs of the pun.) The handsome sales buckaroo in Wranglers cut open a bag of Hog Wild so I could sniff what the manufacturer promised was the "most unbelievable boar draw on the market! BOAR NONE!" Hog Wild had the chemically berry smell of low-end conditioner so popular in middle school locker rooms. I bought a bag of Hog Wild, a jug of Pig Lickkor, and a hog caller that mimics the sound of a "piglet in distress," but held off on the "Handy Spray Bottle" of Sow-N-Estrus Urine & Scent ("WARNING!

Never put hog attractants on your body or clothing. You could be attacked").

We drove west by southwest out of Austin some four hours until we dead-ended at Rancho Grigiot, a Brigadoon of a spread so close to the border that providing *lonche* for illegals passing through is standard fare. The ranch existed in an Old West warp of time and truth where real names don't matter and you're only as good as your last shot. An ascot-clad stiff of the first order appeared wearing a pith helmet (a sure sign that someone has gone troppo, wears Gore-Tex underwear, and/or has troubles in the bedroom). He introduced himself as "Eric von Chesley, of the von Chesley almond fortune. Perhaps you've heard of our line? Uncle Harry's Nuts?" Another punster!

Inside the compound the rest of the hunt club waited. Amidst a clutter of camp followers and baby mamas was Carl J. Dunne, who insisted upon the final *e* in his made-up name. Carl J., with his pleasant, boyish mien; Harry Potter glasses; sweet tooth; AC/DC schoolboy shorts; and hog-slaughtering reputation was the Baby Face Nelson of the gang. They called him Dead Eye.

The alpha male of this pack of curs was J. Boy, a dark and volatile sort with a story for every one of his many tattoos, most involving Afghan warlords, Thai pirates, and drug-running gym teachers. He told a particularly chilling tale of being abandoned by his Maori guide while under attack from a giant New Zealand boar. "I had to finish him off with my cuticle scissors—he was good eating," J. Boy concluded, leaving listeners uncertain as to whether he was referring to the hog or the cowardly guide.

Von Chesley, who'd left to "spend a penny," reappeared, lured irresistibly to the sweet-smelling hog baits. As J. Boy examined the jug of Pig Lickkor, he grunted, "Well, we know the stuff works. Already drew the biggest bore I've ever seen." He tossed von Chesley the hog call and told him he wanted to hear him "squeal like a pig."

"Remember what happened to Harry Whittington?" von Chesley asked, referring to the hapless Austin lawyer who'd been shot in the face by Dick Cheney. He added darkly, "I'm a lot better shot than our esteemed vice president." With his W. C. Fields of a drinker's nose, von C. sniffed the Pig Lickkor and wondered aloud whether to pair it with vodka or gin. The burst capillaries of his great tuber of a proboscis twitched as he sniffed again and decreed, "Tequila! Something in the margarita range."

A brief discussion ensued as to whether one of the concoction's main ingredients, propylene glycol, was or was not antifreeze. Undeterred by such niceties, von C. took a taste of the boar bait and immediately spat it out. "Why, you can't make a decent cocktail out of that!" he said in a tone of outraged betrayal, as if the manufacturer had specifically marketed Pig Lickkor as a sophisticated mixer rather than hog bait.

Carl J. was certain that Hog Wild's granular mix was the key. With a jaunty "It's five o'clock somewhere!," von C. poured a generous helping of Hog Wild and enough vodka to wet it down into his martini shaker.

"A name!" J. Boy exploded, already envisioning legions of boar hunters out in the field quaffing portable juice boxes of his signature beverages. "We need a name!" That the cocktail tasted like Sterno mixed with Berry Blue Kool-Aid did not slow his mad marketeering. "You've heard of the mai tai?" he asked, holding aloft a glass of the fluorescent pink mixture. "This shall be the hog tai."

As Carl J. and von Chesley argued over whether it should be the hog tai or the hogtini, I breathed a sigh of relief. All my requirements for the perfect Texas hunting trip were being met: Gear had been purchased. Jokes had been made about both *Deliverance* and Dick Cheney. Too much alcohol was being consumed. Lies would be told. And my hands would never touch a gun.

MOTHERHOOD

—

Two Seconds after the
Stick Turns Pink

Mombo

AUSTIN AMERICAN-STATESMAN, MAY 9, 1993

M y mom's favorite movie line comes from *Terms of Endearment*. Jack Nicholson hands Shirley MacLaine a cocktail and says, "Here, you need a drink. You need *lots* of drinks to drown that bug in your ass." If I bring my mom a margarita and deliver this line with even a twinge of Jack's snap, she will, invariably, crack up, putting her hand in front of her mouth and laughing like a geisha on nitrous oxide.

I was eight or so when it occurred to me that Colista McCabe Bird, the woman who cut the crusts off my peanut butter sandwiches and made the great vats of macaroni and cheese for me and my five ravening brothers and sisters, was not exactly like the other girdled and white-gloved moms on the Air Force bases we inhabited. That a stranger dwelt within her capri pants, a stranger once known to friends and lovers as Crazy Mac.

The first clue I had were the six engagement rings. Already in training for my brief, inglorious career in journalism, I was a terrible snoop from an early age. I was long adept at jimmying open my little sister's five-year diary, so the lock on my mother's trunk, stored away in the attic, presented no problem. Inside, I found the rings, a stack of love letters, and many eight-by-ten glossies of the six impossibly glossy young men who inscribed their photos with varying degrees of adoration to "Crazy Mac."

It is one of the sad truths of parenthood that your children will never know the hot, hip, and happening person you were before said children made their appearance and changed you so utterly. I wanted desperately to know Crazy Mac. As a twitchy introvert with various "nervous" complaints, my only hope was that I might have a drop or two of Crazy Mac blood mamboing through my tense little veins.

I was treated to brief glimpses of this glamorous stranger in the tiny slices of time left over after the sheer draft-horse labor of keeping six children fed, watered, and relatively disease-free had been accomplished. I saw Crazy Mac in the saucy swing of her gold hoop earrings as she danced a little calypso step to her hi-fi recording of "The Banana Boat Song," her six children replacing the six fiancés: "Day! Missa day! Missa day! Missa day-ay-ay-oh! Daylight come and me wanna go home!" I heard Crazy Mac when I lost one of the engagement rings, a perfect little diamond solitaire that I could weep for even now, behind the bleachers at a Little League game. At the end of our futile search, with my wee peptic ulcer preparing to flare up, Crazy Mac simply shrugged and tossed off the all-purpose absolution that had gotten her through the Invasion of Sicily and a few other rough patches as an army nurse: *machs nicht*. It doesn't matter. Don't sweat the small stuff.

Obviously, Crazy Mac was a Caribbean Islander mistakenly born into an Indiana farm family. Her father died when she was 17, leaving her mother, Sarah Renschler McCabe, with four children and a failing farm just as the

Great Depression hit. She entered nurse's training at a strict Catholic hospital the next year, graduated with the second-highest score on the state boards, and enlisted in the army at the height of the war.

In France, Italy, and North Africa, she worked until she dropped from exhaustion, washed her hair in her helmet, then went out to sing with the USO. She made fudge with a war hero, later to be a movie star, Audie Murphy; hosted a reception for a visiting general in a long black slip when no suitable dress could be found; went boar hunting in Morocco; and met my father at a barn dance in Tunisia.

From army nurse, Crazy Mac became an air force wife. Then there were the six children. And the moves. In fifth grade I attended five different, yet equally traumatizing, schools. Our longest tour was three years in Japan in the early '50s. That was when, thirty-five years ago, Crazy Mac bought Chinese pajamas for her mother back in Indiana. The high-collared ivory brocade outfit, more gown than pajamas, dazzled me.

On her last trip to visit my grandmother, my mother found her gift, still in the box she had sent it in from Japan. The Chinese pajamas had never been worn. My mother asked why. My grandmother answered that she had never had any place "special" enough to wear them. Sarah Renschler McCabe Runyan died a few months later.

My mother brought the pajamas home with her after the funeral, but never took them out of their box because they made her too sad. She gave them to me two Christmases ago and ordered me to wear them. To wear them all the time. She told me to make macaroni and cheese and to cut the crusts off peanut butter sandwiches in them. To sing "The Banana Boat Song" to her grandson and to dance little calypso steps with him in them.

I don't wear the Chinese pajamas nearly enough. But, because I got lucky and Colista Marie "Crazy Mac" McCabe Bird is my mother, I do keep trying to drown that bug in my tight ass.

Nurse Bird

GOOD HOUSEKEEPING, NOVEMBER 2009

Postpartum depression, I was ready for that. But *pre-partum*? From the instant that sperm collided with egg for my first and only pregnancy, I was knocked off-balance. The hormonal lunacy was compounded when my three best friends—the ones who'd pledged that if I went ahead and used the last fifteen minutes of fertility left on my biological clock they would see me through—all abruptly moved away. Then, deep in the grip of Mama Mania, I insisted we leave our cozy little neighborhood and move into a distant exurb with better schools.

Friendless and freaked-out, I felt like a pioneer wife alone on the edge of the frontier. I wanted my mother. We, all her six children, always had. But now, even with the world's sweetest husband and most attentive father-to-be, a deep, atavistic need for my mother took hold. Aside from having her own brood of half a dozen, she'd been a labor and delivery nurse, an army nurse, a school nurse, and had finished out her career at a women's health center. She loved to laugh and appreciated a good margarita. What pregnant lady wouldn't have wanted Nurse Bird?

But I couldn't have her. She was a long plane ride away and couldn't leave my ailing father. So we ran up enormous phone bills dissecting every varicose vein and bout of heartburn. As I lumbered through the Austin heat toward the mid-August due date, my anxiety rose with the mercury. Then miracle of miracles, my amazing sisters patched together a plan for a few days of care for my father that, if our timing was perfect, would allow what I wanted most, my mom to be with me for the delivery.

We were all on Red Alert when I went for a check-up. My doctor told me that I was at least a week away from D-Day. I rushed home to call my mom and tell her to unpack. Instead, a message was waiting for me: she'd had a "feeling" and was on her way. Heartbroken, we picked her up at the airport with the news that she was too early. Her visit would be wasted.

On the glum ride home, Nurse Bird decided that we all needed a drink. We stopped at a diner with a name too perfect to be invented, Mother's Cafe and while my mom and husband slurped margaritas, I sipped a smoothie. Perfectly in tune with my gloomy mood a rainstorm, perhaps the first to ever moisten an August in Austin, commenced pouring down. Halfway through my health concoction, Nurse Bird peeked at the watch she'd taken a thousand pulses with just as I spasmodically gripped the edge of the table. "Mom, only Braxton-Hicks contractions," I told her, proud of my insider knowledge of the term. She smiled and kept timing.

We walked outside to a sight I had never witnessed in all the desiccated summers I'd spent in Texas: a rainbow, violet and pistachio, shimmering across an August sky. An hour later, my water broke. My husband was wonderful during the delivery, but it was my mother's hand that I gripped for dear life.

She has been gone now for two and a half years, yet the luck of her magical appearance when I needed her most remains a facet of the greatest bit of luck of my life: that Nurse Bird was my mother.

Lactation Nation

TEXAS MONTHLY, AUGUST 2008

Nothing can take the fun out of fun bags quite like breast-feeding. Putting the mommy in mommy muffins instantly transforms our hitherto fabulously recreational lady bumpers into no-nonsense, utilitarian dispensers of the Thin White Line, the last best hope for keeping our children from growing up with Joan Crawford intimacy issues and Bubble Boy immune systems.

I was always favorably disposed toward breast-feeding. For my mom, it was an opportunity to sit down with the newest of her six children, put her feet up, and suck down a Falstaff along with a Lucky Strike or two. I liked the idea of these little all-ages happy hours, everyone chilling and slurping down the beverage of his or her choice.

Fast-forward to my first La Leche League meeting, which I attended when I was five months pregnant. It's hard to pinpoint the exact moment when the phrase "lactose intolerant" took on a whole new meaning. Could it have been when the speaker commanded us, brusque as a dominatrix (Mistress Mammary!), that we had to nurse for the entire first year of our child's life, even if it meant divorcing ignorant, unsupportive husbands and quitting work? And beer and cigarettes? Thanks, Mom, you've just condemned your child to a non-Ivy college. Perhaps the decisive moment came when the hostess's sturdy four-year-old son strode up to her, growled, "Nur-nur," unbuttoned her blouse, and plugged in for a loud, lengthy refill. Which we all then had to honor as the very natural, very sacred experience it was.

When I related my time with the hard-line lactorati to a friend, she told me, "You have to meet Kristine. She will completely change your mind." Having not even partially changed my mind in far too long, I made a date with Kristine Kovach, known professionally as the Mobile Mama, Austin's most popular breast-feeding swami.

I met Kovach in the depths of Seton hospital, where she was setting up for class. I can't say precisely whom I was expecting, but it wasn't Pebbles Flintstone, whom Kovach, with her headful of sproingy red curls and petite body full of sproingy muscles, resembled. Except that she had five fingers on each hand, as well as a husband, John, an award-winning musician, and two children: a daughter, Ava, 19, and a son, Severin, 15. And she herself was 42—"Elvis's death age," she informed me. Otherwise, she was the spitting image of Pebbles.

The classroom filled up with couples both well-off (husbands checking BlackBerrys, wives sporting expensive blond highlights and French-manicured toenails) and less well-off (dads in hoodies and oversized jeans, moms with tats and tongue studs). All spoke in whispers and had the awkward air of people trying to avoid eye contact in a proctologist's waiting room. Kovach called the class to order and introduced herself. "I've been a lactation consultant for ten years," she said. "It's a silly job. When I meet people, they either think it's some tech job, or, if they do know what lactation consulting is, the guys ask, 'Do you need an assistant?' So I just say I'm a spy.

"I'm not here to rip on formula. I'm formula-fed. I'm not retarded. I don't hate my mom. I'm just here to give information. I'm sure you all have researched the car seat, the crib, and the monitor. Anybody know how much formula costs?"

Lots of shrugs. No guesses.

"Twenty-five dollars a can. If your baby is average and goes through ten cans a month, that's two hundred fifty dollars. That's a car payment every month. I saw a formula ad the other day that said, 'Now even *more* like breast milk.' You know what is *just* like breast milk? Breast milk."

Kovach's manner, forthright as a public health nurse, funny as a stand-up, melted embarrassment away, and the group warmed up. She moved on to the obstacles mothers wanting to nurse their infants might face. "My mom told me that breast-feeding was a fad. A fad? I'm sure that Joseph was out trying to find a convenience store open at night to buy some formula for Mary. Still, when I had my daughter, I was certain that I wouldn't be able to breast-feed. That I was too little, too redheaded, too something. But she was born and drank like a frat boy."

First-time parents enlarged their vocabularies with terms such as "latch," "colostrum," "football hold," "let down," and "engorgement." Knowledge bases were enriched with new wisdom. "Women have two breasts," she said, "because all mammals have twice as many teats as the average litter and it looks better in a sweater."

A wispy blonde worried that she was too underendowed to make enough milk for her baby. Kovach replied, "I've seen about a thousand moms a year for the past ten years and do you know how many couldn't make enough milk?

Four. Look at me. Obviously I'm not Pamela Anderson. I had two huge babies and I made enough. Saying you won't be able to make enough milk because your breasts are small is like saying you can't see well because you have blue eyes."

A second-time mom groused that her first baby wanted to nurse for ninety minutes at a time. "Yeah," Kovach observed, "and some people want to have sex three times a day. We don't always get what we want, and we don't let ten-pound people make the decisions."

I braced myself as Kovach moved on to the forbidden-substances list and waited for She Who Knows Breast to give us the party line. Instead she related an anecdote. "I heard of a doctor who told a mom that she would have to pump and dump for five days after she had one drink. I'd like to know where the formula company sent that doctor for a cruise. The rule is, if it's in the head, it's in the milk. If you feel drunk, don't nurse. But nursing is not like being pregnant. You can eat sushi, you can change the cat box. Just don't eat the cat box. One six-ounce drink is not going to hurt your baby. In fact, a dark beer might increase your milk volume."

As the class ended, all I could think was how much I wished I could teleport Kristine Kovach back to that La Leche League meeting. She *had* completely changed my thinking. I loved every word out of her mouth. My two favorites were "dark" and "beer"—but oh, Kristine, you had me at "engorgement."

The Q Gene

NEW YORK TIMES MAGAZINE, MAY 1, 1994

As a mother the bane of my existence, the biggest pain in my capacious can, is Recent Studies and Recent Studies' attack dog, Recent Studies Indicate. Although I am a slob and raised my child with abundant messiness, Recent Studies are now indicating that I should have gone the extra mile and provided actual squalor. Recent Studies are telling me the absolute best thing for building antibodies in our offspring is close contact with livestock.

Ah, if only I'd put a goat in the bassinet with my baby, he probably wouldn't have an ear infection right now. But I didn't, so add that to the very long and ever-growing list of my maternal deficiencies. It will have to go somewhere near the bottom, though, because at the absolute top of that list has to be my deeply lamentable failure to stop my child from becoming a gun nut.

This most politically incorrect of flaws came into sharp focus last Saturday at that commercial shrine to all that is right-thinking and green, the Nature Company, when my four-year-old son strafed the baby dolphins in the computer-generated video with his toy Uzi.

A woman standing behind us pulled her own children away as the frolicking Flippers ate hot lead. I imagine that this woman was the sort of mother who had a bumper sticker like the one I had scraped off the back of my own car when the wee one was eighteen months old. A sticker that hectored: "Don't Encourage Violence. Don't Buy War Toys." I imagine that she was the sort of mother who had successfully banned all implements of destruction from her house. You know the sort of mother I mean. The mother of daughters. Or the mother of a son who obsesses about Thomas the Tank Engine rather than battle-axes, nunchucks, hand grenades, throwing stars, dirks, daggers, and catapults.

My boy, however, came hard-wired for weaponry. His first two-syllable word, right after momma, dadda, and backhoe, was scabbard. Scabbard at 18 months? Why did I ever bother resisting?

Why? Because in college, in the '60s, I started Damsels in Dissent, which counseled draft candidates to eat balls of tinfoil and put laundry soap in their armpits to fool induction center doctors. Because I believed that wars were a manifestation of testosterone run amok, much like the purchase of bad toupees and red Miata convertibles. Because I believed that white sugar, commercial television, and guns were afflictions of a sick society and that any child could be immunized against them *if only he had the right mother* to pass along her more highly evolved antibodies.

Parents do not, indeed, live by bread alone. We feast daily on banquets of our own words. My child has never seen an adult touch another adult in anger; he has never been spanked; he has never even watched a Ninja Turtles cartoon—yet he is as bloodthirsty as Quentin Tarantino.

In his toy bin are half a dozen Ninja Silent Warrior Assassin swords, two scimitars, three buccaneer blades, two six-shooters, four Laser Fazer stun guns, a Captain Hook flintlock, the aforementioned Uzi, and a silo full of items he manufactures himself. This inventory is by no means complete. I have lost friends over this arsenal. They cannot allow their children to be exposed to such untrammeled barbarism. Friends? I have lost an entire self-image and my deep Jeffersonian faith in the infinite perfectibility of man.

I resisted at first, certain that if only I stayed the course I would end up with a gentle little boy who named his stuffed animals and found Beatrix Potter a bit brutish. And I was holding the line rather well, too, till he started sleeping with a shoe. Though never one to question too closely anything that encouraged slumber, I did finally ask, why a shoe? He answered, clutching the tip of the shoelace, "So that when the bad things come in my dreams I can shoot them away."

"... when the bad things come in my dreams."

Zen monks could contemplate their koans for years and not come close to the transformation I experienced when my child aimed his shoelace at me. Children are small and weak. The world is big and scary. Gabriel's need to feel safe so outweighed my own need to feel morally correct that the contest ended. From that night on, we began building the armory until we achieved the overwhelming first-strike capability we have today.

I know what drives this war machine. It's a discovery of my own that I call the Q gene. The Q gene is that chromosomal imperative that compels little boys to pick up sticks and hair dryers; to chew their organically grown, wholegrain sandwiches into the shape of guns; to use whatever they can lay their murderous hands on, take aim, and commence firing: "Kyew. Kyew. Kyew." The Q gene.

And here is my awful confession. I passed the Q gene on to my son. As in male pattern baldness, I displayed none of the symptoms myself but carried it from both of my parents. My father an air force officer, my mother an army nurse—I am the daughter of two warriors. I reflect on this heritage as my son stands beside a helicopter at nearby Camp Mabry. We have already examined the tanks and fighter jets parked on either side. Compared relative firepower. Discussed how each would fare in a battle with Tyrannosaurus rex. But my son pats the shark's grin painted on the helicopter and announces: "This is the one, Mom. This one is the best."

Watching him calls to mind a photograph of my father taken in the late '50s. He stands before a plane with a shark's smile painted on it, just beneath the inscription: 6091st Reconnaissance Squadron. My family lived in Japan then, conquerors grinning into the last minutes of a doomed colonialism. The crew gathered around my father have their arms thrown about each other's shoulders, as heedless and glamorous as movie stars, frat boys, RAF pilots, any gang of young men who know they will never grow old, never die.

Thirty years were to pass before I learned what it was my father did when he left us for weeks at a time. He and his smiling buddies would fly their "birds" over Russia and wait to be chased back into American airspace to test Soviet response time. That was when I understood why my mother, alone with six children, would burst into tears whenever an officer in uniform came to our front door.

I watch my son stroke the shark's grin and I want to whisper to him: "It is evil. All these machines are evil. You must never think about them again." But it can never be that simple.

I hear myself sometimes, times like this one right now. I see myself the way the mother shielding her children from the sight of my son opening up on the baby dolphins must have seen me, and I feel like a shill for the NRA. My position is indefensible, illogical, inconsistent. But love makes intellectual pretzels of us all. It's just that I know, long before I would like, there will come a moment when I can do nothing to chase away the bad things in my son's dreams. Until then, if I can give him a shoelace's worth of security I guess I will.

But I'm less worried after an incident that took place just yesterday. We were stopped at a red light and my son glanced over at the driver glowering behind the wheel of the battered truck next to us. This fellow was slouched over, head jutted forward like a vulture. He sported sideburns down to his jaw and a stringy Fu Manchu. The look he was going for was "bad hombre," and he was crushing it.

My son slunk down in his seat. I asked what was wrong and he answered, "That man looks like he has a gun. A real gun."

Nonetheless, I did cave on the white sugar, the TV, the war toys. In my defense, however, there is one moral issue that I have not wavered, have not wobbled, have not waffled on. I swore before my child was born that I would never buy a certain particularly insidious toy, and I am happy to report that I have held that line. There has never been, nor will there ever be, a Barbie doll in my house.

———

From *Mothers and Sons in Their Own Words,* a photo book by Mariana Cook with an introduction by Isabel Allende (1996):

GABRIEL BIRD-JONES: *I like mom because she gives me Apple Jacks and we explore and find specimens. My best specimen was a deer antler, but I found the spot before mom did. Before anyone did. And there was also moss and a blue jay feather and other stuff too numerous to mention. And I like my mom when she screeches the car. You know, when the light is red and then it's green and I say "GO!" and she screeches the car. And she smells like cherries which I like. If she was a manatee and I was a baby manatee we would go in the deep blue Atlantic and see flying fishes and fairies. And that's all I have to say.*

Going Private

TEXAS MONTHLY, OCTOBER 2006

I f you made a list of People Least Likely to Send Their Children to Private School, I wouldn't be at the very tippy top, since Fidel and Che would have those spots sewn up. But I would be close. I grew up believing that private school—unless it was Catholic, in which case you had to go or your parents would burn in hell for all eternity—was a highly suspicious New England Yankee affectation. Private school was for the spawn of robber barons with names like Chauncey and Chatsworth, Whitney and Morgan.

A superior public school system, I believed—and still believe—is the foundation of democracy and the only way to make sure that the person doling out my meds at the Shady Rest Nursing Home will be able to count. But something happened to make me abandon my principles. Something that, had I learned to write from *Bridget Jones's Diary*, might have read something like this:

*Hormonal lunacy takes hold at same instant as pregnancy. Insist we must buy house in neighborhood that, according to TAAS scores, has best public elementary school in district.

*Snap out of it after move long enough to recall that Baby Man won't be attending public school for five years. Have contract to write novel. Must work. Endure several years of babysitters who range from marginally competent to psychotic.

*Search for preschool and find the market cannily cornered by organized religion. Preference and discounts for church members. One "principal" shows me "Jesus Room" and brags about "curriculum." Had thought potty training might be large enough challenge.

*Enroll at Mother's Morning Out run by Presbyterians. Consider Prezzies safely ecumenical until another mother shares her thoughts on "Rapture preparation." Word spreads that I am author of several "anti-Christian" books. Baby Man ostracized.

*Switch to preschool operated by Church of the Old Hippie. No Jesus Room or curriculum. Lots of wild dancing to Motown's greatest hits and back rubs at nap time. Baby Man and I both adore this school. Tuition roughly what I had figured college would cost.

*Enter "best public elementary school in district." Tuition ends; college fund starts. Kindergarten teacher named Mrs. Olsen. In astute early character analysis, Baby Man calls her Mrs. Wholesome. Less thrilled to discover class is in a "portable." Had I wanted my child to spend his days broiling in a double-wide, would have married Bobby Wayne DuPree, had a passel o' young'uns, and gotten addicted to meth.

*First-grade teacher dramatically less cuddly. While helping with student art projects, am instructed to redo all Paper Plate Snowmen: must reapply carrot noses in anatomically correct fashion. Begin to understand uniformity and excellence of all "student" projects. Notice that display of fifth-graders' Greek projects includes sugar cube models of Parthenon that would test architectural skills of I. M. Pei.

*Highlight of second grade is Japanese Garden project. Baby Man works for weeks on adorable tiny clay figures, little curved bridge. Is crushed when project not selected for display in hall. Notice that two projects selected for display still carry price tags from floral shop.

*El Hubbo, the Hub of My Universe, waylaid in deserted hallway by teacher responsible for large dental bill. Considers asking if she could control class with something other than Warheads candy. (Warheads: not just sugar—sugar with two kinds of tooth-dissolving acid.) Before Warheads issue broached, teacher thrusts prodigious bosom in El Hubbo's face and asks if he'd like to "pet it." Horror-induced blindness passes and El Hubbo sees sugar glider squirrel peeking out of breast pocket. Wisely declines invitation to pet.

*Legendary principal quits, takes cream of teaching crop to new school. Disgruntled, un-cherry-picked teachers drive off two subsequent principals. Morale plummets.

*In parent-teacher meeting, head of math department boasts that third-graders are doing algebra. I ask when multiplication tables might be addressed. Moment of silence. Am informed that such mindless, unfashionable "drill and kill" tasks are parent responsibilities.

*Make several discoveries: (1) Junior high school now called "middle school." Common wisdom is that grades six, seven, and eight are lost cause. Best parents can hope for is that child will emerge alive and unaddicted. (2) Student must be in top 10 percent of class to get into University of Texas, the school we'd blithely considered our sure thing. (3) "Best" school in district actually does no better in math on TAKS test than school in El Paso where English is second language. High scores in reading due to upper-middle-class children having been read to in utero. For most, math requires actual teachers doing actual teaching. Tuned-in parents all have children enrolled in Kumon, after-school Japanese program that teaches math using drill and kill exercises.

*Toward end of fourth grade, Baby Man still not doing what was once called "borrowing" in subtraction, now known as "regrouping." Regroup with teacher who says this is "grade-wide" problem but that everyone will be "up to speed" before year is out. Two weeks before school ends, it is announced that fourth-graders are exhausted from taking onerous, anxiety-producing TAKS test. Rest of year devoted to early-American crafts. Baby Man gets good at stamping tin but still can't borrow.

*Decide tin stamping excellent preparation for making license plates in prison; other careers might require ability to subtract. Decide to switch to private school. Must collect grade reports from teachers to apply. Happy duty, since genius child is straight-A student. Peek at teachers' grade books, however, calls to mind moment in *The Shining* when Shelley Duvall finally sees Jack Nicholson's "manuscript," discovers hundreds of pages filled with "All work and no play makes Jack a dull boy." Grade books covered with all A's, apart from two or three B's. Can all students be geniuses?

*Switch to private school, Strip Mall Prep. Ha! Don't have to construct sugar cube Parthenon. But saving for college out of question. Remind self that college is immaterial for applicant who can't subtract. Strip Mall Prep, nicknamed for affordable price and location in old house near electrolysis parlor and nail salon, is miraculous. No library, no gym, no cafeteria, no tax base, no Jesus Room, no Jesus, no institutional support—only great teachers. Baby Man becomes Teen Boy, has best years of education.

*Neighborhood high school rated "exemplary." Teachers inspirational. Whew! Back to public school. Restart college fund.

*By sophomore year, secret of exemplary high school has leaked out. School is flooded with transfers. Already crowded school overwhelmed. Several teachers problematic. Teen Boy learns much more about geometry teacher's belief that Asians are taking over school system than he does about isosceles triangles. Grades, morale, motivation plummet.

*Back to private school. College fund impossible dream. Writing giant checks puts self in very grumpy mood. Rethink stance on tin stamping. Consider how educating one child has strained two fully employed parents with decades of experience in working the system. Wonder about Bobby Wayne DuPrees of the world. Worry about young'uns of Texas.

Pedal to My Mettle

TEXAS MONTHLY, AUGUST 2006

I never wanted a Humvee before; I considered it the automotive equivalent of a Hardee's Monster Thickburger. Then my child started learning to drive. Suddenly, the Humvee seemed a perfectly reasonable mode of transport. In fact, I'm now wondering what a nice, used Sherman tank might be going for these days. Much better than the armored-assault-vehicle option, however, would be the simply-not-driving option. I know this is heresy in Texas. I know that among the inalienable rights and truths that the Texas male holds to be self-evident are life, liberty, and the pursuit of a driver's license the very instant he is physically able to peer over the dashboard, but hear me out. I am opposed to sixteen-year-olds getting driver's licenses for a number of very sound reasons.

To wit: (a) Ever priced car insurance for a sixteen-year-old? (b) The latest research shows that the brain of the average sixteen-year-old boy is composed of the same stuff that's inside Twinkies—a soft, creamy filling that doesn't start to gel until the age of 35 or when hair appears on the ears, whichever occurs first. (c) The horseless carriage is a fad and will never last.

So I recused myself and let El Hubbo, the Hub of My Universe, handle the driving instruction. Okay, I was requested—court ordered—to recuse myself. Mention was made of my unfortunate, though generally entirely warranted, habit of describing all my fellow motorists as "effing maniacs." There were also sniggering references to a certain motor trip I embarked upon—decades ago!—to visit my sister, who'd gotten a summer job working at Fort Courage, Arizona, ninety miles due west of our Albuquerque home, serving Navajo tacos to fans of the deathless TV classic *F Troop*. Much hilarity and mockery ensued simply because I took one wrong turn in Albuquerque and ended up ninety miles due *east*, on the outskirts of Santa Rosa, New Mexico.

I trace all my driving "issues" to the hideous mismatch between me and my own driving instructor, my father. My father: born in Detroit, Motor City, Michigan; flew aerial reconnaissance in World War II and the Cold War; participated in Corvette road rallies. Me: born in Ann Arbor, Pointy-headed College Town, Michigan; never took the training wheels off my bike; screamed in terror and threw up while spinning around in the tea cups. Lifelong fan and connoisseur of the internal combustion engine, my father had all sorts of Indy 500 tips for me ("Goose the g's, double clutch, rev your amps, bank into the turn, warp speed, activate tractor beam"). I had all sorts of loser questions ("Which one do you step on to make it go?").

Though I don't recall ever actually taking a driving test, the word "K-turn" does make my left eyelid twitch uncontrollably. So I was delighted to let El Hubbo be the passenger-side crash-test dummy while practice hours were logged on the learner's permit. He was the right man for the job. The proudest moment in his own Texas boyhood was when, long before being issued an actual license, he borrowed his brother's '56 Chevy Bel Air to drive his Older Woman date to the prom. Perhaps the snappy coat of royal-blue house paint they'd spiffed the car up with caught the officer's attention? Or could it have been, hmmm, that he was *barely five feet tall*? A much bigger question, though, is, Did he get a ticket? Texans, you know the answer. Do other states extend this level of sympathy and encouragement to toddler drivers? I think not.

This, then, is what Hollywood would call the backstory behind the day recently when I drove Teen Boy to the orthodontist to have his braces removed. I was all ready, camera in hand, to record the first smile in two years that wouldn't set off metal detectors. Would it be as beautiful as a sunset over the Eiffel Tower on that Paris vacation we'll never be able to afford? As stunning as the glass tile we won't be buying for the bathroom we won't be remodeling? I can't say, because there was no smile. There was only glower—intense teen glower. The braces had not come off. The orthodontist explained, poking his fingers into Teen Boy's mouth and tapping teeth, "See these guys right here? These guys aren't doing what I want them to do." For what we're paying him, those "guys" should be doing taxes, windows, and quantum physics.

Out in the parking lot, trying to take the edge off of Teen Boy's disappointment, I toss him the keys. Then I get into the passenger seat and have a small, silent nervous breakdown. The Volvo we bought shortly after he was born, mostly for its armoring of Swedish steel, now feels like an eggshell around my precious chickling. The instant my baby is behind the wheel, I want the roads cleared. And dusted, if that's not asking too much.

I control the terror. When he starts the car, I don't clench my "guys" and suck in panicked inhalations like a karate master about to snap a board in two. When he edges into traffic, I don't shoot my arm out in front of him the way my mom did in pre–seat belt days. When a jerk driving a truck with tires the size of satellite dishes won't let him change lanes, I don't go into a Tourette's-like spewing of epithets. Instead, amazed, I state the obvious. "You're a good driver. A really good driver."

The glower disappears, and I get my sunset-over-Paris smile. It reminds me of another smile. Take away the braces and the teeth, add some drool, and it is the same proud smile he beamed at us as he took his first step. Maybe it's the smile all parents get as their child ventures ever farther out into worlds of danger we cannot protect them from. Because I was a POTA—Parent Older Than Average— I knew from the first contraction that the only part of this expedition that was going to last longer than I wanted it to was labor. That I would wish it would slow down to teacup speed. But childhood has its own velocity, and far sooner than most of us are ready, it propels our offspring out beyond the charmed circle we try to draw around them.

So I soaked in that smile for as long as I could, then told him to goose the g's, double clutch, and rev the amps or we were going to get rear-ended by the effing maniac behind us.

Tour de Farce

TEXAS MONTHLY, FEBRUARY 2007

As a Texas mom, I always assumed that college would be a no-brainer. If you wanted your child to get a world-class education, you sent him to the University of Texas. If you wanted him to have unnatural congress with barnyard animals, it was off to Texas A&M. Something for everyone. But like so much else about parenthood, from potty training to the home tonsillectomy, it turned out to be vastly more complicated than I'd been led to believe.

My first shocking discovery was that the majority of the kids UT accepts are in the top 10 percent of their class. I take that on faith, since a quick stroll across the Forty Acres reveals myriad flip-flopped chuckleheads who look to have been in the top 10 percent of their class in, maybe, Gap Sweater Folding for Condescending Teens. In any event, UT is not the given it once was, and now that Teen Boy is a junior in high school, I have been forced to consider the roughly one squidgillion colleges outside the state.

This necessity presented a particularly brutal learning

curve, since my own college preparation fell somewhere between blithe and comatose: I stepped out of a giant public high school, walked a few blocks up the street, and entered a giant public university. The concept that there was much difference between one college and another only penetrated my consciousness when I spent a summer as an intern in Washington, DC (far less spicy than one might hope). Everyone I met took an inexplicable interest in where I'd gone to school. I found this quirky Back East trait endearing until I figured out that conversations tended to stop dead after my bright and peppy answer, "University of New Mexico! Go Lobos!" On the other hand, intense friendships involving weekends sailing on Chesapeake Bay developed when the answers were "Princeton," "Harvard," or "Yale."

The next shocking discovery was that getting into college has become reminiscent of snagging a seat on the last lifeboat leaving the *Titanic*. It's a frenzy driven by fear—the fear that if your child doesn't get into a "good" college, he faces a lifetime of janitorial work sweeping up at China Intergalactic, and the far greater fear that your tennis partner's child will get into a better school than yours and make it obvious that you have failed as a parent. The damn Brits have it so easy: You're born. You get the coat of arms. Case closed. Now stressed-out parents have to club their children's way into the meritocracy with lacrosse sticks and Suzuki violins.

So there I was, facing a mountain of depressing consumer research about a purchase that, in year one of four potential years, could end up costing us—literally—what our first house did. Luckily my mantra is the writer's mantra: when the going gets tough, the tough retreat into a fantasy fugue state. I decided to write a novel about the college search. My main character would be female, a straight-A overachiever dying to go to an Ivy League school. Which meant that I had to hie myself east and actually tour a few campuses. After much nuanced, artistic deliberation about where I had friends I could stay with for free, I decided to investigate Harvard and Princeton.

The surprise was how much I learned while playing pretend. Not wanting this great research to go to waste, and being nothing if not service oriented, I now offer these tips to Lone Star parents on how to survive a Back East college tour.

*Number one with an armor-piercing bullet: leave your own child home. Do as I did and take along an imaginary teenager. Take the one who loves to share her thoughts and listens raptly to yours. Who digs it when you dance and sing along to "Who Let the Dogs Out?" Who is not going to be embarrassed by your dopey questions, dopey shirt, dopey shoes, your dopey insistence on breathing. Rory, that animatronic poppet from *Gilmore Girls*, would be perfect.

*Next, a bit of fashion advice for parentals as you head east: leave the pastels behind. Your Southwest connection in Dallas is the last time you'll see clothing in any color that an Italian widow wouldn't wear. This tip is especially crucial if you screwed up royally and brought your own, actual child along. The more you approach a ninja-level of invisibility, the happier your teenager will be. Parents, you can't go wrong with the official fabric of the dorky dad and misguided mom: polar fleece. You can't go right either, but isn't that parenthood's essential conundrum? And, students, should you accidentally be invited along, you are going to be tempted to look presentable. Don't. If you need fashion tips on touring the Ivy League, head out to the nearest highway intersection. Your style gurus will be holding signs offering to work for beer. Seriously, pajamas and shower shoes are top fashion items in elite prep school classrooms.

*Develop filtering systems capable of fuzzing out tour guide phrases that begin with words like "interdisciplinary" and "process oriented." Also immediately route to the lint trap comments like "In assembling our freshman class, we're looking for more than _____." Fill in and ignore "grades," "test scores," "freakish brainiacs," "thirteen-year-old Nobel Prize winners," "big fat bank accounts," and "colossal endowments."

*All right, let's say that worse has come to worst and your offspring is with you. Take immediate action! Before you open your mouth, you must, must, must attach yourself to someone else's child. Yes, Dad, go up to the nearest child who is not your own and put your arm around her. Trust me, the years you spend in the slammer nicknamed Short Eyes will be nothing, the merest blip on the parental radar, compared with the agony of watching your own daughter incinerate from embarrassment—literally spontaneously combust and burn to cinder—after you ask the hottie student guide, well, essentially anything. But do try the question one mother in my Harvard tour group posited: "Will we be able to examine the sprinkler system in the dorm?"

My favorite parent question, though, came from a Korean dad on the Princeton tour. After the admissions counselor—herself a recent grad with, perhaps, a bit too much Ivy in her high-fiber ego—told us that P'ton admits roughly one out of every nine million applicants, he made up his mind. Treating her like a particularly cagey used-car salesman who'd somehow managed to close the deal, he gravely announced, "Okay, my son go this school. Where I pay?"

Craigslust

TEXAS MONTHLY, DECEMBER 2007

I emerged from the vegetative coma I'd slumped into while finishing my last novel, stretched, looked around, and discovered that (a) our house looked as if the Collyer brothers—the notorious pack rats overcome by towers of their own junk—lived there and (b) our only child was turning eighteen the next day.

I had probably suppressed this last bit of knowledge, since buying presents had become such a fraught activity. In the early years, it was a breeze—a very cost-effective breeze. I would wrap up whatever I found lying around the house: pepper mill, stapler, bag of charcoal briquettes. The Birthday Boy would delight in shredding off the wrapping paper, toss the "gift" aside, crawl into the box, and have the "hours of fun" promised by commercials that actual toys failed to deliver (possibly because his mother had neglected to buy sixteen D batteries).

All too soon, however, he wised up, and actual gifts were forced to enter the equation. Thank God for those crafty Danes and their Legos. Many a happy birthday rolled by with the Lego robot giving way to the Lego log cabin, the

Lego starship, the Lego particle accelerator. Then there was the year when, like most parents around the world, we participated in the pyramid scheme that was Pokémon cards and paid exorbitant sums for pieces of cardboard. It would have been cheaper to simply draw Pikachu's picture on $50 bills and wrap those up. Had I only known. After Charizard and Squirtle left our lives, we entered the years when the answer to "What do you want for your birthday?" was invariably "A new computer." From there it escalated alarmingly to this year's request: "A car." Fairly certain that the B'day Boy didn't mean a squared-off yellow-red-and-blue Danish model he could snap together himself, I conveniently forgot the whole matter.

Until the day before the monumental eighteenth, when I came to and went straight from hibernation to hysteria. Fortunately, I had a clue: I'd glimpsed Internet searches for "motorcycle jacket" on the B-Boy's computer. Unfortunately, I'd also glimpsed price tags. Price tags high enough to explain why Joey Ramone apparently owned no clothing other than his iconic jacket. In any case, there was no time for shipping. Frantic, I defaulted to my solution to all of life's tough problems: call girlfriends and sisters. One of the first responders suggested that I try Craigslist.

I was dubious. Several years ago, when a friend I was visiting in Boston introduced me to this phenomenon, I misheard "Craigslist" as "Kegelist." I couldn't understand why there would be a website devoted to strengthening the pelvic muscles. My misapprehension was reinforced when my friend drew my attention to the "Casual Encounters" section. I left Boston believing that "Kegelist" was a specialty site catering to young men with time, and so much more, on their hands—young men who enjoyed posting cell phone photos of attributes whose most winning qualities were being "disease-free" and available at no cost to any lucky lady or gent wishing to rush over and claim them.

Then, like so many innovations, from the Dewey decimal system to Elfa shelving, Craigslist under its proper name wormed its way into my consciousness. I warily typed in the words "motorcycle jacket." To my amazement, one popped up at exactly the price I wanted to pay: dirt cheap. I fired up my regulation Suburban Mom gray Volvo station wagon and raced over to meet the seller.

Scott was waiting on the porch of his subdivision bunga-low. He'd just finished mowing his lawn and was drinking a beer. He looked like Ricky Gervais but with a slightly larger paunch and no twinkle in his eye. Or anywhere else. In fact, Scott was twinkle-free to the point of outright grumpiness.

Undeterred and eager to make my first Craigslist friend, I bounded up the porch steps and stuck my hand out. He ignored my hand and, without a word, languidly waved his Shiner longneck toward the jacket, a perfect Joey Ramone model, hanging from the screen door.

"Is that it?" I asked brightly.

"Uh, yeah," he answered, his tone adding, *Dumb ass*. He pointed again with the Shiner bottle. "I saw Sonic Youth, Jane's Addiction, Beastie Boys, Smashing Pumpkins, and Nine Inch Nails in that jacket."

"Wow. Great bands."

He looked from me to the Volvo and narrowed his eyes. A thought bubble appeared above his head that read, *The last "great band" you heard was backing up Enya.*

Scott didn't seem terribly interested in selling the jacket, and that worried me. "Can I check out the size?" Without waiting for an answer, I slipped the jacket on. It was exactly too tight around my middle and too long in the sleeves. It would fit B-Boy perfectly.

I had to close the buy. "Well, Scott, you'll be happy to know that it's going to a good home. My son will carry on the bad-ass attitude."

"Lady, I'm selling the jacket. The attitude stays with me."

From inside the house came the sound of young children squabbling. Their mother screamed at them and turned on cartoons. The volume was loud. Really loud.

Scott turned toward the open door and yelled over *Beavis and Butthead*, "I'm only SELLING the jacket because SHE told me I HAD to sell THE JACKET!"

B&B was turned up even louder. It was clear by then that the words "my youth" could be substituted for "the jacket." At this point, a decent person would have backed delicately away and allowed the crisis intervention team to step in. I wasn't that person. I was a person who had to come home with either a motorcycle jacket or a car.

Desperate, I pulled up a little trick I'd learned for dealing with balky toddlers: the illusory choice ("Bun-bun, would you rather brush your teeth with the Mickey Mouse toothbrush or the Batman one?"). With more pep than a Longview coed rushing Pi Phi, I asked, "So, Scott, should I write you a check or would you prefer cash?"

Still wearing the jacket, I backed off the porch, stuffing twenties into Scott's hand, jumped into the trusty Volvo, and gunned her out of there like the sweet, smokin' getaway car she was.

The jacket was the biggest birthday hit since I wrapped the rice cooker in a refrigerator box. B-Boy put his present on and didn't take it off for the next three days. As for me, I had had my first Craigslist encounter. It wasn't casual, but I did come out of it wearing more clothes than I'd gone into it with, and I considered that a major score.

Ranch Blessing

TEXAS MONTHLY, AUGUST 2009

T wo words—three, depending on how you feel about hyphens—have changed my life and net financial worth: "mid-century modern." If you're a fan of *Mad Men* or martinis, you probably already know about mid-mod, the rekindling of love for all things '50s: sunburst wall clocks, dinette sets, tail fins, Tang, and, most significantly, the suburban ranch house. This infatuation with the brawny, ebullient time following World War II, when America was in love with space travel and clam dip, was not in play when we were house hunting twenty years ago.

I was pregnant and therefore in the thrall of intractable cravings for salty food and real estate in supposedly good school districts. Two seconds after the stick turned pink, the walls of our once cozy eight-hundred-square-foot bungalow began closing in on me. Far worse, the formerly charming elementary school down the street morphed into a scene out of *Deliverance*. The second I imagined my offspring enrolled there, all the children devolved into six-fingered throwbacks picking head lice off one another. Desperate to save my only begotten from marrying his cousin, I hit the Multiple Listing Service with a vengeance.

Fortunately, my mental implosion coincided with the late-'80s collapse of the Austin real estate market. This allowed a couple of sorry subprimers like my husband and me to obey the realtor's credo—"Worst House, Best Neighborhood"—and weasel our way into an allegedly topflight school district. The house itself, a suburban Ranchburger of dun-colored brick, was almost beside the point. Two distinguishing features barely saved her low-slung anonymity from total invisibility: she had been built by a Melville scholar who'd equipped her with a staggering acreage of built-in bookshelves, and she was in our price range (i.e., insanely cheap). This helped us ignore the gold-flecked, mandarin-red Formica counters, the ancient venetian blinds, and the Sputnik-inspired light fixtures.

Once our son was born and the house hormones had been flushed out of my system, I realized that I should have been paying a lot more attention to potty training than TAKS scores, since he was five years away from having to worry about schools of any quality. I also noticed that I had exiled us to the kind of neighborhood that looked as if it had been hit by one of those bombs that kill the people but leave property values intact. The only humans I ever saw were operating leaf blowers. This was in vivid contrast to Bungalow Land, where everyone did their own yard work and we always knew when the bars had closed from the sounds of alfresco fighting and retching.

On our first night in Ranchburger, I discovered that, even with all the *I Love Lucy*–era venetian blinds shut tight, our house still glowed like a bad nuclear rod. I turned to El Hubbo and asked, "What's that?"

"I don't know. The midnight sun?"

We peeked out. Crime lights blazed from tall poles beside our nervous neighbors' houses, lighting the block up like a prison yard (this, in spite of the fact that the only crime that ever occurred on the street was that our election signs—first Clinton, then Gore, then Kerry—got stolen).

Ranchburger came to seem like a mistake. Behind her back, we started to see other houses. It's not as if we didn't try to make it work; we ripped out the speckled linoleum and installed tile the exact color of the fawns that capered through our yard. We battered down a wall, and the galley kitchen—named for the galley slaves who'd died in similar cramped conditions—opened into a space large enough for a counter that a grown man could lie down and make snow angels on. But the paint we slapped up was always in the neutral tones that realtors advise for maximum resale value, and the tile we covered the mammoth counter with came from the low end of the spectrum. Still, faithful Ranchburger, though she knew we had commitment issues, never complained or even asked us to go into counseling with her.

Gradually, though, something changed. As the original owners on our block left, they were replaced by groovy young couples: designers, architects, music producers. Stylish individuals who had been to Italy, they immediately ripped out the déclassé Saint Augustine and replaced it with the sorts of grasses and ground covers that my old neighbors would have treated with Round-up. They painted the brick siding of their ranch houses goulash brown and army-jeep-olive drab with kicky splashes of battleship gray. They chipped out Saltillo tile, stained and buffed the exposed concrete floors, threw in fiberglass and vinyl furniture, and invited us over for a highball. If only they'd added a Ping-Pong table and a meat freezer, they would have duplicated exactly the look my mother was going for with our garage when I was in high school. They all seemed to be going for Hugh Hefner's ultimate, cool daddy-o bachelor pad, complete with hi-fis, swag lamps, and Chex Mix.

Overnight, property values skyrocketed. Realtors who advertised that they specialized in mid-mod asked if we were interested in selling. Secret suitors were eyeing Ranchburger? Like the straying husband who finds out that the little missus is getting some on the side, I took a whole new look at our domicile. For the first time, I saw that Ranchburger, asking nothing in return, had given us everything. I needed to not feel trapped in a suburban neighborhood, and she gave us patio doors across the entire back side of the house that faced a greenbelt where squirrels, raccoons, armadillos, foxes, doves, blue jays, cardinals, waxwings, owls, and whip-poor-wills cavorted among cedars fuzzy with shaggy bark and towering live oaks twisted into exquisite bonsai shapes. Our son and his friends needed a house that wasn't cherished, a house that they could colonize and slosh Big Red on, and Ranchburger offered herself without reservation. My husband needed to never eat a weed, and Ranchburger supplied an untendable thicket of scrub oak and herds of deer that would have gobbled AstroTurf.

Most of all, we needed to be lazy slobs, and Ranchburger has ended up enabling that too. All those Sputnik-inspired light fixtures and ancient venetian blinds—the stuff we were too uninspired to update? They're no longer signs of neglect. They've been transformed into highly sought-after "original architectural elements." Magically, we're no longer slipshod. We're mid-mod!

And, since we owe it all to you, Ranchburger, let me put it in terms you'll understand: you're a real gone chick, and we dig you the most.

The Goodbye Boy

TEXAS MONTHLY, DECEMBER 2008

The last place I expected to have a full-blown existential crisis was in the middle of the sing-along version of *Mamma Mia!* I mean, how seriously is anyone supposed to take a movie in which Meryl Streep, dressed in white Keds and bib overalls, bounces around like a toddler on a sugar high? *Mamma Mia!* is all about sneaking thermoses of margaritas into the theater to share with the G Friends, singing along to "Dancing Queen," and pretending that any one of us could have blown off Colin Firth, Pierce Brosnan, and that Scandinavian guy with the potbelly and owned an adorable little B&B on a sun-splashed Greek island that the colorful locals love to clean for us. And that the world would find it irresistibly intoxicating if we kicked off our shoes and danced like trained bears. All fine in a campy, no-wire-hangers, *Mommie Dearest* sort of way.

So there I was, waiting for Meryl either to tell me that I was the dancing queen—young and sweet, only seventeen, et cetera, et cetera—or to deliver that puzzling message to the equally enigmatic Fernando about something in the air that night and stars being bright. But instead of allowing as to how I can dance, I can jive, having the time of my life, she began singing, as her daughter was dressing for her wedding, about time slipping through her fingers and "an odd melancholy feeling and a sense of guilt I can't deny." As Meryl crooned that she was losing forever the little girl with a schoolbag in her hand, the margarita merriment drained away. All I could think about was my only begotten leaving in less than a week for a college 2,400 miles away. By the time Meryl asked what had happened to all the wonderful adventures she had planned and admitted, "Well, some of that we did, but most we didn't," I was blubbering and grieving for Family Game Night. I had fully intended to make Family Game Night a tradition but hadn't, and now it was too late to drag out the Chutes and Ladders.

Until that moment, I believed I had successfully inoculated myself against empty-nest syndrome. As a POTA (Parent Older Than Average), I already knew that time doesn't slip, odd and melancholic, through your fingers. It gushes in undammable, hemorrhagic torrents. Consequently, from the get-go I had consciously clung to as many drops as I could. I had also been careful not to bake too much of my identity into the cupcakes I took to school so that I wouldn't end up bleating out the question I'd heard other mothers of college-bound kids ask: who am I if I'm not Jason/Sophie/Caitlyn's mom? And I was certain I'd delivered a decisive preemptive strike on the empty nest by getting a puppy—an adorable puppy that didn't mind appearing with me in public and never missed curfew. So there would still be messes to clean up and a dependent being to bend to my implacable will. What was my problem?

A few days after the ABBA-activated meltdown, however, I once again started leaking the salty wet ones. This time the trigger was a lone can of Cherry Vanilla Dr Pepper and the realization that it would be the last one ever to grace my refrigerator. Now, had *I* seen a woman sobbing over a soft drink, I'd have advised her to get a life. One that included some topflight professional help. With special attention to nutritional counseling on exactly how evil Cherry Vanilla Dr Pepper is.

Then, like everyone else looking for the big answers to the big questions, I turned to my Spirit Guide, that ultimate repository of all human wisdom: Shri Googlenami. I tried typing in "empty nest," but Mr. Left Ring Finger, that maverick, kept hitting an *x* instead of an *s*.

I finally got the spelling right and found Shri G to be teeming with expert reports about empty-nest syndrome being a myth and with parents blogging about the joys of the child-free house: less laundry, fewer groceries, being able to have sex anywhere, anytime. And, they all pointed out, the kid comes back, you never stop being a parent, he still needs you, yada, yada. All right, maybe Life After Boy *was* going to be an unwashed, low-cal key party, but it still felt as if I'd gotten it right the first time, when I typed in "empty next."

Though I enjoy a moment of maudlin self-indulgence as much as the next person with an Internet connection, it was time to snap out of it. What I needed was a Black Ops team that could parachute in and scrub my house of all evidence of Boy the instant after he left. I was certain that I could handle this empty-nest thing swimmingly if the nest were truly empty.

The team could start by removing that Wallace and Gromit tape we watched when he had chicken pox. Also on the seek-and-destroy list would be the mutant collection he created by snipping toys in half with bolt cutters and glue-gunning Polly Pocket heads to Tyrannosaurus rex bodies and Power Ranger bodies to Inspector Gadget heads. They should also vaporize the possum skeleton, deer horns, sand dollars, ninja sword, cool rocks, arrowheads, and dagger-shaped icicle saved in a jam jar in our freezer for the past nine years.

If the team could scour off the green glitter-glue rectangles on the coffee table, those ghostly frames of crafts projects past, that would be useful as well. It would also be great if they'd eliminate the particular sunbeam that slants into the kitchen window and hits the spot where his supergroovy blue plastic high chair used to sit as he chased bits of pear, slippery as goldfish, around the tray, giving me toothless, drooly grins of triumph whenever he got one into his mouth.

And his smell. Yes, I'm certain that this emptying nest would not have to become a syndrome if the nest didn't still smell so much like Boy. Should the team want to widen their sweep, they might also consider ensuring that I don't have to see a skinny boy shivering at the edge of a pool, his hands tucked into his armpits, yelling, "Mom. Mom! Watch me dive, Mom!"

I know that what everyone tells me is true: the kid comes back, you never stop being a parent, he still needs you. And I know that when he returns, he'll be brighter, funnier, and kinder than when he left. And I'll put on white Keds and bib overalls and dance almost as well as a trained bear. But for just this moment, just right now, I'm going to be a little sad. Then I'm going to go out and teach that new dog to take forty-five-minute showers and drink Cherry Vanilla Dr Pepper.

WRITING

—

Use It in Your Work

For Keith

FOR AIDS BENEFIT "QUEER VOICES," SEPTEMBER 1998

K eith and I were brought together by the alphabet. If you think I refer here to a shared love of fine literature, you flatter me. No, my last name is Bird. His was Benavides, so we ended up sitting across a library table in study hall at Highland High School in Albuquerque, New Mexico. The study hall was commandeered by one Herr Schmitt, a punctilious German teacher who clearly believed that the wrong country had prevailed in the Big One.

I was a senior, enduring my last year of purgatory encapsulated behind a bulletproof shield of sullen cynicism designed to beat everyone to the punch of rejecting me. Keith was a sophomore who ate cynicism for breakfast. He had the face of a cherub by way of Alfred E. Neumann, and was a social provocateur back when Camille Paglia was still ratting her hair and wearing white lipstick. Keith, I would learn, was an imp who loved fucking with the system.

But I didn't know any of that when I took my assigned seat across from him. At first I dismissed Keith as just another part of the Highland High School landscape that I had to fuzz out as much as possible. Besides, he was a sopho-more, and if you don't remember what a colossal difference two years in age used to make, congratulations, you have succeeded in blocking *your* high school experience better than most. So Keith got nothing from me beyond a stoic deadpan. Until that first note he slid across the table after Herr Schmitt checked us off and goose-stepped on past.

That amazing note read: "Hold down the hilarity. Your constant laughter really bugs me." I was the last survivor of an Arctic expedition trapped in a doomed igloo with no one on earth receiving my transmissions and, BAM!, the shortwave crackles to life? Keith, of all the oddball long-shots, had picked up my frequency.

Keith's father, who'd been paralyzed in a car wreck when Keith was a toddler, had dealt with his disability by exhal-ing cynicism and bitterness like bad air. That was the rea-son Keith could bump off my high school version without even trying, but it would be a long time before I found all that out.

In the meantime, Herr Schmitt's study hall came to life. Keith and I got our own low-tech, non-virtual email thing going immediately, shoving notes back and forth across the library table. As a shy unto catatonic individual mistakenly born into an air force family that moved way more than was really good for my mental health, I'd learned early to make up more pleasant worlds to live in than those I was forced to physically occupy. With Keith, for the first time, I had a buddy in these parallel universes.

The study hall became Reichmaster Schmitt's Study Gulag. We invented a rich and vivid life for the unsuspect-ing martinet. Die Schmitt became infinitely more bearable the instant that Keith suggested he might be wearing an eighteen-hour, Cross Your Heart Bra beneath his rumpled, chalk and dandruff–dusted, mustard-colored corduroy jacket. I thought I detected the outlines of a long-line panty girdle lurking beneath the Schmitt's trim-fitting Sansabelt slacks.

But Keith's greatest moment of guerrilla agitation came during the hemline showdown. The school board had just handed down a directive forbidding female students from wearing skirts that did not touch the floor when the wearer in question was kneeling down. Now, two things about this embargo appealed irresistibly to The Herr: it was a rule, naturally, and even more enticing, it offered the prospect of having a female student kneel before him. Thus did Herr Schmitt appoint himself High Lord Guardian of Morals and Master of Hemlines.

Every day, in a show as ritualized as kabuki theater, he would scrutinize the girls as they entered study hall, jotting down the names of those wearing skirts of questionable lengths. Then he would cull out each potential offender, have her kneel before him, and either send her back to her seat or to the principal's office. One did not require an advanced degree from Vienna to hear the squirmy cuckoos chiming out from this guy's clock.

The third time I was cut out of the herd and made to kneel before this twerp, Keith began thinking revenge. That very afternoon, we both cut our last classes and walked over to the Disabled Veterans Thrift Store three blocks away. Keith ran up and down the aisles, scanning swiftly past the polyester pull-on pants and acrylic turtlenecks to home unerringly in on the exact prey he was stalking: a dress with décolleté to die for. A dress that Dolly Parton at her hydroponic heights could barely have filled. A dress with a neckline that plunging only barely began to describe.

Keith, his sweet troll doll face radiant with glee, informed me that this, *this*, was what I was going to wear to school tomorrow morning. How does one argue with the Che Guevara of the suburbs? I wore a sweater all day, until that crucial moment when I had to parade past the Herrball. Of course, I was singled out. And, of course, Keith had made sure that the dress was long enough to absolutely billow around my knees when I assumed the position. You almost had to feel sorry for Schmitt, glaring down at my overexposed chest, the excessively hardwired circuitry of his brain straining for the precise rule I had broken. But there wasn't one. He had to send me back to my seat.

Did I only imagine that everyone in the whole study hall whistled "Bridge on the River Kwai" as I marched back triumphantly to my seat? I did. But Keith definitely whispered "Beauty, babe," to me as I sat down and put my sweater back on.

Since Keith helped *me* out of the closet, helped me to realize that I could speak out in a voice that, while not technically homosexual, was still queer as hell, and that someone would get it, someone would understand, it was only fair that I help him out. I started taking him to the Wednesday night dances at the university where I had discovered worlds of other weirdos who had survived high school on synthetic cynicism. Keith and I would start off the evening dancing together. Then we'd cruise and he'd point out the guys he thought I should zero in on.

After the dance, we'd go the Frontier Restaurant on Central Avenue, drink coffee consciously left black just to be sophisticated, eat the sweet rolls they used to bill as "the world's biggest," and debrief. Keith never officially came out to me, we just gradually let the charade of him telling me which guys he thought *I* should think were cool slide. So, halfway through a sweet roll the size of a catcher's mitt, we were suddenly squealing about which of the black basketball stars the Lobos had imported from Philadelphia was the cutest. Gay, straight, we never put that fine a point on the issue: Keith was just Keith, my bud.

His father killed himself halfway through Keith's junior year and his mother moved them to Asheville, North Carolina, to be closer to her family. Keith was not as good at letters as he'd been at notes. He wrote that if God were going to give the world an enema, he'd put the nozzle in at Asheville. Then I didn't hear much more.

Years rolled by. Keith was one of those people who liked to get drunk and call old friends. When the phone rang at three a.m. on New Year's Morning, I'd know it was Keith. He'd moved out to Venice, California, and was working as a waiter at Le Dome until he could sell a screenplay. Keith regaled me with celebrity gossip from the restaurant, tending to concentrate on Richard Gere.

The phrase T-cell didn't penetrate my awareness until one evening almost a decade ago. Always a trendsetter, Keith was once again ahead of the curve. I never understood how sick he was. My name was on a list of friends he wanted notified. That's how I found out. I suppose, if I could ever be mad at Keith for anything, it's that. He didn't let me say goodbye.

On this evening consecrated by and to community and understanding, I would like to say goodbye to Keith Benavides and to thank him for the voice he helped me find. He lives on still in it.

Flash Back

THE *ALCALDE* (THE OFFICIAL PUBLICATION OF THE TEXAS EXES), MAY/JUNE 2011

T he best thing that the University of Texas ever did for me was to stick a camera in front of my face and officially justify what I already was: an observer, a recorder, a voyeur, an introvert driven by insatiable curiosity.

It was the summer of 1974. I had a freshly minted BA in anthropology from the University of New Mexico, a temporary job at the LBJ Library that was about to end, and a boyfriend who was leaving me for Scientology. I needed a plan.

I took to wandering the campus on my lunch hour, as awed by the power and the might and the marble as a peasant from the provinces come to Imperial Rome. The journalism building called to me with its air conditioning and drink machines. I ambled around the cool, empty halls, sipping my Diet DP and entertaining vague fantasies about being a girl reporter.

On one of these rambles, I made my way to the third floor, where I stopped to peruse a bulletin board. As I was considering whether to pluck a phone number off of an ad for "Roommate Needed," or one from the equally plausible "Passenger to Seattle Wanted," a thin, cracking voice from an unseen source startled me, "May I help you?" It was summer break. The only open door on the entire floor led to what I'd taken to be a broom closet. I peeked in.

It was a small, windowless office upholstered from floor to ceiling with teetering piles of books and papers. At its center was a slight, elderly man, his pronounced buckteeth displayed in a friendly smile. His manner was courtly in an old-fashioned way, more southern than Texan, more country than city. The old gent seemed to have all the time in the world and an inexplicable eagerness to spend every second of it chatting with a clueless stranger from New Mexico. I took him to be some sort of emeritus presence, a former professor so beloved that he was allowed to linger long after retirement.

Though I left feeling as if I'd had an audience with a skinny Buddha, I didn't take the application he'd given me for his "program" seriously. I stuffed it in my backpack and forgot about it. Until three days later. I was at work on the fifth floor of the LBJ Library, unloading big brown boxes of miscellanea—photos of Lynda Bird's makeover for her date with George Hamilton; letters from schoolchildren outraged that President Johnson had lifted his beagles, Him and Her, up by their ears; recipes for Lady Bird's Bunkhouse Chili—cataloguing the contents, and repacking them into mandarin red buckram boxes for display.

I had just finished cataloguing the last of several red boxes that I'd filled with small, heart-shaped boxes holding pieces of Lynda Bird's wedding cake—long since dried into leathery pucks—when I opened a box packed with photos of the First Lady. And there, right on top, was the professor who had been so kind to me receiving an award from Mrs.

Johnson. I quickly dug that application out of my backpack, applied, and was awarded a fellowship to the graduate program directed by one of the legends of Texas journalism, the skinny Buddha himself, DeWitt C. Reddick.

The very first semester, though, I discovered my big problem with journalism: facts. I would go out to "cover" a "story" and return knowing everything about my subject: why she and her husband were breaking up, how bad her ragweed allergy was, and how much she hated pimiento cheese, but not, necessarily, her last name. Or what was in the dreary bill she was sponsoring.

Photojournalism, however, was another story altogether. A story where the facts reshuffled themselves with every click of the shutter, no one could ever say they'd been "misquoted," and you owned whatever corner of the world you could put a frame around. I was electrified by a sense of discovery. Of capturing places, people, moments that no one had ever seen before. Certainly not in quite the way that I saw them. The thought that popped into my head most frequently was a gleeful: "No one is going to believe this shit!"

Best of all, a camera gave a shy person like me permission and a reason to talk to anyone. Delighted with this new superpower, I undertook as one of my first student projects photographing shoppers at a nearby mall, Hancock Center. My subjects taught me my first lesson in portrait photography, which was that, if I asked directly if I could take their picture, they immediately stiffened into taxidermy. On the other hand, if I inquired if I could photograph their extremely fetching sunglasses, or cool trucker hat, or super adorable earrings, they would instantly relax, becoming the proud possessors of such stylish items, flattered by every click of my shutter.

Back at the University of New Mexico, I'd dreamed of being an anthropologist studying exotic cultures, and now I was. A camera was my passport to anywhere I wanted to go. And there were so many places I wanted to go: Wurstfest, a quinceañera, the snow monkey ranch in south Texas, shows at the Armadillo World Headquarters, the dayroom at the state mental hospital, an old lady beauty salon, and rodeos. Especially rodeos. My first was the Huntsville Prison Rodeo, where I sat in front of a row of French sailors in their Donald Duck uniforms muttering, "Quelle barbare!" to each other.

It was barbaric and I was hooked. Not on the actual sport but on the unique subcultures that blossomed around what I came to think of as "mutant rodeos," hybrids that refashioned mainstream rodeo into expressions of their communities. Off and on for a few years, I photographed and interviewed the ropers and riders in prison, police, kids', women's, gay, African American, and old-timers' rodeos. I even heard about a nudist rodeo held, naturally, in California, but I never got close enough to that one to learn the true meaning of bareback riding. To say nothing of rawhide.

I had found my place in journalism and that place was not in the rusty monolith on Guadalupe and 26th. No, my home was a dank, toxic-fumed darkroom located in the basement of the Geography Building. There, in the amber glow of a safelight, I experienced that Christmas-morning moment that digital photographers will never experience. That moment after you've rushed your film to the lab, loaded it onto canisters, swished and swirled it in developer solution, then pulled your coils of negatives out for the moment of truth. Was the exposure right? The shutter speed? Focus? Had you captured the magic you'd seen through your view finder? Was it there? Did you get the shot?

The photographers who gathered to develop film and make prints from the negatives with a series of chemical baths and precise sweeps of light reminded me of the crews my navigator-father flew with during the Cold War. Aggressive, funny, glamorous, filled with bravado. We were shooters. We were badasses. If you needed to be inside the rodeo arena when they turned out the bull, on the dirt, fully exposed to hoof and horn, then that's where you were. Our photos were the prize catches we brought back to the darkroom, and each one was a challenge to the others to step up their game. My group had a bounty of especially talented members who went on to win Pulitzers, own their own studios, and fill the pages of every important publication in the country with their work.

But the clock was running out on my fellowship. My master's thesis was due. It was made clear to me that my extensive forays into the graphic world would not be tolerated as the main topic of this final project. I wasn't ready, however, to emerge from the amber glow and step back into the harsh light of facts. Through some marvel of academic double-speak, I managed to get a proposal approved that would let me continue photographing at my latest visual paradise, the Hyde Park Beauty Salon.

If I were ever to design a writing program, I doubt I could come up with a better project than my beauty salon thesis. It brought together everything I'd learned in anthropology—figuring out how a culture affects an individual—and photography—focusing on the details that tell that individual's unique story. I had a sense of urgency about capturing this world, since the owner had confided to me that she was selling the shop. She was too old to be on her feet all day and, besides, most of the clients she'd had for decades were dying or had already passed on.

In the thesis I eventually submitted, illustrated with as many photos as the department would allow me to cram in, here's how I described the shop. "The Princess Beauty Shoppe is a cozy, tacky place cluttered with the affectionate debris of forty years. A tray of brownies brought by a patron combine their sweet chocolatey smell with the ammonia stink of hair dyes, straighteners, and permanents. The shelves are lined with dusty jars and bottles filled with beauty products from another era. The chairs in the shop are filled by the users of those products who come once a week to have their hair washed, rolled, dried, and teased into the styles they've always worn: beehives; a bouffant pageboy; perms as curly and tight as poodle fur. 'Just say we're an old lady shop,' states the owner, Miss Faith, in a proud apology."

The salon did close, eventually replaced by a custom-framing shop. I went on to rediscover the perfect synthesis of all my impulses to capture worlds and people when I returned to writing fiction. I put my camera aside and never set foot in a darkroom again. And now, except in the world of rarefied art photography, darkrooms are gone as well. Chemicals, film, and light have been replaced by pixels. But sometimes, when the writing is going especially well, when it takes me somewhere I could never have gone on my own, an exhilaration that seems bathed in a familiar amber glow overtakes me, and I think again, "No one is going to believe this shit!"

Shrines to a Common Good

SPEECH TO THE TEXAS LIBRARY ASSOCIATION, JULY 2017

I'd like to start off by saying how happy I am to be with you today. I know, most speakers say that, don't they? In my case, however, it is absolutely true. I promise, you will not find another person in all of Austin who appreciates, who frankly *needs*, librarians more than I do. I appreciate you Austin librarians so much in fact that I have been carrying on DALLIANCES with many of you ever since I first arrived in Austin way back in 1973. I know that my current home branch, Old Quarry, *thinks* that it is the only one, my only library family. That it and it alone fulfills all my book and periodical needs. The truth is, though, I am a library polygamist. Yes, Old Quarry, you might as well know the truth, I have been checking out the goods at other branches all around town. Yarborough, I love you for your glamorous past as a screen star. Faulk downtown, who can deny your colorful, walk-on-the-wild-side clientele? And all the rest of you—Howson, Willie Mae Kirk, Twin Oaks, Terrazas, Windsor Park—we've all had our moments together and I have loved each and every one of you in different seasons for different reasons.

And now the moment I've always feared has come and you're all here together, finding out I've been seeing other branches behind your backs. My worst fear, though, is that you, my beloved Austin librarians, will discover that I have also become involved with the University of Texas libraries. All eleven of them. What can I say? I have my needs and they can't be filled by just one library. Or even by all twenty-one of you.

Okay, I feel better now with that confession off my chest, so, let me get serious and say what I really want to say, and that is, "Thank you, all of you, Austin librarians. Thank you for always being there for me."

Because it's true. Since I first arrived in Austin, the most reluctant of Texas transplants, you have been there for me. You have been the mainstay of my career. Every novel, magazine article, and screenplay I have ever written started at an Austin library. I have researched offbeat rodeos, flamenco dance, the burial practices of ancient Okinawa, Bob Wills, the Buffalo Soldiers, the snow monkeys of south Texas, a lady anatomist in sixteenth-century Italy, marathon dances of the Great Depression, and orangutans in Borneo at Austin libraries. No matter how obscure, no subject has ever stumped you. For my entire writing life, Austin librarians, you have been my most constant, most unfailing, most trusted partner.

And, may I just say, a very open-minded and tolerant partner.

You never judged me. Not once. Not even last year when I checked out "Overcoming Your Crystal Meth Addiction: An Essential Guide to Getting Clean."

No, you didn't bat an eye or turn a hair. Not for that, nor for "Body Contouring: Your Complete Guide to Breast Augmentation." Austin librarians, I so appreciate that you didn't alert the IRS when I reserved: "Tax Cheating: It's Illegal, but Is It Immoral?" Or notify the DEA when I picked up "Pissed: How to Clean Your Urine for a Drug Test."

I am also deeply, deeply grateful that you didn't betray even the slightest hint of pity when I requested: "Spying on your Spouse: A Guide for Anyone Who Suspects A Partner Is Cheating."

Austin librarians, I cannot tell you how much it's meant to me that you never made me say, "It's for research. It's not for me, it's for a character. My *character* is a meth-addicted tax swindler with fake boobs and a cheating dog of a husband. Not me. Really. Ya gotta believe me. It's not for me."

A few years ago, I was interviewed by *Good Housekeeping* magazine, along with a dozen other novelists, for an article in which they asked "What are you most grateful for?" Very sensibly, Jodi Picoult said she was grateful for her children. The great and wise Abraham Verghese answered, "True love and good health."

Mega-bestselling author Dean Koontz rhapsodized: "I am every day grateful for the gift of life. I glimpse eternity in the coral sky of a dawn drenched in silence, in the mystical eyes of my golden retriever, in my wife's lovely hands as she chops vegetables for dinner, in the diamonded night sky, and in every humble thing."

Namaste, Dean Koontz. Namaste.

My answer to the question, "What are you most grateful for?" was "My library card." I explained that "Every hurdle I have ever faced in life, I have researched my way over at a library. I am deeply and eternally grateful for that part of the American spirit that believes every citizen should have access to books."

That statement was true when I said it. It was true when I was an intensely shy child growing up in a military family that moved far too frequently for my temperamentally tense nature, and librarians turned me on to the friends I would never have to leave behind when the air force transferred us from base, to base, to yet another base: Jo March. Anne of Green Gables. Nancy Drew. Scout Finch. And the patron saint of kids who are constantly uprooted and thrust into strange new worlds filled with odd and frightening strangers: Dorothy Gale of Oz.

And it is so much truer today—in this highly fraught historical moment in which we find ourselves—when, for so many, a library card gives access not just to books but to a better life. Clearly, libraries are so much more than the place where they keep the books. Just as clear is that our budget-slashing legislators don't understand how necessary libraries are.

For the digitally denied, libraries mean access to the online world of jobs, educational opportunities, and relationships. They also mean access to librarians, who will separate real information from fake news. And libraries are more important than they've ever been in accomplishing one of the missions that Benjamin Franklin had in mind when he established the first public library: the mission of turning colonists, immigrants to America, into citizens versed in the fundamentals of democracy.

In short, libraries are shrines that we Americans have always built to the concept of a common good. Supporting libraries and educating those who control funding is not a "left" thing or a "right" thing. It's not a progressive or a conservative thing. Libraries are a common good thing. In speaking out for libraries, we honor the belief that, if we pool our resources and work together, we, and more importantly our children, will have a better life.

Passion Victim

TEXAS MONTHLY, MAY 2005

At times I've been invited to speak to aspiring writers about my "career path." This always seemed like asking Hannibal for tips on mountain travel. Yeah, he did cross the Alps, but, damn, it would have been a heck of a lot easier without all those elephants.

Let's say, though, that you're attending one of our more prestigious writing programs, dreaming of that Nobel Prize in literature, that cozy interview with Terry Gross, the dazzling soirées, clinking glasses with big-name literary luminaries. Should you be taking advice from someone who got her start writing pesticide brochures, true-confession stories, and romance novels? Is this route going to lead you to Guggenheim grants? Yaddo fellowships? I wouldn't bet any boxed sets on it.

No job counselor pointed my way to the first-ever Romance Writers of America Conference, held in the Woodlands in the summer of 1980. Romance novels had just come out of the Harlequin closet and were emerging as a publishing phenomenon. Intrepid young freelance journalist that I was, I thought I'd be able to wring a story out of this burgeoning new genre. So I cornered one of the many real-life New York editors who'd flocked to the conference to recruit authors. What she had to say stunned me. She spoke of translations into dozens of languages. Of print runs in the hundreds of thousands. Of advances in equally enticing figures.

I swapped my official cub reporter notebook for an armful of the samples publishers were giving away and started reading. I went to bed that night a girl and got up a woman—a woman who knew a thing or two about "shuddering fulfillment" and "aching chasms yearning to be filled." Shoot, I'd written about pesticide runoff for the EPA; surely I could churn out a few thousand words on the "throbbing evidence of male desire."

I left the conference with a nom de whoopee, Tory Cates, and a contract to write a novel for a new line to be called Silhouette Special Edition. *Handful of Sky* would be set in the "glamorous" world of rodeo. Yes, I actually convinced a New York editor that rodeos were glamorous. After only one night in the Pink Ghetto, I knew that Silhouette was not going to be interested in a novel set in the manure-stinking, pill-throttled world of real rodeo. Yee-*haw*! Write 'em, cowgirl!

Over the next few years, Tory Cates paid my rent and supported my "serious" writing habit by penning four more Silhouette Special Editions. These editions were special in the way that education can sometimes be. They covered the basics. And the most basic of all basics was the first kiss. Romance editors have specific requirements for what kids at movies used to call "the mushy parts." But editors know that, rather than hiding their eyes and groaning, readers want the hot and heavy stuff, and they want it strung out for as long as possible. They think five pages is a good length for a first kiss. I think five pages is a good length for a first conquest of Mount Everest.

As I cranked out those first books, I happily, then increasingly not so happily, arranged and rearranged romance boilerplate. On Tory's watch, "knees turned to jelly," "touches trailed liquid fire," "secret inner cores of womanhood moistened," "deltas dampened," "groins surged," the blind saw, and the lame walked.

I guess the problems started on book four of the Cates quintet. Around this time, Silhouette discovered oral sex, and my editor ordered me to insert three such scenes into the manuscript. Set at the Albuquerque International Balloon Fiesta, this airy little confection was titled *Cloud Waltzer*. I came to think of it as "Blown in a Balloon" as I worked in tedious variations of the newest phrase to be added to the romance writer's lexicon: "She tasted the sea." *Ewww*.

By the fifth one I knew I wasn't long for the Pink Ghetto. I winced when strangers, upon discovering how I paid the rent, joked about the nudge-nudge, wink-wink "research." Truth be told, I had become as detached as a gynecologist in the face of reproductive details.

Oh sure, I zipped through the easy stuff—plot, characterization, foreshadowing, theme. I created that instantaneous, knee-buckling magnetism that must then slam immediately into the contrivance necessary to keep my yeasty young couple, Matthew and Lissa, from fulfilling their titanic biological urges and hopping into bed shortly after page 1.

I went through the entire book pleading headache after headache. The prospect of yet another scene involving touches that trailed paths of liquid fire and kisses that stirred whirling vortices of passion was more than I could stomach.

I didn't know just how frigid I had become, though, until I reached that pivotal moment in number five when Matthew and Lissa must share their first kiss. The first one is a biggie. If you don't get it right, none of the pulsing need that follows will make any sense. Try as I might, though, I couldn't pencil in so much as a pucker. I struggled for days, totally blocked, then simply scrawled "Insert here: first kiss, five pages," then jumped back on the barreling freight train of the narrative.

My entire manuscript was riddled with flaccid notations: "Second kiss: three pages." "Breast cupping, etc.: four pages." "Everything but: seven pages." I ignored the mounting total of shirked pages until that awful moment when there was, gulp, no more story to write. I had to go back and fill in all those blanks, those aching chasms yearning to be filled that I had scattered so blithely behind me. I had to, as I once heard a frenzied female patron yell to a male stripper, "put the meat on the table!"

So there I was, staring at that crucial "First kiss, five pages," feeling no tingles beyond a vague numbness in my butt from sitting too long. Worse, I was having profound doubts about setting Lissa and Matthew adrift on such dark carnal seas. All those fluttering pulses and surging groins and dampening deltas? How much more sensible to simply take an aspirin, lie down until the more alarming symptoms pass, then get up and go look for a solid citizen with good manners.

But that is not what readers wanted. They wanted those pulses to pound, mouths to go dry, hearts to flutter, innards to heave. Where could I turn for inspiration?

Personal experience? Puh-leeze.

I have no doubt that, all over the world, at this very moment, couples are surrendering to first kisses that make the earth move and knees wobble. First kisses worth five pages. My own initial osculations, however, had leaned much more toward teeth cracking together, excess slobber, guy wires of spit looping from mouth to mouth. Toward discovering saliva tacky as rubber cement and breath worse than an old dog's. Of course, in a few miraculous instances, we both survived and went on to kisses more sublime. But, for the most part, first kisses for me have been many more parts embarrassment than ecstasy.

Then I came across a theory that held that women seek in romance novels what they don't get enough of in life, and it's not sex, it's mothering. It's that luxurious illusion of being the center of the universe rather than some celestial maid keeping it all orbiting around boyfriends, husbands, children. For most women the mothering stops with mom. Never again are we so extravagantly nurtured and attended to. Never again do we take precedence.

Except in the contemporary romance novel. Here we become the absolute focal point of some strong-jawed man's existence. Gone are the bodice-ripping pirates of old-school romances. The heroes of "contemporaries" care. These fierce yet loving, hard yet soft Treys and Lincs, Derricks and Forrests really, *really* care. The heroes spend their every waking hour tormented by visions of the heroine. They ache for her bewitching body while puzzling over her tantalizing psyche. They buy her expensive presents. Often in colors that match her eyes, such as the ever-popular cornflower blue. Her whims are indulged, her fantasies fulfilled. And the reader is vicariously nurtured, vicariously mothered.

This was the first explanation of why romances are consumed so insatiably that made sense to me. It filled me with a new sense of purpose. I determined that I would write that five-page first kiss.

But then I felt burdened, oppressed by unfulfilled expectations. By Hollywood dreams dying on the set of everyday life all over America. By the world of women starved for magic with only me to serve it up.

Alone, I was supposed to send the flowers they yearned to receive. I had to titillate them with banter drenched in innuendo, desire them with a blazing passion that turned bones and stern resolve to jelly. It was my job to caress millions of neglected thighs, fondle the peremptorily treated breasts, to court, cajole, coax. My readers wanted to know again the incomparable power to make a strong man weak, and they wanted to wobble a bit themselves. They wanted foreplay that wasn't meagerly doled out as stingy prepayment. They wanted acres, prairies, veldts, tundras of foreplay. They wanted dazzling galaxies of foreplay. They wanted, by God, that five-page first kiss.

It was too much. Performance anxiety paralyzed me.

Far worse, I realized that it wasn't less sex I wanted; it was more real life. I wanted to write love stories that didn't have to end happily and might not even always involve the more popular gender and species configurations. I wanted to concoct plot complications that couldn't be resolved with the words "She's my sister." I wanted to create messy characters with messy lives and "problems" far, far messier than a heroine cursed with boyishly slender hips.

And then, powerful inspiration arrived in the form of my editor calling to say that if I didn't come across with the goods, I could just start thinking about how I would be paying back the advance I had already frittered away on rent and groceries. Yes, indeed, at that very moment I felt the fires of passion ignite deep within the moist and secret core of my own hidden delta. I stopped balking at romance boilerplate. I began to think of myself as an ethnomusicologist transcribing the songs of a primitive tribe that chants notes only they can make.

Within seconds I had Lissa trembling with, quaking with, quivering with, shimmering with, shivering with, shuddering with, and being transubstantiated by, lust. Matthew likewise blazed with, smoldered with, flamed, flickered, FLARED with, and was immolated by, desire. When all was in readiness, when "Passionate Illusion" was as tumescent as a saguaro cactus at sunset, Matthew and Lissa puckered up and . . .

SMACK, the five-page first kiss began.

This time, however, as my lovers began their windup, I knew it would be the first kiss for Matthew and Lissa, but a long kiss goodbye for Tory Cates.

Read 'em and Weep

TEXAS MONTHLY, OCTOBER 2005

T he first rule of Book Club is you do not talk about Book Club. The second rule of Book Club is you DO NOT talk about Book Club. The final rule of Book Club is, if this is your first night at Book Club, you have to actually read the book.

After the first night, the true purpose of Book Club will reveal itself. Unlike *Fight Club*, it is *not* to see Brad Pitt with his shirt off, though that is, indeed, a worthy aim. No, the real reason Book Club exists is to get together with your girlfriends, drink cheap white wine, eat snacks—both salty and sugared—and talk about old boyfriends, new diets, and whether to go with Corian or beveled granite counters in the kitchen. But most of all, Book Club exists to get you the hell out of the house with no guilt.

This no-guilt motif unites the dozens of book clubs I have visited all across America, in homes, bars, libraries, and one beauty parlor. From these clubs I've learned that books have become the magic pass that women use to skip out on domestic duties right around grub-rustling time. Wielding their passport to freedom—some worthy doorstop by David McCullough, maybe a Toni Morrison classic, but more than likely *Girl with a Pearl Earring, The Red Tent,* or *The Secret Life of Bees*—they clump out the front door pretending that Book Club is a tedious chore, a sort of Bible-study-and-Pilates-class combo. As soon as our escapees have backed out of the driveway, however, *Snow Flower and the Secret Fan* gets heaved to the rear of the minivan and the pedal hits the metal. There's a glass of chardonnay waiting, and it's got Mama's name on it.

"What?" you're saying. "At my book club we always read and discuss the book."

Oh, dear. So sorry. Clearly you didn't have the proper guidance in selecting a book club. Try this: Which of these clubs is most likely to be fun? Quill and Swill; Wine, Women, and Diphthong; Happy Bookers; Reading Between the Wines; The Book Bags; Overreaders Anonymous; Let's Be Friends Fun Book Club; or the East Wickinsham Literary Society? If you picked the last one, prepare to hear phrases like "underlying theme" and "character development." Brace yourself for piercing insights into the multilayered motivation of the Ya-Ya sisters. Worst of all, be resigned to learning nothing about your friends' old beaux.

Other tips? Try not to join any club so large that extra chairs have to be dragged into the living room. No one sitting on a metal folding chair will ever tell about her First Time. Be careful to evaluate the quality of the eats. Beware both the sit-down affair and the can of Pringles; a happy balance somewhere in the containers-of-takeout-from-Whole-Foods range is what you'll be shooting for. Be alert as to the presence of bossy types who would turn Book Club into homework. Exasperated harangues will be the tip-off here; if a suspected martinet begins any statement to the group with the word "people," run. Likewise, should mention be made of the "discussion questions" that publishers print at the back of their hopefully marketed book club selections, flee. I recently visited a book club which had read one of my deathless classics and was barraged by a flurry of such questions that, unbeknownst to me, had been tucked at the back of my book. To every general question about the "author's intention," I had to answer "No earthly idea." To the more specific "What was the author thinking when . . ." questions, I had to fess up that more than likely the big question I had been pondering was, "Is there any of that pasta left over from last night?"

Above all else, it is essential to go with the all-female group. Introduce one straight man and Book Club will turn into, well, a book club. Husbands will read and discuss dutifully. Nonfiction will be favored. Pithy comments will be made, and none of them will concern anyone's old flames. The all-male club is an even less jolly kettle of fish. Remember that college seminar where one guy knew more than the professor and asked excruciatingly long "questions" intended to display the full extent of his knowledge? Every guy in the all-boy club will be that guy. In the one estrogen-challenged club I visited, I was told several times what an exception had been made for me. The group never read "chick" books (i.e., novels). It took only a few minutes before I cracked under their withering cross-examination and admitted that, yes, it was true, I hadn't really written the book in question. Furthermore, I'd not only never *written* any book, but I'd never *read* one either. Case closed. Good wine, though.

This is not to say that there is *no* discussion of books at a Quill and Swill–style book club. In fact, I recall quite a spirited colloquy during my visit with the Readin' 'n' Eatin' group. In keeping with the Far Eastern setting of my novel

The Yokota Officers Club, all the members had brought Asian delicacies. So, after sake and sushi, we tackled tough topics such as the ways in which the hero was just like a guy one of the members had dated and would my heroine be doing the Paleo or the South Beach diet? This was a great club, and not just because almost everyone there had bought a copy of the book.

I came to cherish this book-purchasing aspect of Readin' 'n' Eatin' after the next bunch I visited. This club met in an ultraswanky neighborhood: a fleet of Range Rovers and Lexi were parked outside. As it was their holiday gathering, sixty members and guests waited inside. I spent the evening putting on my little floor show and answering questions. At the conclusion, the organizer asked if anyone would like their book signed. Two members had actually purchased copies of the novel. Three others asked me to sign their library copies. A dozen members told me how interesting the book sounded and that they would be borrowing Ashley's copy just as soon as Heather, then Whitney, then Jennifer finished with it.

Let me now add another rule for Book Club: if you've managed to inveigle the author to visit, buy the damn book. This isn't third grade, where stars are awarded for simply reading. Writers love what they do and want to do it again. The only way they'll be allowed to publish another book, though, is if they sell enough copies of the one you just borrowed from Whitney.

In general, though, book clubs are the last ferny growth keeping midlist dinosaurs like myself alive and we *love, love, love* book-buying book clubs. As a reader, however, I don't get them. Like my love life, reading for me is a solitary activity. (Kidding, just kidding. Not about the reading, though.) The fatal flaw of book clubs for me is this: The only time I'm truly interested in what someone else thinks about a book is *before* I read it. It's a little late to tell me that *The Corrections* is an overhyped, self-indulgent piece of drivel *after* I've wasted days of my life on it.

Which is exactly why Book Club is so brilliant. A guilt-free evening getting a little buzz on with *les* girls that doesn't end with you loading the dishwasher? Perfect. Just don't let a book muck it up. And . . . DO NOT talk about Book Club.

Say "Cheesy"

TEXAS MONTHLY, JANUARY 2006

Certain professions almost guarantee a minimal level of physical attractiveness: astronaut, actor, trophy wife, anyone who handles a pole, whether fireman or exotic dancer. With their vigorous, active lives and multiple cosmetic procedures, these are humans other humans *want* to see.

Writers? Not so much.

Our lives are spent plopped on the gluteal upholstery for eight hours a day with only imaginary friends for company, spinning lies, marinating in envy, and wondering when the Pulitzer committee is going to twig to our brilliance. This is not the route to the body beautiful. This is the route to the complexion phosphorescent and the eye bag intumescent.

Why, then, the author photo? Shouldn't authors be read and not seen? This is my firm position, taken as I contemplate a contact sheet of photos intended for use on the jacket of my next novel.

Let us now consider legendary authors and *their* photos. The burly macho of Hemingway. The Jazz Age elegance of F. Scott. The dewy depravity of Truman Capote.

The neurasthenic splendor of Virginia Woolf. The craggy magnificence of Lillian Hellman. Let us now consider this contact sheet I have before me. Hmmm. Seems all I really got right are the crags—that and a hint of macho around the mustache I probably should have waxed.

Once, in a kingdom long ago and far, far away, Eudora Welty was what a serious female writer looked like. You didn't study Welty's transcendentally compassionate face and wonder, "You been hitting the Botox, babe? Had some 'work' done?" Now we have Zadie Smith. Super writer. Supermodel. Probably an extraterrestrial.

Best not to dwell on Zadie as I address my current dilemma: I need an author photo for a book that is completely serious. I need a pensive, staring-out-the-window shot, a classic pose based on Rodin's *The Thinker*, angsty enough to warn readers that there is no yukfest in store. I need Marion Ettlinger, famous photographer of famous authors, who seems to have revealed to her subjects right before clicking the shutter, "You've got pancreatic cancer and three months to live. Now, stick your chin in your hand and deal!"

Okay, maybe I don't absolutely have to look as if I'm trying to decide who I'm going to leave Mama's china to, but this current author photo must communicate a lack of funny-osity. I don't want disappointed readers around the world, misled by my grinning mug, asking, *"Pas du yuks?" "Vo ist der yuks?" "Donde estan los yukos grandes?"* Or, most plaintively, in the poignant glottal clicks of the bushmen of the Kalahari, *"N!xau/!+?"*

Still, as I review the bags and crags, I find myself trapped between two competing desires: that of every woman who ever gets in front of a lens, to appear fifteen years or fifteen pounds lighter, and that of the Serious Arthur, to project the kind of gravitas that gets her reviewed in *Important Books Weekly*.

On one hand, I need to look like Lillian Hellman after a bad bender, yet I still yearn for the diffusion filter, that special gift to women that makes it appear as if we were photographed in a steam bath. The pound-of-Vaseline-on-the-lens quality of the filter erases crow's-feet, laugh lines, complexion irregularities, mouths, noses, and ethnic identity. With enough filtering and eye makeup, the subject can end up looking like Casper the Friendly Ghost. Just two heavily outlined and mascaraed holes floating in a sheet of white. The diffusion filter, however, creates its own set of wrinkles. No writer wants to show up at a book signing and have some fevered fan ask when her *daughter*, the smokin' soft-focus babe on the jacket, is going to appear. Nor does she want to discover a walker and an oxygen tank waiting.

The problem is that I outsourced. As with all my other author photos, I should have done this one in-house. Intrepid young photojournalist that I once was, I loved cooking up self-portraits. The head shot was my idea of a major yawn, which is why, in the photo on the back of my first novel, I'm having a tea party with my dog. In the second, I am "washing the dog": it's a saucy snap of me at a Laundromat measuring Tide into a cup while the same long-suffering dog sits, disgruntled, inside a washer.

I tried full nudity in the next attempt. As part of a story *Texas Monthly* was doing about the state's writers, a genuine celebrity photographer, Mark Seliger, was dispatched to my backyard. Because I had stupidly revealed that, like Voltaire, I accomplished much of my writing in bed while wearing jammies, minions set up an antique bed and perched an antique typewriter and an increasingly antique writer upon it. They dressed me in striped cotton pj's from

Neiman Marcus that cost $150 and told me not to sweat on them, since they were going right back. Ditto for the striped sheets. The eight-month-old baby going through separation anxiety who whined all day in the background was mine; I got to keep him.

You wouldn't think there could be that many ways to photograph an increasingly sweaty woman perched on a bed set out in the broiling sun. But an entire day passed with lights being readjusted and shiny noses (mine) being patted with powder and my baby boy whimpering miserably. At last, Seliger finished. I begged for just one picture with my child, and he was scooped out of the wading pool where he'd been splashing for the last shot. As reflectors were adjusted to focus even more blinding sunlight into my eyes, my baby boy, naked as the day he was born, his back to the camera, crawled onto the expensive sheets with me and I managed my first real smile of the day. As much as Teen Boy now hates this photo of the cutest tushie on the planet, I love it. The stripes. The sweat. The postpartum depression. My golden-haired boy. It captures motherhood perfectly: a prisoner doing hard time on the euphoria chain gang. It's my idea of a good author photo.

Meat, My Maker

TEXAS MONTHLY, JULY 2012

"Hey, be my date for the Film Hall of Fame deal." This irresistible invitation to Austin's annual swankorifico salute to Texas filmmaking luminaries such as Renée Zellweger, Richard Linklater, and Dennis Quaid was offered by my buddy and my only movie-star friend, the exceptionally swoon-worthy Brett Cullen. (Yes, one of *those* Cullens. But the "middle-class" side of the family, he's always quick to add.) "They're inducting Meat Loaf for his movie work, and I'm going to introduce him."

Meat Loaf. I first encountered the Dallas-born actor and singer in *The Rocky Horror Picture Show*, the movie about a "sweet transvestite from Transsexual, Transylvania." It was 1977, and my brother was a co-owner of the first theater outside New York to run the cult favorite as a midnight costume party and yell-along. As Eddie, an Elvis-bewigged, cryogenically frozen biker, Meat Loaf was a baby-faced bolt of plushly upholstered, primal rock energy—and, like everything else in that movie, he electrified me. It's hard now during this, the fourth season of *RuPaul's Drag Race*, to convey the sheer thrill we felt at the sexual free zone that *Rocky Horror* opened up. Sure, David Bowie had been prancing around in a unitard with a streak of lightning painted over his eye, but that was in Manhattan. Not Texas. *Rocky Horror* took the word "transgressive" out of doctoral theses and made it play in neighborhood cineplexes.

Meat Loaf went on to seduce a nation into "paradise by the dashboard light" with the fifth-biggest-selling album of all time, *Bat Out of Hell*; to play more than fifty roles in everything from *Fight Club* to *Glee*; and, in the past season's *Celebrity Apprentice*, to unleash what might have been the most epic meltdown ever witnessed on reality television. Still, the Grammy Award winner was important to me, not just because he told off the preternaturally annoying Gary Busey and showed the world that chubby boys in bad wigs could be objects of intense lust but also because he helped me write my sixth novel.

Backstory on How My Life Intersected With Meat Loaf's: I was the most accidental of screenwriters. A writing exercise had led me to this black art. I had lost my way on my second novel, *The Boyfriend School*, because I didn't truly know my male protagonist. To understand him better, I decided to rewrite the entire book from his point of view. I was pricing carpal tunnel surgery when I happened to behold, for the first time ever, a screenplay. Here's what I immediately loved about screenplays: acres and acres of glorious white space. Most of a script is a narrow tube of dialogue tunneling between occasional thin planks of stage direction along the lines of "Jebediah picks up the gun." The magical part was that I didn't have to decide what Jebediah was wearing or how his hair was cut. Nor did I have to spend days at the library researching whether the gun he picked up was a musket or an Uzi.

Since the prop, hair, and wardrobe departments would be doing all the heavy lifting, my first screenplay puffed up before my eyes like one of those tiny sponge capsules that transforms into a dinosaur with just a few drops of water. A surprisingly short time later, my exceedingly mediocre screenplay was made into an exceedingly mediocre movie. Released in 1990, it starred deathless thespians Steve Guttenberg and Shelley Long. Inexplicably, an entire decade's worth of assignments in Hollywood followed. There was much to love: getting paid whether the movie was made or not; the minimal public accountability (as a non-famous screenwriter, I was almost never mentioned in bad reviews when the movie *was* made); and, best of all, the fact that someone else came up with the story ideas. Once hooked, though, I did keep working on my own ideas on the side and produced several original "spec" scripts (short for "spectacularly minuscule chance that anyone will buy them"). One of these speck-imens, set in the tumultuous world of flamenco dance, caught the attention of Brett and his amigo Meat Loaf, who were partners in a production company. They optioned *Flamenco* and embarked on the Sisyphean struggle required to get a movie made.

I never met the rock icon during the lamprey-esque process of getting "elements" (in Hollywood speak, famous actors and directors) "attached" to a "project." Still, having the Meat Loaf Meteor crash upon my distant shore was one of those fantastical anomalies that made my years as a screenwriter feel like being trapped inside a video game. Without a rule book. During all my wanderings through Planet Pretty People, I never knew which beautiful princess could kill me and which evil troll might offer a bag of magic powder. Or, more likely, had already consumed far too much magic powder. Fortunately, Brett and I had bonded immediately over that strongest of Filmland adhesives, shared nemeses. United by our loathing of certain nameless individuals who'd behaved abominably and, in the best Hollywood tradition, never suffered the slightest consequence, he acted as my guide to this strange world. For example, I called up to brag that a director had sent me a shrub-size bouquet with a note thanking me for all my "hard work," it was Brett who decoded the floral tribute: "Honey, you've just been separated from the project." Further translation ensued. "Separated from the project" meant that my can had been canned.

Maybe because I hadn't always dreamed of being a screenwriter the way I'd always dreamed of being a novelist, these Hollywood experiences ran off me without soaking into my psychic water table. Whatever the reason, the sense of surrealism was so strong that when my time in Hollywood was over, it was as though that very long chapter in my life had happened to someone else. A lucky acquaintance, perhaps, whom I was fond of in a remote, distant-relative sort of way and exceedingly grateful to for buying me a house and providing me with exceptionally good health insurance. Which is why, when I told my husband about the Film Hall of Fame invite—that I'd be a movie star's date and even get to sit at the same dinner table with Meat Loaf, *the* effin' Meat Loaf—I felt like an impostor, if not an outright liar.

As this massive collision of my bygone secret life with my real life approached, I worried more than a bigamist whose other family was about to show up on his doorstep. I told a thoroughly therapized friend about my apprehensions, and she said I should "embrace this opportunity to integrate your two selves" and "get some closure by bringing that life into the one you consider real."

"But," I countered, "most of my HWood experiences were so *un*real."

"Such as?"

Such as: going to a rodeo in Kingsville with an Oscar winner who'd been "attached" by Warner Bros. to direct the adaptation I wrote of my novel *Virgin of the Rodeo* and alienating her almost immediately by expressing sympathy when she kept touching the "cold sore" about to bloom on her upper lip. I knew how painful they were; I got them myself. Bull riding, calf roping, and all the details of rodeo subculture that I adored and yearned for her to capture on film were ignored as she poked obsessively at what turned out to be botched collagen injections. She cursed her incompetent dermatologist and wondered whether cotton candy was allowed on her fat-free diet.

Such as: spending two weeks in Borneo with Isabella Rossellini doing research for a *National Geographic/* Hallmark film collaboration about a primatologist who'd been studying orangutans in the wild for the past twenty-five years. The scene that greeted us as we were introduced to our subject's husband, a Dayak tribesman, and his extended clan was out of *Heart of Darkness* by way of *Apocalypse Now*. We were not comforted to learn of her in-laws' prowess as headhunters and the untraceability of the poison they used in their blowguns. But the moment that caused the light in Rossellini's famously incandescent face to flicker out came when we visited the rehabilitation compound, theoretically devoted to returning these great apes to the wild, and were met by an orangutan mom sharing a can of Coke with her big-eyed baby. I think we all knew then that this would not be the song we'd teach the world to sing.

Such as: always flying first-class when on assignments.

Although writers who don't create HBO franchises are generally Hollywood's coach class, the Writers Guild of America, our union, does insist that, at least on airplanes, we fly first. These Queen-for-a-Day upgrades allowed me access not only to scented hand towels, hot nuts, and unlimited drinks but also to, on one memorable flight home, an unimpeded view of Sandra Bullock and her beau at the time, Matthew McConaughey. They waved away the chateaubriand in favor of a Tupperware container of vegan goulash, then made out like teenagers after the prom. Thank you, WGA!

The glamour! The fantasy! The craven name-dropping! Maybe my encounters could all be integrated into an episode of *TMZ*, but my own Bartleby the Scrivener ink-stained-wretch existence? I was dubious. The two were literal worlds apart. Then it dawned on me that, aside from Brett, Meat Loaf was, in fact, the one person who had ever bridged my screen- and novel-writing selves. Although *Flamenco: The Movie* never materialized, his optioning of my screenplay financed the research and writing of my novel *The Flamenco Academy*. If anyone could set the stage for the far-fetched mash-up I envisioned going down at the ceremony, it would be the Bat Out of Hell himself.

The day of the Texas Film Hall of Fame extravaganza was lovely in its early spring Austin mugginess. However, thanks to our state's stunning ability to put the mercurial in the mercury, the temperature plummeted thirty degrees after I left my house. During the walk from my distant (yet free!) parking spot to the event, my diaphanous frock and I were pelted with icy rain. By the time I met Brett, I was drenched and shivering, puddles of mascara under my eyes and my hair plastered to my head. I'd kept up with my pal through his work on *Friday Night Lights*,

Damages, Justified, Castle, The Mentalist, and dozens of other shows, so I already knew that he'd remained an actor in high demand. Brett probably wondered when I'd become homeless.

"Meat's got food poisoning," he informed me. His friend had been felled while on tour in England. Adding to the doubt about whether he'd be appearing that night was the man's history of avoiding award ceremonies; he'd had his daughter pick up his 1994 Grammy. As the lights dimmed in the vast hall, the seat beside me remained empty. I clutched the copy of the novel his patronage had allowed me to write and regretted that I wouldn't be able to present it to him.

And then he appeared beside me, and I met the least divalike human imaginable. Even though he has sold 43 million albums and counting, is a god in Austin for his work in the 1980 film *Roadie,* and was coming off five days of food poisoning and a transatlantic flight that would have flattened a man half his age, he didn't demand so much as one non-green M&M. Whether he expected it or not, however, the adulation flowed. A parade of women dramatically oversharing their new breastesses passed by, leaning in to whisper in Meat Loaf's ear about the "giant crushes" they'd had on him back in the day, their husky tones promising instant reactivation of said crushes should he be so inclined. (And, yes, the adorable and adorably age-appropriate Mrs. Loaf *was* seated right beside him.) The ultra-suave tequila and shampoo gazillionaire John Paul DeJoria sidled over as well to kneel beside Meat Loaf's chair and welcome him to Austin. Busboys and servers abandoned their stations simply to catch a glimpse of the only headliner that night that they cared about seeing.

Amid the fans and supplicants, I presented Meat Loaf

with a copy of my flamenco novel. He received it with the dignity of an ambassador from a country that was once, almost, my own. I wanted to ask him what on earth had ever attracted him to a screenplay about flamenco dancers, but clips from Meat Loaf's many movie and television roles were already playing onstage. Brett introduced his friend Marvin Lee Aday, and, as one, the crowd leaped to its feet for the only immediate, universal standing ovation in an evening packed with big names.

Meat Loaf took the stage and—discarding his prepared notes, ignoring the teleprompter—pointed to the screen where his life in acting had just unfurled and said, voice quavering, "Watching that . . . it's unbelievable how much acting is about truth. And that's what I think we all attempt every time we walk on a movie set." Seeing Meat Loaf openly surrendering to tears, talking about "growing up a poor, fat boy in Dallas," I wished that I could take back whatever dopey, flustered sentiment I'd inscribed in his book, because I finally knew what I should have written.

When I last glimpsed my benefactor, Brett was running interference, trying to spirit his exhausted friend out of the hall before he collapsed or was tsunamied by fans. As they neared the exit, they were intercepted by a phalanx of gala crashers who'd managed to sneak into the high-dollar event. Meat Loaf insisted on stopping for the interlopers, guys still wearing their rent-a-cop uniforms from their security jobs and their girlfriends, who had the signs of the zodiac decorating their press-on nails. Treating each fan as if he or she were a gazillionaire kneeling at his feet, he nodded, fully engaged, as they told him of the moments of transport and pure fantasy that his music, his performances, had caused to bloom in their lives. Then, across the bottom of their *Rocky Horror* posters and *Bat Out of*

Hell albums, he signed the only name they had ever known him by: Meat Loaf.

The opening lines of the novel Meat Loaf helped me write are "Flamenco has Ten Commandments. The first one is: *Dame la verdad*, Give me the truth." In the Venn diagram that represents the bizarre intersection of my life with Hollywood, this—the struggle to make something heart-stoppingly real out of words on paper—seemed to be the place of overlap. I wished I had thanked Meat Loaf for giving us his truth.

Was it closure? It was close enough.

The Big Sleep

TEXAS MONTHLY, OCTOBER 2013

A year ago this month, I was nervously preparing for my star turn at the 2012 Texas Book Festival. Two hundred and sixty people in my line of business—torturing the alphabet for fun and profit—were converging on the Capitol grounds, and I was going to play the big room, the Senate Chamber, at high noon. I would be moderating my dream panel, "War and Absurdity," with two authors I admire extravagantly: Ben Fountain, who wrote the best book I read last year, *Billy Lynn's Long Halftime Walk*, which looks at America's disturbing tendency to conflate war and spectator sports, and David Abrams, who wrote perhaps the funniest, *FOBBIT*, about the inhabitants of a forward operating base in Iraq. Both novels had been dubbed the *Catch-22* of the Iraq war, and since I'd been beavering away on my own tome, *Above the East China Sea*, concerned with how the price of empire is always borne by the young, I was doubly excited to have this conversation.

Anxious about being the dim bulb amid the illuminati, I had labored mightily over an exhaustive list of questions that ranged from penetrating to hard-hitting. Just to make absolutely certain that I would be the sort of steely, unflappable examiner not seen since the Spanish Inquisition, I dropped my trusty bottle of the public speaker's secret friend, propranolol, into my purse. Like many actors and musicians, I'd long relied on the blood pressure medication to ward off the pounding heart, fluttering pulse, and clammy hands of stage fright. Armed with pills and pages of high IQ–affirming questions, I felt relatively calm.

And then, as my car approached the Capitol grounds, I recalled that the festival attracts 40,000 book lovers—*40,000!*—and a squadron of kamikaze butterflies hit. As I spiraled upward through a parking garage, I snaked a trembling hand into my purse, felt for the bottle of pills without glancing down, extracted two, and popped them in.

Should I note at this juncture that I'd accidentally tossed a bottle of Ambien into my purse rather than harmless blood pressure meds? Or that I'm such a lightweight that on the occasions when I do use the sleep aid, I hold one pill in my hands like a squirrel with a nut and chip off a flake with the tips of my incisors so small that I can make a single blue beauty last through a week of otherwise sleepless nights? Or that parking my car is the last thing I recall from my big day at the Texas Book Festival?

From this point forward, we will have to rely on deduction and eyewitness accounts to piece together the suspect's activities on the day in question. After getting out of my car, I must have crossed several busy streets, made my way over to the Capitol, and ascended the fairly steep flight of stairs into the building. Friends told me later that they hailed me but that I ignored them. That I had an odd "blank" expression on my face and that they sensed "something was wrong." The word "zombie" appeared in some reports. Apparently, I made it through the rigorous security screening at the entrance. Because an official Author/Moderator badge was found later on my person, I know I must have checked in at the private apartment just behind the House Chamber that Speaker Joe Straus was kind enough to make available to the festival as a green room. And that I had settled in—taken root—there.

It was around then that a festival volunteer approached literary director Clay Smith to report that "a moderator is asleep." Smith, besides dealing with sick moderators, malfunctioning microphones, and prima donna authors demanding cappuccinos and Brazilian blow-outs, was also contending with the fallout from Hurricane Sandy. Thanks to that Frankenstorm, six authors, including the main attraction, Pulitzer winner Junot Díaz, had been forced to cancel at the last minute.

In the Speaker's apartment, the already-beleaguered Smith found his moderator, the one who was supposed to facilitate a high-brow, paradigm-shifting discussion in less than half an hour, slumped on a bench, mouth open, eyes glazed. Visualize your favorite alcoholic aunt ten nogs into Christmas dinner, and you'll have a fairly accurate picture. When he roused me, I insisted that, in spite of the drool, I was ready to get out there and kick some panel ass. To prove it, I'm told, I attempted to make myself a mug of hot tea. Instead of my usual dollop of milk, however, I poured in orange juice until the cup overflowed onto first the table, then the floor.

Maybe it was the scalding tea dribbling on his feet or perhaps it was my bovine gaze that convinced Smith that his moderator was not ready for prime time. With assistance from a heartier-than-average writer, he was able to wrangle me into a room in the back, where I could achieve the total horizontality I'd been teetering toward like a rhino with a tranquilizer dart between the eyes.

Fortunately, the quick-witted Smith promptly found my sheet of questions and enlisted as my substitute the writer Amanda Eyre Ward, who filled in so beautifully that friends sitting in the balcony later wrote to tell me what a great job I'd done. Michael Merschel, of the *Dallas Morning News*, even said that the animated remarks occasioned by my questions were "still worth talking about a couple of days later." Obviously, comatose is my best moderating mode.

My steadfast husband, George, was summoned to rescue me, and after sleeping the rest of the day away, I came to and, for a few buoyant moments, shielded by Ambien's blessed amnesiac properties, remembered nothing. In fact, I was bemused both by the outlandish dream I'd had and by the fact that the special panel outfit I'd planned to wear that day was scattered all over the floor. Why, I thought, it almost looked as if someone had undressed me and just dumped the clothes wherever.

It wasn't until I began rushing to get ready that George entered the room and sketched in the outlines of a day I could remember nothing about. Each new, increasingly humiliating detail sent me skittering further down the ex–Catholic schoolgirl's well-greased chute into the Vortex of Shame. Mortification crushed me.

As I always do when feeling like the world's biggest loser, I called my sisters. Of course, they tried to snap me out of my funk. The younger one, Kay, said, "This sounds like something from a Sarah Bird book. You can use it in your work." Ah, yes, the writer's all-purpose ticket to redemption: use it in your work. That bucked me up a bit, until I recalled that this incident sounded like something from a Sarah Bird book because it had already been *in* a Sarah

Bird book. *How Perfect Is That*, to be precise, the one where the thoroughly reprehensible caterer protagonist drugs a party of socialites with a mixture of grain alcohol, Welch's grape jelly, and Rohypnol. That was so not the art I had ever wanted my life to imitate.

We all have our daily humiliations, the first drafts of life that we fix in editing before we step out the door and face the world. But this? Passing out in the state Capitol? It was so irredeemably public. I considered the standard means of seeking redemption: going into rehab or finding Jesus. But those were the easy ways out. No, defaulting again to all I'd learned from the nuns, I decided that confession, a public mea culpa, was my only hope for salvation. That evening I composed a Facebook post admitting to the world that I had roofied myself and offering apologies and thanks to Ben Fountain, David Abrams, Amanda Ward, and Clay Smith. "I will get over my embarrassment," I wrote, "but it's going to take a while." Before I sent it, I hesitated and considered my new life as a known loser so pathetic that not only was she dependent on a gaudy array of chemicals to function but she couldn't even keep her pharmaceuticals straight.

Sitting there, I recalled my only other experience of blacking out. It had occurred more than forty years ago, when I was nineteen and working as a summer intern in a hospital psychiatric unit in San Diego. Most weekends my surfer boyfriend and his gang of whoa-dude buddies would drive down from Seal Beach in an Econoline van and pick me up from the flophouse for retired merchant marines where I was renting a room. (Here's a detail that I usually omit because it sounds so entirely made up. The name of the hotel, occupied almost entirely by men, was the Knox Hotel. The "n" in the neon sign that advertised this fleabag was burnt out, leaving it to read, all-too-aptly, The Kox Hotel.) The instant the getaway van appeared in front of the Kox, I'd jump in and me and the Whoa Dudes would head south to Mexico.

In those years before "cartel" became synonymous with "chain-saw beheading," a favorite destination was an undiscovered stretch of beach between Tijuana and Ensenada. We'd camp out on the hundred-foot-high cliffs above the waves, eat Dinty Moore stew out of the can, smoke weed, and drink Ripple or some other wine-adjacent beverage. I favored an impertinent little vintage known to oenophiles and bag ladies alike as Pagan Pink; I could almost finish off an entire glass without throwing up. My inability to party hearty nearly disqualified me from being an official beach bunny. Early most mornings, the Whoa Dudes would clamber down the steep cliffs to surf the southern swell while I stayed up top reading books by R. D. Laing, Erving Goffman, and other radicals in the anti-psychiatry movement and working on the baby-oil-and-iodine-annointed tan required of all surfer girlfriends.

Then, one memorable evening, a smoky Mexican stranger joined our merry crew: Jose Cuervo. Tequila, which went down as easy as water, with just as few immediate effects, appeared to be the golden river that would carry me to full beach-bunny status. The last words I recall saying were "I've found my drink!" I came to late the next afternoon as I was being driven across the border in the back of the van, wedged in among a sodden pile of wet suits. Confinement had been necessary because of my inebriated insistence upon dancing along the hundred-foot cliff. The surfer boyfriend said he'd had to literally sit on me to keep me from boogalooing off the edge. In this feral band, that passed for tenderness. I was touched and interpreted such protectiveness as proof of a love eternal. It lasted right up until the moment when I walked in on him in bed with one of my friends.

I had a similar loved-and-lost feeling—combined with crushing embarrassment—after my day as a zombie moderator when I finally hit the "Post" button on my Facebook confession and apology. I cringed, expecting my screen to fill with invitations to twelve-step with friends who'd gotten sober, maybe a few stern Scripture citations from the high school pals who were wont to impart such advice whether requested or not. Or, worse, nothing. Simply the silence of friends politely turning away.

Instead, dozens of posts flooded in, all with the same message: we're human, we make mistakes. Not long after, Ben Fountain emailed to say he'd quoted one of my questions in an essay he was writing for a British magazine. David Abrams got in touch to ask if I would interview him for Booktalk Nation. A kind friend came by with a gorgeous bouquet and a card with a photo of a dog about to pounce on a cat above the caption "Life is one damned thing after another."

As I crawled out of the spiral of shame, I thought about that long-ago boyfriend sitting on me, and tears filled my eyes. Was it because forty years had passed since I was a teenager dancing on a cliff? Or was it because I'd burned my mouth and ruined my blouse with scalding orangey-brown tea? Maybe a bit of both. But mostly it was because I realized that a little humiliation is a very small price to pay for learning how many friends stand ready to catch you when you fall.

Paisano

TEXAS HIGHWAYS, NOVEMBER 2018

My personal slice of Texas paradise lies fourteen miles southwest of Austin, tucked into the idyllic canyon that cradles an immaculate stretch of Barton Creek. The Dobie Paisano Ranch is a 258-acre retreat owned by the University of Texas and it has been awarding fellowships to a few select writers every year since 1967. My lucky number came up in 2010 when I spent three blissful summer months nestled in this sanctuary.

I'm returning because, well, who wouldn't want to return to paradise? Given the chance, I'm certain that Eve would have been rethinking the whole apple thing if it meant more time in Eden. But I have another reason for wanting to plunge once again into a swimming hole so soul-rejuvenating that my husband George and I call it Liquid Xanax. I still have an obligation to fulfill: when I lived on the ranch eight years ago, I made a promise to a ghost I encountered there, and I need to tell her that I have kept it.

The first day of summer, the solstice, when pagans once celebrated the power of the sun over darkness, seems the perfect time for the mystical encounter I have in mind. My husband, George Jones—*not* the dipsomaniacal, lawn-mower-riding, no-show legend—and I set out in the most *un*-ranchlike vehicle imaginable, a sage-green Prius. A torrential rainstorm has swept through, leaving the sky lushly upholstered with soft gray clouds. The downpour has both dropped temperatures to unseasonable lows and raised our hopes that our favorite swimming hole will be full.

We hum south on MoPac. In the backseat is our faithful dog, True. Though True would be recognized as a cowdog back in his ancestral Wales, where his stumpy-legged sort was bred to herd cattle, here in Texas he's just a borderline foo-foo, fluffy-butted Corgi. No matter—all of us are ranch veterans, car and dog included, and now, eight years later, we are on our way to see how much Paisano we still have left in our souls.

The ranch's guiding spirit and most famous occupant was the first great supporter of Texas letters, J. Frank Dobie. He was a folklorist, professor, columnist, prolific author of dozens of books, recipient of the Medal of Freedom, celebrator of the open range, and savior of the longhorn—a breed he immortalized in one of his most popular books, *The Longhorns*. Dobie and his wife/writing assistant, Bertha, bought the ranch in 1959. They didn't purchase his country spread as a place to work, however, but rather as a clubhouse.

With that in mind, Dobie christened his "country place" Paisano, not because it meant roadrunner in Spanish but more for its secondary meaning, "compatriot." Dobie opened Paisano to friends near and far. On long nights sweetened by the melodious calls of chuck-will's-widows and nighthawks, J. Frank, Bertha, and all their pals would gather on the "gallery," the long, stone porch running the length of the front of the house, and discuss life, literature, and the layers in between.

After Dobie died in 1964, his friends throughout Texas sought a way to honor their compatriot. A conversation between Bertha Dobie and two of her husband's friends, Frank H. Wardlaw, director of the University of Texas Press, and Lon Tinkle, a book critic and professor at Southern Methodist University, spawned the idea that the best way to remember Dobie would be to purchase Paisano and use it as a writer's retreat. Funds were raised to take Paisano off the market and the operation was turned over to UT, who facilitates the writing program and maintains stewardship of the grounds.

In 1967, the university established a fellowship program to "stimulate creative endeavor in the arts." By 1993 the focus had shifted entirely to writers, and in the intervening years, the list of fellows has grown long and illustrious. It includes the cornerstone of Chicana literature, Sandra Cisneros (*The House on Mango Street*); National Book Critics Circle Award winner Ben Fountain (*Billy Lynn's Long Halftime Walk*); bestselling author Stephen Harrigan (*The Gates of the Alamo*); National Book Foundation honoree ZZ Packer (*Drinking Coffee Elsewhere*) and Pulitzer finalist Philipp Meyer (*The Son*). Altogether the fellows have produced more than one hundred books of fiction, non-fiction, and poetry, as well as numerous feature films, PBS documentaries, and prestige television series.

As George Jones, True, and I head south on MoPac, construction slows our progress to a crawl and George and I—as is required by law of all old-time Austinites—bitch about how bad the traffic has gotten and reflect on what a handicap it is to have known the city back when it was an entirely manageable hippie hamlet. Soon enough, though, we are zipping along nearly deserted roads that still qualify as country. We turn off at . . . let's call it Branding Iron Trail so as not to zero in too precisely on the location of this writers' sanctuary, and traffic all but disappears. The only creature we encounter for miles is a fiberglass longhorn that gazes forlornly at us from the yard of a ranchette. I wonder if Dobie would be pleased to see that his favorite bovine has not only been saved from extinction, but elevated to the status of a graven image for all true Texans.

A few seconds later, True's nose begins twitching, his foxie ears perk up even higher, and whining expectantly, he paws at the window button. We are at the exact spot where, back in our ranch days, True had always signaled that tantalizing odors, more feral than fiberglass and undetectable to the suburban human nose, had invaded the car and it was time to let that wild wind blow free. We lower all the windows. True scrambles up on his stumpy Corgi legs to poke his nose out the window. Panting with the sort of doggie excitement that looks like a gigantic grin, eyes slitted in bliss, he hoovers up all the delicious, uncivilized smells and howls a low-pitched, growling song of return.

The pavement ends at a twelve-foot-long gate of rusted pipe with a stylized roadrunner scampering across the sign reading "Paisano." Without a word spoken, I slip back into the routine we'd perfected years ago and hop out of the car, grab the heavy chain and lock that are holding the gate closed, dial in the combination, sweep the gate open, and allow George to enter, before locking out the world behind us. Once we are parked, True, who's not as springy as he once was, waits to be lifted out. The instant we are on private land, the three of us are simultaneously overtaken by every Texan's God-given right to sprinkle the thirsty land. As I squat beside True, who is lifting a leg on the rusty gate post, the pagan sun of this summer solstice bursts through the clouds and cuts diamond-sharp shadows across our faces just to remind us who truly owns this state. At that moment, I could not have felt more like a cowgirl if I had been clamping a pigging string between my teeth while doping calves for screwworm.

As the road winds down for a mile and a half into Barton Canyon, the cedar and scrub oak thicken, occasionally rising into a canopy above the road we're crawling along now, mindful of ruts and thankful that it's not washed out. The ranch's sentinels, several towering limestone bluffs, rise up to greet us, a spectacular background for all the greenery.

At the wheel, George puts on a burst of speed, anxious to reach what was, for us, the heart of Paisano: Barton Creek. "You think it's running?" he asks.

"It has to be," I answer, certain that the recent deluge will have sent the creek flowing over the low-water crossing that had kept us trapped a couple of times during our stay. Not that we minded. Getting "creeked-in," being stranded on the wrong side of a flooded creek, preferably with no groceries and a sick dog for added drama, is a badge of honor among former fellows.

"It's not flowing," I moan when we reach the narrow passage across a disappointingly low and ominously stagnant creek. This does not bode well for our cherished swimming hole. We stop and strain for a glimpse of the pristine pool where we'd enjoyed the finest moments of every day we'd spent at Paisano. But weeds now choke the creek, blocking our view of the swimming hole. What water we can see is an unmoving brackish yellow. It appears there will be no swim.

Wilted with disappointment, we drive on to the ranch house. If we are to believe the *Handbook of Texas*, and I see no reason not to, the cabin made of hand-hewn cedar that still remains at the heart of the current, six-room ranch house was built by the original owners in 1863. Handsomely remodeled in 2010, the house still features Dobie's gallery, the long, stone porch sweeping across the front. In his fluffy-butted way, True wiggle-waddles across the length of the gallery, pausing to shoot a glance back at me that I anthropomorphize into the question, "Do you remember?"

I do. The three of us had celebrated our first night at the ranch with a swim followed by a cocktail on the gallery. Dive-bombing hummingbirds had already found the feeders we'd hung and the liquid trilling of canyon wrens filled the air. As night and a sweet alcoholic buzz descended upon us, I settled in, deeply contented, only to be jerked into high alert by the loudest, most booming roar I had ever heard.

"It's only the old lion," George said, reminding me of the stories we'd heard about the ancient, retired giant cat that resided at the Austin Zoo on the far side of the sound-amplifying canyon.

I relaxed, but at the next roar True levitated and shot me an accusing look that demanded, "Hey, you with the prehensile grip and car keys, do something! Now!" After much futile comforting, True, trembling with each roar, beelined into the house and refused to emerge. He'd done what he could to save us, and if we humans were stupid enough to ignore his warning, we deserved to be a lion's amuse-bouche.

But it's high noon now, the ancient lion long gone to that Serengetti in the sky, and the only sounds to be heard are the peaceable gabbling of a mother turkey, out of sight in the underbrush, talking to her chicks.

"Walkie?" I ask True. Of the three of us, True, a rambunctious toddler during our residency, had gloried most in our time at the ranch, adopting the leash-free, country-dog life and never looking back. Our daily walk to the ruins of a cabin built by German settlers circa 1836 had been the highlight of our day. Now, though, eight years older and starting to slow down, he answers by plopping down in the deep shade beneath what I'd thought of as Bertha Dobie's fig tree. I know better than to invite George along. Being the true Texas boy he is, he possesses DNA that is encoded to embrace the wonder of air conditioning and shun the folly of so much as a short stroll in the blistering sun.

It's better that I go alone anyway: I've got a reckoning with a ghost.

Strolling to what remains of the tall log cabin takes less than half an hour. When I turn off the main road onto a heavily wooded path, first years, then decades fall away. The shady path is so quiet that a blue jay's piercing call, *jeer*!, startles me. A moment later, the reverie that most often overtook me on this path settles in. Once again I am transported back in time and I imagine myself to be the bride of the German pioneer who built the cabin. And now, following her new husband along this silent, shaded path, she is about to behold, for the first time, the home that has been built for her in the middle of such vast loneliness.

At the cabin, I bat away a web spun by a shockingly large spider and, stepping gingerly since many of the floorboards are either rotted or missing entirely, I enter the small main room that once contained so many lives. I touch the expertly chiseled and chinked logs and try to imagine raising a family in this confined space, so far from friends, so close to enemies. During the Civil War, Southern marauders ravaged the anti-slavery German settlers, and as late as 1869, Comanches took scalps along Barton Creek.

Imagining the fears and loneliness of a woman surrounded by deadly foes affected me strongly, and fed directly into the novel I worked on during my time at Paisano, *Above the East China Sea*—the story of young women, past and present, caught up in their country's deadliest conflicts. Still, it wasn't that young German wife of my fancy who made the deepest impression on me. No, she only prepared me to meet again the ghost who, in 2010, had already been haunting me for thirty years: Cathy Williams.

I first heard the true story of Cathy Williams, the only woman to ever serve with the Buffalo Soldiers—the legendary African American regiments formed after the Civil War—at a Juneteenth rodeo in 1979. At that time I was doing research for a photo book about what I referred to affectionately as "mutant rodeos," those magnificent hybrids of mainstream-meets-every-subculture in Texas. They all had their charms, but my favorites were the African American rodeos, especially the jubilant Juneteeth affairs such as the one where I first learned about Cathy.

Though this American heroine, largely unknown until recently, seized my imagination from the first moment I heard her name, for various reasons I pushed the story away for decades. And, for the decades that Cathy Williams and her achievement as the first woman to enlist in the peacetime US military went unrecognized, I felt the burden of an obligation left unfulfilled.

In 2010, I was tramping Paisano's more remote stretches when that obligation to Cathy came back to me with a vengeance. I was sweating hard enough to imagine how brutal it would have been for a woman, disguised in the heavy, woolen uniform of an infantry soldier, to march across this endless state. I felt as if Cathy Williams had not only returned but had inhabited me.

She reminded me that she was still waiting to take her rightful place in history. Why, she asked me, did the entire world know the name of Annie Oakley, who was famous for ... what? Shooting over her shoulder using a mirror? Cathy was not impressed, and demanded to know when she would be recognized.

On that day eight years ago, I promised Cathy that I would one day tell her story. And now, as I hike back to the ranch house where George and True wait, my mind quiets. Call it a writer's overactive imagination, call it schizoid affective disorder, call it what you will: I feel Cathy's presence again as surely as if she is marching beside me. I give her the news that the historical novel I've created from the very limited documentation available about her life and service has just been published: *Daughter of a Daughter of a Queen.*

With the lightness that comes from a forty-year-old obligation being lifted, I hurry back to the house. By the time I reach the low water crossing, however, I am soaked in both sweat and a futile desire for the magical swimming hole of the past. I am about to speed up the hill when True, clearly in thrall to a genetic imperative to herd, emerges from the undergrowth to deliver a series of git-along-little dogie faux-nips to my heels. He corrals me, the straggler, then guides me to, of all places, the swimming hole. Following his joyous yips, I crash through the snarl of greenery to find George, dipping as skinny as a good Texas boy is required to, in "our" clear, nearly brimming swimming hole.

I plunge in. The spot has the otherworldly feel of a grotto, shaded as it is by an enormous cottonwood arching over to nearly meet the fern-covered limestone bluff on the opposite bank. The cool, chest-high water is so clear that every glittering scale on a pair of smallish bream is visible as they nibble at our toes planted on the limestone bed.

Liquid Xanax, indeed: this pristine bit of Barton Creek still has that same narcotizing effect. Arms outstretched, I float on my back, staring up into J. Frank's boundless Texas sky. As I think of the ninety-nine other fellows who, inspired by Dobie's embracing spirit, have sheltered beneath this same patch of sky, a surprising sense of kinship comes over me. High overhead, a vulture cuts its inky calligraphy into the endless blue. I drift down the creek, feeling honored to be a member of Dobie's happy community of professional isolates, my obligation fulfilled at last.

Acknowledgments

A few words now about a rare sort of relationship that exists somewhere between that of mother and child, confessor and penitent, marine drill instructor and terrified recruit. Also, in some cases, elements are present of a tapeworm sucking the life and best ideas out of a host and never giving credit. I speak of the connection between a writer and her editor.

I have been exorbitantly lucky in this regard. (Except for you, you priggish martinet, you know who you are, with your Holy Crusade against both the hyphen and the serial comma. Dude, what was up with that? Oh, right, and you, the one who sprinkled my copy with Swisher Sweets "cigarillo" ash, red grease pencil slashes, and squawks of "Awk!" written in the margins. Big Reveal: The only changes that I ever made to those stories were brushing off the ash and retyping them, unchanged. Then, after I thanked you for your invaluable guidance, off the original story went to the printer.) But aside from Swisher and Holy Crusade, oh, and the ones who never paid, I have wandered an editorial orchard filled with nothing but the most luscious of peaches.

Me and the editors of my novels, those relationships have been like marriages, long, contractually bound unions where we ended up finishing each other's sentences and arguing about whose turn it was to take out the trash. I'm not talking about them. I'm talking about the one-night affairs, the flings, the brief (mostly), beautiful interludes that spawned the pieces in this book.

If I ever knew the names of the first editors I worked with, the ones at the true confessions magazines, they dropped out of the memory bank long ago. Like the editors of the romance novels that I'd meet later, they functioned more as quality-control technicians, making sure that the stories were just lurid enough, that sinners had to suffer and then repent, and that no one ever shopped at any hoity-toity J. C. Penney's. Those editors were exactly what I needed back then, because they made sure that the paralyzing question of literary merit, if I was or was not an actual writer, never entered the picture. As long as I followed specs and created a uniformly blue-collar product with a heartwarming message at the end, "Awk!" was never a concern.

The essays and articles I wrote for magazines like *O, Cosmopolitan, Mademoiselle, Good Housekeeping, Ladies' Home Journal*, and *Seventeen* make only the briefest of appearances in these pages since, well, tips on "This Season's Kickiest Lip Liners" have a very short shelf life. Learning the names of the junior assistant editors I worked with was an exercise in futility, as they left as soon as the next eager young graduate from Brown or Bard learned how to make coffee.

Third Coast, on the other hand, was a Brigadoon of a magazine that graced my life and Austin through much of the eighties with a take on our city that was as smart and expansive as its 14-×-11-inch, black-and-white format. There, I met and was fortunate enough to work with my first true editor, John Taliaferro. Along with the other brilliant boys, David Stansbury, Jerome Weeks, and Ernest Sharpe, John made *TC* into a clubhouse with Algonquin Round Table aspirations where the winner was always the one who got the most laughs.

Great editors help you find the lead you buried in the tenth paragraph, point out that you've used the word "just" eighteen times, and help you see what the story or essay is really supposed to be about. They also accept that all writers are pathologically insecure but almost never use that knowledge against you. And then there is that rarest of great editors: the great editor who can edit humor. I had the outlandish good luck of working with just such a unicorn for six years when I wrote back-page columns for *Texas Monthly*. Yes, Evan Smith, come on down.

Editing is a left-brain activity that looks at a piece of writing like an equation with the goal of ensuring that it all adds up. That the beginning and ending, along with all the random bits in the middle, balance out. Sadly, the surest way to kill an attempt at humorous writing is to apply logic to it. I will be forever grateful to Evan for, when looking at some piece of disjointed absurdity, never asking "Why?" For never making me whimper the deadliest words known to whimsy, "Because it's funny?"

This is my second book with the University of Texas Press and no writer could have had two better publishing experiences. Casey Kittrell was the structural virtuoso who took the disparate found objects—pieces of writing that span more than four decades—adroitly knocked off most of the rust, and assembled them into a collage with a new life all its own.

Lynne Chapman, what you contributed went far beyond even the everyday marvels wrought by the finest of copy editors. Titles, Lynne! You found section titles! And so much more.

Finally, there is no way that I won't acknowledge Gianna LaMorte. Is Gianna the funniest person I know? Possibly. Certainly, she's the funniest person who's also brilliant and brilliantly passionate about both books and the book business. Though she's never touched a word I've written, Gianna is the editor every writer dreams about.

Thank you, all my five-star editors, for making me look far better than I am. But not you, Swisher. Not you.

SARAH BIRD is the author of ten novels, most recently the historical work *Daughter of a Daughter of a Queen*. In addition to working as a screenwriter, Bird has served as a columnist for *Texas Monthly* and as an occasional contributor to numerous national publications, including *O, The Oprah Magazine*; the *New York Times Magazine*; *Salon*; the *Daily Beast*; and *Glamour*. Her many accolades include induction into the Texas Literary Hall of Fame in 2012.